CAMOUFLAGE, MARKINGS, AND SQUADRO
AMERICAN VOLUNTEER GROUP'S AIRCRAFT

TIGERS OVER CHINA

**History and Artwork
by Thomas A. Tullis**

EagleFiles #4

Color Notes

Color interpretation from black and white photographs amounts to educated guesswork, at the very best. The advent of computer technology has greatly aided in this endeavor. The computer has, through grayscale comparison and analysis, eliminated much guesswork from the evaluation of true colors.

ISBN 0-9660706-7-4

Library of Congress Catalog Number 2001093125

First Edition

Copyright © 2001 by Eagle Editions Ltd.

Printed in Korea

Library of Eagles

Eagle Editions Ltd.

Post Office Box 580
Hamilton, MT 59840 USA
www.eagle-editions.com

We are interested in hearing from those who may have
photographic or data material for use in future publications.

INTRODUCTION

ver the last ten years I have been involved in several projects for which I needed to illustrate aircraft of the American Volunteer Group. Each time I searched in vain for an accurate reference book on these aircraft, but came up short. Much has been written about the men and mission of the A.V.G., but little has been published documenting the machines they flew.

In 1999, I was commissioned by the National Aviation Hall of Fame to produce a series of limited-edition lithographs commemorating the A.V.G. receiving the NAHF's "Spirit of Flight" award. I spent the better part of a year interviewing surviving pilots for the project, and amassed a large amount of reference material on these beautiful airplanes. After completing the project, a suggestion was put to me to publish the research I had been gathering. The decision was then made to combine that research with the artwork I did, to create the type of reference book I have been longing for these many years. This book is intended to be a supplement to the histories and biographies that have been published on the A.V.G, and I am confident that the aircraft illustrations in this book are among the most accurate yet produced of these famous aircraft.

Thomas A. Tullis
November 17, 2000

DEDICATION

his book is dedicated to my son, James Harrison Tullis. May you always appreciate the sacrifices and service of your country's veterans.

ACKNOWLEDGMENTS

 work such as this would not have been possible without the generous support and contributions of the following people and organizations: Dana Bell, Mike Bobe, Charles Bond, Jerry and Judy Crandall, the Curtiss Wright Historical Association, H. "Bud" Golem, Roy Grinnell, David Lee "Tex" Hill, Ken Jernstedt, Bob Layher, Chuck Older, Dick and Lydia Rossi, Erik Schilling, the United States Air Force Museum, and Peter Wright.

Special thanks to Allan Erickson, for kindly providing access to his A.V.G. photo archive which includes photos from the R.T. Smith collection. Additional thanks go to researcher Dana Bell for providing me with information regarding the DuPont paints used by Curtiss.

CONTENTS

INTRODUCTION .III

DEDICATION IV

ACKNOWLEDGMENTS IV

HISTORY 6

CAMOUFLAGE COLORS 32

SQUADRON MARKINGS 40

SHARK'S MOUTHS 42, 52

COLOR AIRCRAFT PROFILES 43

B&W AIRCRAFT PROFILES 49

NATIONAL MARKINGS 54

FLYING TIGER INSIGNIA 54

STENCILS .54

REFERENCES 87

History

The American Volunteer Group, or "Flying Tigers," represented the United States' first covert military operation against a foreign nation in World War Two. It was formed by a secret Executive Order issued by President Roosevelt in the spring of 1941. A.V.G. per-

sonnel were all ex-Navy, Marine Corps, and Army pilots and ground crew members, who had temporarily "resigned" from their respective branches of the U.S. military and hired on with the Chinese Air Force. Led by Colonel Claire Lee Chennault, the A.V.G. achieved an incredible record of 286 downed Japanese aircraft during its extremely short career. The A.V.G. was operational from August 1941 to July 1942, when it was absorbed into the 23rd Fighter Group, USAAF.

Above: Curtiss Hawk 81-A2 #47, after being transferred to the 3rd Pursuit Squadron and having new squadron markings applied. Originally flown by John Petach of the 2nd Pursuit Squadron, the aircraft wore a blue fuselage band and blue lips on the shark's mouth. New markings include black lips, a red fuselage band, "Hell's Angels" insignia, "Flying Tiger" insignia, and pilot R.T. Smith's name and victory markings under the cockpit.

Right: A close-up view of R.T. Smith's cockpit markings on aircraft #47.

A good shot showing cockpit details of the P-40, including the reflector gunsight.

Below: One of the six original P-40E aircraft obtained by the A.V.G. in March 1942. These E models were ferried from Takoradi on the African Gold Coast.

Ken Jernstedt's #88, P-8121.

Excellent view of #77's shark's mouth; the aircraft was flown by R. T. Smith. Note stenciling on propeller.

A close-up view of Tommy Haywood's #49. This aircraft was originally assigned to the 2nd Pursuit Squadron, but later was obtained by the 3rd P.S., and flown by Haywood. The "Tiger" decal is a replacement for an earlier one that peeled off, just forward of where this decal is applied.

Pilot R.T. Smith poses on the spinner of his Hawk 81-A2 #77.

Flight Leader Paul J. Greene poses next to his Hawk 81-A2 #84.

Pilot Tommy Haywood on the wing root of his #49. The "Bulldog" was applied to both sides of the aircraft. The partial head of a "Tiger" decal remains, and a new complete decal has been applied just aft of it.

Another view of Flight Leader Paul J. Greene and his Hawk 81-A2 #84, P8195.

This page and opposite: Three views of aircraft #6, P-8187, flown by Flight Leader John Dean. Note the mis-matched alignment of the camouflage demarcation line where the wing assembly meets the fuselage. This was due to the way Curtiss painted the aircraft in sub-assemblies prior to mating them, resulting in frequent non-alignment of the color edges.

Left: Unidentified Hawk 81-A2. Note the single-colored wheel hub, and chipping paint on forward edge of the shark's mouth upper lip.

Opposite page, top: Arvid E. Olson in the cockpit of his fighter. Note the detail visible under the wings.

Middle left: Chuck Older's #68. Note odd camouflage demarcation on the vertical fin.

Bottom left: Bill Reed in front of his aircraft #75. Prior to painting the shark's mouth, each pilot would sketch the rough outline in chalk. Still visible is an early sketch of a very differently-shaped mouth. Note that barrels on the fuselage guns extend further out than normal.

R.T. Smith in the cockpit of aircraft #77.

Aircraft #99 of the 3rd Pursuit Squadron.

Below: Aircraft #91, P-8150. See color photo of the aircraft elsewhere in this book for details of the unusual shark's mouth colors.

Above: A group of 3rd Pursuit Squadron aircraft standing in readiness along the flight line.

Far right: "Hell's Angels" insignia of the 3rd Pursuit Squadron.

Right: A mixed line-up of Hawk 81-A2s, and a single P-40E.

Line-up of three A.V.G. P-40E fighters.

An excellent close-up view showing details of drain pipes and shell ejection chute.

"Moose" Moss in front of his Hawk 81-A2.

Aircraft #77 after having bellied-in. Note the repair patch on the vertical fin just forward of the serial number.

This and the following two photographs: Three views of aircraft #74, after a belly landing.

This and the following two-page spread:
Various views depicting A.V.G. aircraft mishaps.

A close-up view of R.T. Smith's #77. Note the barely visible "77" just above the shark's eye.

Jesse Crookshanks, next to R.T. Smith's #77.

Left: Tommy Haywood in aircraft #94. Some researchers have confused this aircraft with Haywood's #49, thinking this photo was of the latter.

Below: Flight Leader Paul J. Greene's Hawk #84.

CAMOUFLAGE COLORS

See color profiles on pages 43 through 48

The Curtiss Hawk 81-A2 was the export version of the P-40B/C. The first aircraft received by the A.V.G. were Hawk 81-A2 fighters originally intended for the RAF, and as such they were painted according to RAF guidelines. While Curtiss did not have actual RAF paint stocks on hand, they used DuPont paints that approximated the color descriptions given to them by the RAF.

The upper surfaces were to be painted Dark Green and Dark Earth, and the DuPont paints used were fairly close to the specified RAF colors. In some cases the brown color used had a slightly more yellow hue to it that the RAF color, which became more evident when fading occurred in the field as shown in several color plates in this book. The DuPont paints used were 71-065 (Dark Brown), and 71-013 (Dark Green).

Probably the most confusing and disputed area of research on the colors of these aircraft concerns the paint used on the undersurfaces. While the RAF used a greenish-blue color called "Sky Type S" for their fighters, there wasn't any DuPont color that closely matched it. A cool gray color was used instead, and this was likely F.S. 16473 Aircraft Gray, which has a very slight blue-green hue to it. Some color film and photos seem to show a much bluer color on some aircraft. Whether this is a legitimate variation, or simply the effects of time deteriorating the film over the last fifty years is unknown. During the course of my interviews, most crew members clearly recall a neutral or slightly cool gray as having been used. The idea of blue undersurfaces may have originated with a color photo of a group of 3rd Pursuit Squadron aircraft dispersed on the ground.

In some publications, the undersurfaces have reproduced as a very definite powder blue color. During my research, I obtained an early generation copy of this photo from an A.V.G. pilot. After scanning and digitally enhancing this photo, I believe it is more likely that the color had shifted during numerous copy generations and subsequent color separations for four-color printing, resulting in the incorrect blue-gray interpretations.

The wheel hubs were painted in either Aircraft Gray, Dark Earth, or a scalloped design consisting of the three squadron colors.

The propellers were black with yellow tips, and had data stencils applied in white near the propeller base.

All aircraft were factory painted in sub-assemblies using large masking mats, which resulted in very hard-edged demarcation lines between the camouflage colors. Frequently the edges of these colors did not match up when the assemblies were finally mated together, resulting in a very patchwork appearance. Some researchers have mistakenly stated that the large round areas of Dark Earth on the wings and fuselage were the previously-applied RAF roundels that had been painted out. That is not correct. The masking mats had large circular cutouts where the RAF roundels were to have been applied, which resulted in large Dark Earth circles on the wings and fuselage. This was done to aid in aligning the decals of the RAF roundels when they were to be applied at a later date. Photos of Curtiss workers painting wing assemblies clearly show these round areas on the masking mats. In some cases, the mats were reversed, resulting in a "mirror" image of the

text continues on page 51

Three 3rd Pursuit Squadron aircraft over China. Older's #68 is nearest the camera.

A color photo of Chuck Older's fighter, P-8109.

Group shot of 3rd Pursuit Squadron pilots. Standing are Haywood (left) and Olson. Sitting are (from left) Smith, Jernstedt, Prescott, Laughlin, and Reed. Behind them is aircraft #68.

A beautiful shot of aircraft #47 in flight over China. This shot shows the aircraft during a transition phase for the squadron markings. Originally flown by John Petach of the 2nd Pursuit Squadron, the aircraft had a blue fuselage band and blue lips on the shark's mouth. In this photo the lips are now black, the "47" on the forward cowl is painted out, and the blue fuselage band over-painted with red. This aircraft would eventually have a "Flying Tiger" decal applied along with a "Hell's Angels" squadron insignia, and R.T. Smith's name and victory markings as shown in another photo in this book.

Above: A color shot of 3rd Pursuit Squadron fighters. By this time the numbering system had broken down due to transferring aircraft between squadrons, as demonstrated by aircraft #35 and #22 in 3rd Pursuit Squadron colors and markings. This is the color photo that most people who support the use of light blue for the undersurfaces refer to. The center aircraft does appear to have a slight blue tint to the under-surface, and even more so in other reproductions of the photo. This photo has been digitally corrected using the teeth as a white point to remove any color cast. Even with this process a very slight blue hue remains, possibly indicating at least a few aircraft had such a color applied.

Opposite page, bottom:
Chuck Older and R.T. Smith in
Kunming, China, 1942.

A shot of R.T. Smith in front of
aircraft #40. Note the data plate in
the aft cockpit scallop. The dark
area around the "Flying Tiger"
decal is from a varnish that was
brushed over the decal to prevent it
from peeling off during flight.

Pilot R.T. Smith in his aircraft #77. Note that the "Hell's Angels" insignia is only a white outline at this time, and has yet to receive a red fill. Compare this shot to the other close-up views of #77 elsewhere in this book. The progression of the markings application is interesting.

Aircraft #91, P-8150. Note colors used to paint the shark's mouth. The tongue is an exact match for the "Dark Earth" camouflage color. A red cheat stripe is used to separate the tongue and the badly faded "Chinese Blue" upper portion of the mouth. The eye consists of a black pupil within a "Chinese Blue" disk.

Probably the best color photo of Chuck Older's #68. Note staining from spilled fuel below the two fuel caps. R.T. Smith stands in front.

SQUADRON MARKINGS

Once assigned to the A.V.G., the aircraft were divided up and painted in individual squadron markings. Initially the aircraft were divided into numerical divisions, with aircraft numbers 1 through 33 going to the 1st Pursuit Squadron; 34 through 66 going to the 2nd P.S; and 67 through 99 to the 3rd P.S. But that identification method rapidly fell apart due to aircraft being shifted between squadrons, which in the many years since resulted in photos being incorrectly identified in various publications due to the author relying solely on the aircraft's number to determine its squadron affiliation.

Each aircraft had its number applied to the fuselage in white, 20 inches tall. In the beginning, the aircraft also had the number repeated on the forward cowling just in front of the exhaust stacks in white, 5 to 6 inches tall. The serial number was applied in white on the vertical stabilizer.

The First Pursuit Squadron, as described above, started out with aircraft numbers 1 through 33. The squadron color was white, used to identify 1st P.S. aircraft via a stripe on the aft fuselage. The 1st P.S. was known as the "Adam and Eves." It adopted an insignia featuring a green apple with a man and woman, often depicted in stick figures, running across it. A black sash running across the lower half of the apple had "1st Pursuit" written on it. As the badges were all hand-painted, numerous variations exist between individual aircraft. Most aircraft in this squadron had "open" style shark's mouths, in which only the tongue was painted in, leaving the camouflage color showing through the upper portion of the mouth area.

The Second Pursuit Squadron initially had aircraft numbers 34 through 66. The squadron color was "Chinese Blue," and as with the 1st P.S. above, this color was used to identify the aircraft via a stripe on the aft fuselage. The 2nd P.S. was known as the "Panda Bears," and some aircraft featured a small painting of such a bear on the fuselages. Each of the "Panda Bears" painted on the aircraft was quite different from the others, and many 2nd P.S. aircraft carried none at all. Some 2nd P.S. aircraft used the squadron color for the lips on their shark's mouths, but as mentioned above, this color was very prone to fading and later was usually painted over with black. Several color photos of Erik Shilling's #52 with blue lips have been published over the years, confirming this practice.

The Third Pursuit Squadron, as outlined earlier, started out with aircraft numbers 67 through 99. The squadron color was red, applied to the aircraft via a stripe on the aft fuselage. The 3rd P.S. was known as the "Hell's Angels," and adopted an insignia featuring a winged woman painted in red having a thin white outline. Each individual "Angel" was unique in her pose, and some aircraft carried one on each side. The shark's mouths from this squadron often had completely filled-in mouth openings, using either Aircraft Gray or "Chinese Blue."

1ˢᵗ Pursuit Squadron

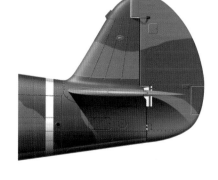

1ˢᵗ Pursuit Squadron

2ⁿᵈ Pursuit Squadron

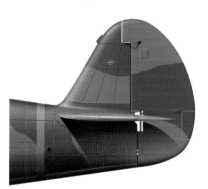

2ⁿᵈ Pursuit Squadron

3ʳᵈPursuit Squadron

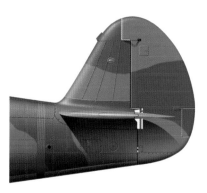

3ʳᵈ Pursuit Squadron

SHARK'S MOUTHS

See related text on page 52

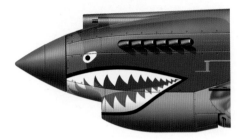

Type 1

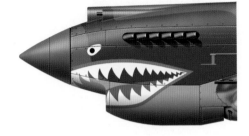

Type 2

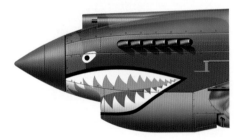

Type 3

Type 4

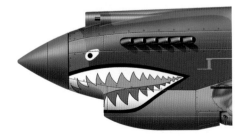

Type 5

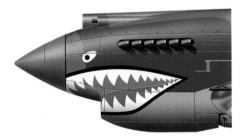

Type 6

Curtiss *Hawk* 81-A2 #3

P-8103 flown by Dick Rossi of the 1st Pursuit Squadron. A small Chinese roundel was applied under the starboard cockpit in the same position as the USAAF roundel shown on the port. The shark's mouth is provisional, as no photos of the aircraft with this marking could be found. The shark's mouth applied is the result of several interviews with Dick Rossi, and this rendering received his approval.

Curtiss *Hawk* 81-A2 #21

P-8182 flown by Greg Boyington of the 1st Pursuit Squadron. Note the repainted area of the fuselage just forward of the cockpit, resulting in a deviation of the standard camouflage pattern. The white "21" on the rear fuselage has faded considerably.

Curtiss *Hawk* 81-A2 #47

Curtiss *Hawk* 81-A2 #47

P-8127 early version, flown by John Petach and Bob Layher of the 2nd Pursuit Squadron. This aircraft is a good example of the 2nd Squadron's use of "Chinese Blue" for the lips on the shark's mouths. The small illustration on the side of the aircraft is not a "Panda Bear," as some publications have stated, but rather a caricature of Petach riding a bicycle with a camera slung around his neck. This aircraft was later transferred to the 3rd Pursuit Squadron and flown by R.T. Smith.

P-8127 later version, flown by R.T. Smith of the 3rd Pursuit Squadron. Formerly with the 2nd Pursuit Squadron, the aircraft now carries new squadron markings, including a repainted shark's mouth. Note the areas repainted with Dark Green on the cowl, mid-fuselage, and tail areas. The dark area immediately below the victory markings is simply where the fuselage had been washed prior to their application. A portion of the rudder has been repainted with fresh Dark Earth.

Curtiss *Hawk* 81-A2 #49

P-8133 flown by Tommy Haywood of the 3rd Pursuit Squadron. This aircraft was formerly attached to the 2nd Pursuit Squadron. The "Bulldog" insignia was applied to both sides of the aircraft as a reference to Haywood's days as an USMC pilot. Of particular interest are the partial remains of a "Flying Tiger" insignia that peeled off during flight. The outline of the "Tiger" is still visible, due to the discoloration of the surrounding area by the protective varnish applied to secure the decal. A new decal complete with blue victory "V" has been applied.

Curtiss *Hawk* 81-A2 #52

P-8147 flown by Erik Schilling of the 2nd Pursuit Squadron. This aircraft was converted to a photo recon platform by removing the wing guns and cutting a 10-inch hole for a camera in the bottom of the fuselage directly under the fuselage access hatch. Several excellent color photographs have been published over the years showing the shark's mouth of this aircraft with "Chinese Blue" lips.

Curtiss *Hawk* 81-A2 #75

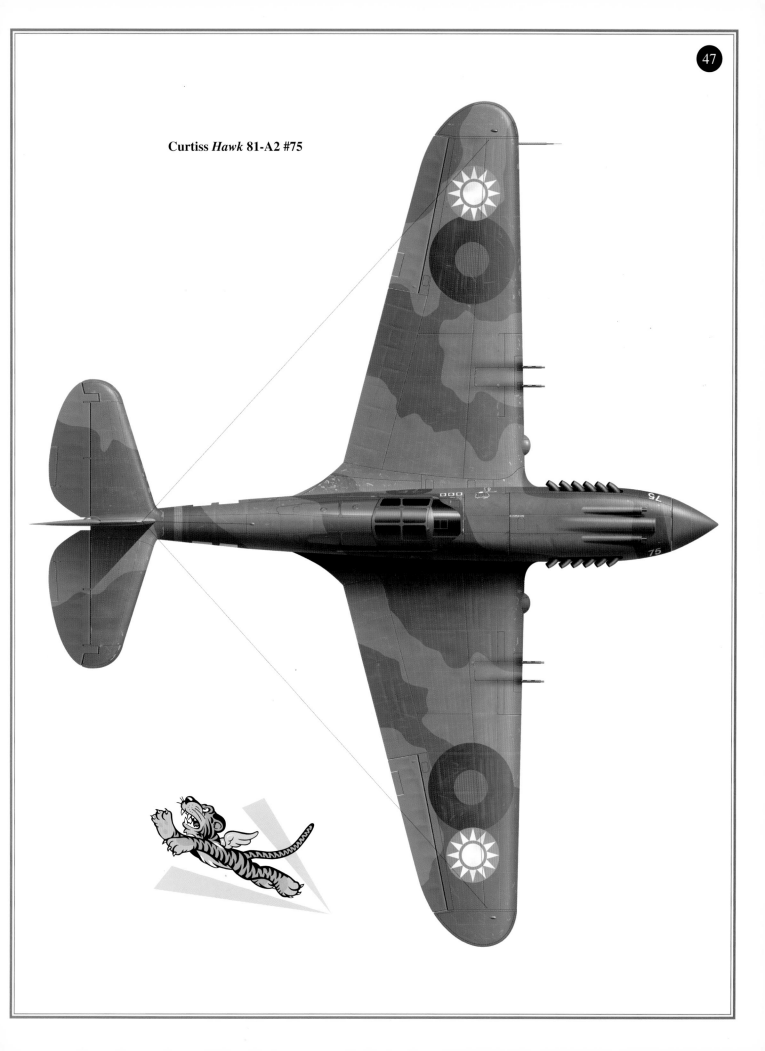

Curtiss *Hawk* 81-A2 #75

P-8186 flown by Bill Reed of the 3rd Pursuit Squadron. Note the chalk outlines of mouth styles that were drawn prior to the painting of the shark's mouth. Probably the most interesting feature of this aircraft is the application of RAF roundels to the upper wings, undoubtedly applied at the Curtiss factory and simply not removed prior to shipping to China. This could very well be the only aircraft of the 99 Hawk 81-A2s flown by the A.V.G. with these markings. RAF roundels were not applied to the lower wings. No good photos showing the "75" on the rear fuselage could be found, so the marking was constructed using other aircraft in the "70-79" number range as references.

Curtiss *Hawk* 81-A2 #68

P-8109 flown by Charles Older of the 3rd Pursuit Squadron. This profile represents probably the final stage of the marking evolution for this aircraft. Note the repainted area on forward cowl and spinner. While it is extremely faded in most reproductions, the interior of the shark's mouth was painted "Chinese Blue." The small "FIRST AID INSIDE DOOR" stencil just forward of the fuselage access hatch is in red, rather than the more common white lettering.

Curtiss *Hawk* 81-A2 #1

P-8125 flown by Peter Atkinson of the 1st Pursuit Squadron, prior to squadron insignias and shark's mouth being applied.

Curtiss *Hawk* 81-A2 #5

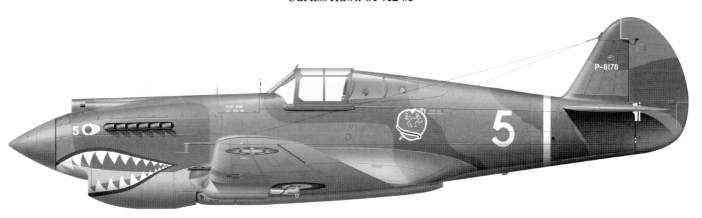

P-8178 flown by Charlie Bond of the 1st Pursuit Squadron. This profile represents an early version of Bond's markings, prior to any victory flags being applied.

Curtiss *Hawk* 81-A2 #7

P-8194 flown by Robert Neale of the 1st Pursuit Squadron.

Curtiss *Hawk* 81-A2 #11

P-8164 flown by Robert J. Sandell, Squadron Leader of the 1st Pursuit Squadron.

Curtiss *Hawk* 81-A2 #48

P-8134 flown by David Lee "Tex" Hill of the 2nd Pursuit Squadron. This illustration was constructed from a starboard view of the aircraft and several interviews with "Tex" Hill, to confirm various details such as the "Panda Bear" illustration.

text continued from page 32

camouflage pattern (aircraft #42 is a good example of this). Since the aircraft were to have been painted with RAF fin flashes, the vertical stabilizers had to be camouflaged once the decision had been made to divert the aircraft to China. The stabilizers were painted prior to the attachment of the rudders, resulting in the camouflage demarcations of the two not aligning when mated. The stabilizer camouflage consisted of the two upper surface colors being applied in equal amounts, usually divided by a horizontal or slightly angled demarcation line. Some were simply painted in a single solid coat of either color.

A color unofficially known as "Chinese Blue" was used by the A.V.G. for various markings as outlined below. This color faded extremely rapidly, almost giving the impression that multiple blue colors were used on the aircraft. The "fresh," unfaded color was a close match to F.S. 35095. After some fading, it began to resemble F.S. 35180 or F.S. 35183, and eventually lightened to a color that is similar to F.S. 35250, but much less saturated.

The P-40Es that were later obtained by the A.V.G were painted in the standard USAAF scheme of Olive Drab 41 upper surfaces and Neutral Gray 43 lower surfaces.

Bill Reed's #75. Unlike the top wings of this aircraft, the lower wings do not carry RAF roundels.

SHARK'S MOUTHS

Shown in color on page 42

The famous "shark's mouth" of the Flying Tigers came in many styles. The more common are listed below, and color examples of each can be found in the markings section of this book on pages 33 through 48.

Type 1:   This style consisted of an unpainted or "empty" mouth area above the tongue. The lips, teeth, and tongue were the only areas painted in. Almost all 1st Pursuit Squadron aircraft were of this type.

Type 2:   These were identical to "Type 1" mouths, with the exception of having "Chinese Blue" color lips. The only examples I have found are from the 2nd Pursuit Squadron. Color photos have confirmed this style.

Type 3:   The "empty" area of the"Type 1" mouth is filled in with Aircraft Gray. Other features are the same as above.

Type 4:   The "empty" area of the "Type 1" mouth is filled in with the "Chinese Blue" color. Other features are the same as above.

Type 5:   These are the most "refined" of all the mouth styles. They have the "filled in" upper mouth areas of either Aircraft Gray or "Chinese Blue," as do Types 3 and 4. In addition, they feature very fine black pin-striping around the details of the tongue and teeth.

Type 6:   This style has been positively documented only on a few aircraft, one of which is shown in a color photo in this book. The tongue is painted in the same Dark Brown as the upper fuselage, but has a red cheat-line along the top edge. The color photo shows the upper portion of the mouth to be a very faded "Chinese Blue," but other aircraft with this style may have had the same area painted Aircraft Gray instead.

Two shots of a five-ship formation. Aircraft include (from front) #68, #46, #49, #81, and #74.

NATIONAL MARKINGS

Shown in color on pages 44 and 47

The Chinese roundels on these aircraft were all painted using the "Chinese Blue" color. Since this color faded extremely fast, the result was a very light blue roundel on the upper wing and a darker, unfaded roundel on the bottom. Some publications have incorrectly attributed this to the use of two different colors for the upper and lower roundels, but interviews with crew members have positively confirmed the use of a single color.

FLYING TIGER INSIGNIA

Shown in color on pages 35, 44, and 47

Henry Porter of the Walt Disney Studios designed the now-famous "leaping winged tiger" emblem of the A.V.G. The artwork as applied to A.V.G. aircraft was actually an adhesive decal that was printed in the United States and sent to China. Initial flights with the decals revealed that they peeled off in the airstream, so a new method of application was devised. Once applied, a varnish was brushed over the entire decal to permanently affix it to the aircraft. The procedure resulted in a dark patch surrounding the marking, which is quite evident in many of the photos reproduced in this book.

STENCILS

Shown in color on pages 33 through 48

The stencils on these Hawk 81-A2s were applied as decals, resulting in a dark rectangle around each individual stencil. In some cases the color of the type changed between aircraft, but the size and shape remained the same.

R.T. Smith leans on the wing of his aircraft #77. This view clearly shows the size and position of the upper wing roundel. Note the antenna wire coming from the wing tip and running just behind Smith.

*One of the best (of a very few) photos showing the position
and size of the underwing Chinese national insignia.*

One of the A.V.G.'s P-40E aircraft.

Ken Jernstedt, Tommy Haywood and R.T. Smith strike a pose in front of Smith's #77.

Below: Aircraft #92 of the 3rd Pursuit Squadron. Note the area of the underwing just inboard of the Chinese roundel. The area where the RAF roundel would have been applied had been masked off during factory painting, and is still visible. This was probably a very light gray color.

Two views of Older's #68, P-8109.

Line-up of 1st Pursuit Squadron aircraft, prior to the application of unit insignias or shark's mouths.

This shot of Older's #68 was taken prior to the repainting done on the spinner and forward cowling, depicted in the color photos elsewhere in this book. Note the area just above the "eye" where the white "68" has been painted out.

P-8115, # 69, of the 3rd Pursuit Squadron.

Henry Geselbracht's #38, of the 2nd Pursuit Squadron.

A rare view of the starboard side of Chuck Older's #68.

A close view up of Ken Jernstedt's #88. Note the mis-matched camouflage edges on the gun port covers.

Bill Reed's #75. Note the RAF roundel still on the upper wing inboard of the Chinese national insignia.

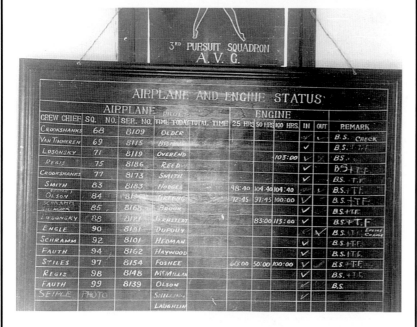

3RD PURSUIT SQUADRON A.V.G.

AIRPLANE AND ENGINE STATUS

CREW CHIEF	SQ. NO.	SER. NO.	PILOT	TIME TODAY	TOTAL TIME	25 HRS	50 HRS	100 HRS	IN	OUT	REMARK
Crookshanks	68	8109	Older						✓	✓	B.S. Check
Van Timmeren	69	8115	Bishman						✓		B.S. T.F
Losonsky	71	8119	Overend					103:00	✓	✓	B.S.
Regis	75	8186	Reed						✓		B.S. T.F
Crookshanks	77	8173	Smith						✓		B.S. T.F
Smith	83	8183	Hodges			98:40	104:40	104:40	✓	✓	B.S. T.F
Olson	84	8184	Geffro			72:45	97:45	100:00	✓		B.S. T.F
Schramm	85	8168	Brouk						✓		B.S. T.F
Losonsky	88	8171	Jernstedt				83:00	113:00	✓		B.S. T.F
Engle	90	8191	Dupouy						✓	✓	B.S. T.F Engine Change
Schramm	92	8101	Hedman						✓		B.S. T.F
Fauth	94	8162	Haywood						✓		B.S. T.F
Stiles	97	8154	Foshee			68:00	50:00	100:00	✓		B.S. T.F
Regis	98	8148	McMillan						✓		B.S. T.F
Fauth	99	8139	Olson						✓		B.S.
Seiple	Photo		Shillin						✓		
			Laughlin								

Left, top: A close-up view of the markings on Older's #68.

Left, center: Aircraft status board for the 3rd Pursuit Squadron.

Left: A close-up view of aircraft #36, P-8123 flown by Ed Rector of the 2nd Pursuit Squadron. Note the faded "36" just above and forward of the shark's eye.

Shown in the above line-up is aircraft #98 standing with others on the 3rd Pursuit Squadron's flight line.

Aircraft #92 of the 3rd Pursuit Squadron.

This spread: Aircraft #98 on the 3rd Pursuit Squadron flight line.

Right and below center: Two views of R.T. Smith's Hawk 81-A2.

Chuck Older in the cockpit of his aircraft, P-8109.

This and the following page: Four in-flight shots of Tommy Haywood's #94.

A close-up view of the markings on R.T. Smith's #77. Note that in this photo the angel insignia is painted red. Compare this to the color photo showing the same insignia prior to the application of the red fill.

Excellent view of Chinese roundel under the wing of Older's #68.

Smith in the cockpit of #77. Note the "PRESTONE" decal just forward of the canopy.

R.T. Smith's #77. Note the shell ejection chute, drain pipes, and repainted patch just inboard of the wing guns.

Aircraft #68, #46, and #24 in flight over China.

*Two views of aircraft #90
undergoing routine maintenance.*

R.T. Smith in the cockpit of his #77. Note the excellent view of the reflector sight and the offset mounting of the ring sight.

R.T. Smith poses next to his aircraft.

Another shot of Smith and his Hawk 81-A2. Note the repainted patches on the underwing.

Tommy Haywood's #49, in 3rd Pursuit Squadron colors.

Another of the E model P-40s ferried from Takoradi in 1942.

A line-up of Chinese pilots in front of aircraft #42. Note that the camouflage pattern on this aircraft is reversed or "mirrored" from the standard scheme. This was simply due to the Curtiss factory workers reversing the masking mats, which were used when spraying the camouflage colors.

Yet another shot of the shark's mouth on #68. This is an early shot, taken prior to the repainting done on the forward cowl and spinner. Still visible is the white "68" just above the shark's eye.

Another of the A.V.G.'s P-40E aircraft. Note that the lower wings still carry the "U.S. ARMY" markings, along with the Chinese national insignia.

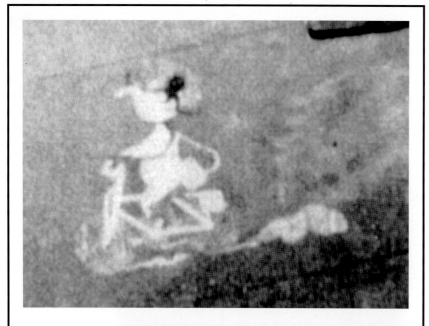

A close-up view of the painting on John Petach's aircraft.

A close-up view of the 1st Pursuit Squadron insignia, the "Adam and Eves." Numerous variations of this insignia have been documented, with the man and woman ranging from simple stick figures to fully-rendered illustrations.

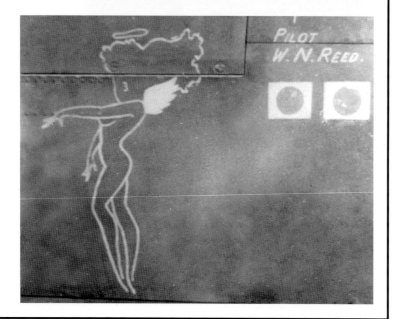

A close-up view of the markings under the cockpit of Bill Reed's #77, showing the "Hell's Angel" insignia of the 3rd Pursuit Group.

Two group shots of the "Hell's Angels" squadron pilots.

Bill Reed's #75. Note the chalk outlines of a shark's mouth sketched on the cowling visible just above the painted mouth.

Pilot R.T. Smith in the cockpit of his #77.

Aircraft #15, P-8132 awaiting repairs.

Aircraft #99 of the 3rd Pursuit Squadron.

Chuck Older's #68. Note the wheel hub markings.

R.T. Smith again poses with his #77. Note the repainted patch just inboard of the inner wing gun.

Excellent view of the top air intake and gun ports. Note propeller stenciling.

One of the original six P-40E aircraft obtained by the A.V.G. in March of 1942.

Henry Geselbracht's #38 of the 2nd Pursuit Squadron.

A stunning, in-flight view from the cockpit of an A.V.G. Hawk 81-A2.

Port-side close-up view of R.T. Smith's #77 Hawk 81-A2, showing American Air Corps star insignia on fuselage.

Left, above: Pilot Bob Layher poses next to a 2nd Pursuit Squadron P-40. Note the medium gray lips on the shark's mouth, believed to be blue like aircraft #47's.

Left: Bob Layher in front of aircraft #47 which he sometimes flew, along with John Petach. Painted on the side of the aircraft is a rendering of Petach riding a bicycle, which has frequently been mistaken for a "Panda Bear" insignia of the 2nd Pursuit Squadron.

Opposite page: P-40Es from the March 1942 ferry flight.

Below: Probably the best photo of Greg Boyington's aircraft P-8182. Note the non-standard camouflage pattern on the mid-fuselage, and the faded "21." Some publications have incorrectly identified faded fuselage numbers such as this one as being yellow. No information supporting this theory has surfaced, nor has any A.V.G member interviewed by the author ever recalled any color other than white being used.

One of the few known photos of Ken Jernstedt's P-40, #88.

Detail of a 2nd Pursuit Squadron aircraft. Note the blue lips on the shark's mouth.

REFERENCES

Interviews conducted by the author with members of the A.V.G. including: Charles Bond, Ken Jernstedt, Bob Layher, Chuck Older, Dick Rossi, Erik Schilling, and Peter Wright.

Air Classics (various articles, issues).

Air Force Colors Vol. 1, by Dana Bell. Squadron Signal Publications, 1979.

American Volunteer Group: The First Aces. Aeromaster Decals.

"Curtiss Camouflage Schemes for RAF P-40s," by Dana Bell. *Fine Scale Modeler* Magazine, Jan. 1995.

Curtiss factory documents for camouflage application on the P-40.

Curtiss P-40 in Action. Squadron Signal Publications, 1976.

Days of the Ching Pao, by Malcolm Rosholt. Rosholt House II, 1978.

Famous Airplanes of the World #39, Curtiss P-40 Warhawk. Bunrin-Do Co., Ltd. 1993.

Flying Tigers—A Pictorial History of the American Volunteer Group, by Sydney P. Chivers. Challenge Publications.

Original photographs provided by A.V.G. members.

P-40 Hawks at War, by J. Ethell and J. Christy. Charles Scribner's Sons, 1980.

The Pictorial History of the Flying Tigers, by Larry Pistole. Moss Publications, 1981.

The Real Flying Tigers. 60-minute video shown on TV on The History Channel.

Special thanks to the Curtiss Wright Historical Association, for technical assistance with my original P-40C/ 81-A2 scale drawings.

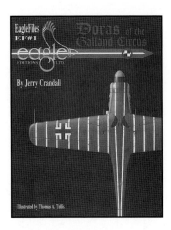
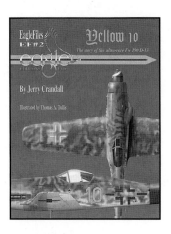
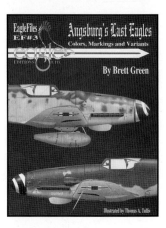
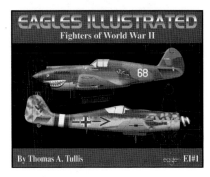
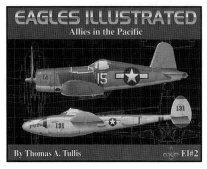

TRUE COLORS

WORLD MASTERS OF NATURAL DYES AND PIGMENTS

TRUE COLORS

WORLD MASTERS of NATURAL DYES and PIGMENTS

KEITH RECKER

Foreword by Lidewij Edelkoort

PUBLISHER: Linda Ligon
ASSOCIATE PUBLISHER: Karen Brock
EDITOR: Carol Karasik
COPY EDITOR: Katherine Bright

DESIGNER: Susan Wasinger

ON THE COVER: Juana Guitérrez Contreras, Teotitlán del Valle, Oaxaca, Mexico. Center photos by Joe Coca and Heidi Gustafson. Upper and lower photos by Keith Recker.

BOOKS

4420 Roaring Fork Court
Loveland, Colorado 80538
USA

Printed in China by Asia Pacific
ISBN 978-1-7335108-5-1
Library of Congress Control Number: 2019902328

OPPOSITE:
Shades of indigo, dyed
by Andro Wipplinger
using the formulas and
methods of Michele
Wipplinger.

ACKNOWLEDGMENTS

Deepest thanks to the talented, inspiring, and colorful subjects of this book. Their generous sharing of work, stories, and time has moved me deeply—not to mention the breathtaking hues they create. A special prayer of thanks to Porfirio Gutiérrez, Juana Gutiérrez Contreras, and Antonio Contreras, who opened their Teotitlán del Valle home and studio to us. I look forward to more cochineal, chocolate, mezcal, laughter, and affection in the future.

The team at Thrums Books communicates at wavelengths I have not often experienced, and I could not be more grateful for their patience and steadfast support in the process of making this book. Linda Ligon steers this ship with remarkable wisdom and perspective. Thanks to Mary Anne Wise for the connection.

An important part of my life in color and culture has unfolded in the company of the artists, artisans, staff, volunteers, leaders, and board members of the International Folk Art Market, whose annual event in Santa Fe, New Mexico, continues to delight and educate me. I am so deeply thankful for the good work of this organization, and for the devotion and talent that make it so vibrant.

The crew at *HAND/EYE Magazine* also bring the world's colors and textures alive in connective and constructive ways, and I salute them—as I do my friends at Pantone, who spur me on into applying what I learn about the rainbow in ever-new and ever-inventive assignments. A special nod also to Li Edelkoort and Philip Fimmano for their insight and intellect and warmth, to Sherri Donghia for her great eye and loyal friendship, and to Katharine Kuharic, who has been teaching me things about color since 1980. And, of course, a wave of gratitude to my parents, Brooke and Bill Recker, for their unique genius, and my siblings, Kevin and Kirsten, for theirs.

I dedicate this book to my partner, James, and our daughter, Katherine, without whom my life would be colorless, and to Clare Brett Smith, who set me off on a wild and life-changing cultural trek almost thirty years ago.

FOREWORD

Whenever I have encountered color in my life it has made a lasting impression. Even now, color can trigger memories of my childhood (my mother in a hand-painted skirt), of art school (learning elaborate color concepts), of the magnificence of nature (incandescent green rice fields in India dotted with bright saris), or of the splendor of humanity (a fisherman dressed in different shades of gray sampled from discarded suits).

The deep color of food, the moving shades of the ocean, the glow of a certain variety of pumpkin—and so much more—have all been inspirations, sometimes sensational, always emotional, often personal. But working as a colorist has also led me to encounter the abstraction of color, and today it seems that color has started to live its own life, to evoke a holistic identity with many facets to its personality. Color unifies and divides, it symbolizes and materializes, it codifies and simplifies. Color talks loud and clear as it descends into the streets: when pink beanies fight for emancipation or when yellow umbrellas and vests fight for human rights and equality. Color is universal—yet local at the same time.

Nowadays, the public at large has learned how to discern color perfectly. Like curators of their homes, they have understood how to handle color choices and reinterpret their cultural identity through color. They know that green can be pistachio, avocado, spinach, or wasabi; that red might be coral, that pink

could be flamingo, that brown will be chocolate, and that flesh-tone is anything but a weird type of salmon. It almost seems as if our retinas are evolving, enabling us to see more shades of each hue.

Just last year, it was revealed that the ever-popular "millennial pink" is actually a shade of the oldest color on earth! More ancient than the dinosaurs, this natural pigment was unearthed after a billion years by Australian scientists analyzing shale rock from the Sahara Desert, suddenly giving pink a completely archaeological and cultural dimension. The mines carved out by the very first humans were exploited in order to extract minerals for making color: color to paint their bodies and illustrate their society, color to dye cloth and embellish food, color to cover walls and decorate their abodes.

These first uses of color are also why the book of Genesis recently inspired me as a metaphor to conceive colors, able to describe all the harmonies in our world and their tactile aspects: from the soft browns

Bark and bark-dyed cloth
by Boubacar Doumbia

The color yielded by avocado
pits varies with the mineral
composition of
water sources

of animals to the crisp greens of plants to the metallic translucency of fish scales and the textured golds of the sun and moon. Not to be forgotten are the dense notes of darkness, harking back to anti-material, as if born before the Big Bang. Equally important in that biblical story is the color of our own skin. Ranging from porcelain white to ebony black, the scale of human tints is endless and demands specific colorings for specific incarnations. In this sense, color's range is truly inclusive of all human beings.

In the Genesis narrative, splendid colors come from the Earth (through mining), modified by the waters (through washing), embellished by the sky (through bleaching) and taken from roots, plants, and insects (through dyeing). It is in this last process that the culture of color has influenced creative beings the most. The discovery of color as a means for expression, and as a need to feel singular and unique, is as old as we are and has forced the human race to discover using feathers and pigments, grasses and bark, blood and urine, and many more plant-derived dyeing techniques. Today, peoples' keen interest in natural dyes is growing to counterbalance and eventually eradicate the detriment of synthetic colors. The fight for our survival as an endangered species is declared, and endeavors to save the planet are getting more attention. The liveliness of the tints and their capacity to transform, having lives of their own as we do—including rusting, crinkling, and fading—makes these colors feel like companions, with us forever, for better or worse.

Just last year, it was revealed that the ever-popular "millennial pink" is actually a shade of the oldest color on earth! More ancient than the dinosaurs, this natural pigment was unearthed after a billion years by Australian scientists analyzing shale rock from the Mauritanian Desert,

This is why I love color. And this is why I believe color is a language we have lost and one that we must all learn to speak again. Learning this language is what Keith Recker has wholeheartedly embraced over a lifetime. His evocative visual vocabulary and his acquired dialect in design distill the lore behind true color: whether searching for indigos around the world, tracing purple back to snails along the distant coasts of Oaxaca, or collecting botanical ingredients in local hillsides. Even in the most sacred Hindu temples, tales of blessed marigold, hibiscus, and rose petals bring color to printed textiles—a horticultural impression that is as unique as Mother Nature's own fingerprint. This book is testimony to his personal quest for color that is human in scale and individual in its storytelling, yet unanimous in its power.

Enjoy!

Lidewij Edelkoort

TABLE OF CONTENTS

vi
FOREWORD *Lidewidj Edelkoort*

1
ENGAGING WITH COLOR: *An Introduction*

4
Chapter 1 **A POINT OF SILENCE**
*Birgitta de Vos creates space
for contemplation*

8
Chapter 2 **TRADITION AND PROGRESS**
*Boubacar Doumbia uses mud cloth to create employ-
ment for young people*

18
Chapter 3 **BACK TO BLUE AND BEYOND**
*Aboubakar Fofana revives Yoruba indigo in a farm-to-
studio practice resonant with far-reaching intentions*

34
Chapter 4 **WANDERING INTO THE BLUE**
*Han Shan rejected life in industrialized China to create
blue the way his Miao foremothers taught him*

40
Chapter 5 **BLUE REVIVAL**
*Guided by fair-minded principles, the revival of indigo
production in Bangladesh counters bitter memories of
repressive colonial-era practices*

50
Chapter 6: **INDIGO GENIE**
*Indigo and porcelain explored by this mother-and-son
team Deborah and Lucas Osburn*

54
Chapter 7: **LAYER UPON LAYER**
*Artist Mary Hark dyes her handmade papers with
African indigo*

60
Chapter 8 **NEVERTHELESS
WOAD PERSISTED**
*Dyer, weaver, and teacher Aviva Leigh works exten-
sively with Europe's earliest blue dye*

66
Chapter 9 **THE LAST PURPLE**
*The ancient sea-snail purple of Mexico's coastal
Mixtec dyers and weavers is severely endangered.
Tixinda holds the future.*

74
Chapter 10 **SERIOUS SYMBOLS**
*Logwood resurfaces in the 21st century in the sustain-
ability-conscious designs of Buro Belén*

80
Chapter 11 **AUTHENTIC VOICES**
*In keeping with Zapotec tradition, Juana Gutiérrez
Contreras and Porfirio Gutiérrez employ ancient
cochineal and other natural dyestuffs in their weaving*

102
Chapter 12 **BUKHARA RED**
*Master dyer, teacher, and weaver Fatillo Kendjaev
works with millennia-old madder reds in
modern times*

110
Chapter 13 **RED RISES AGAIN**
*The Institute of Khmer Traditional Textiles helps save
the lac reds of Cambodian ikat in the post-Khmer
Rouge era*

118
Chapter 14 **IN THE WATER**
*María Elena Pombo explores the pinks of avocado pit
dyes, and along with the color variations created by
water sources around the world*

124

Chapter 15 **STALKING WILD COLOR**

*Mycologist turned natural dyer, Alissa Allen knows
how to extract gorgeous (and responsible)
color from fungi*

130

Chapter 16 **OLD WAYS, NEW TECHNIQUES**

*Australian artist India Flint draws brilliant patterns
with just eucalyptus leaves, and water,
and a little science*

142

Chapter 17 **IN THE BEGINNING**

*Like our most ancient ancestors, Heidi Gustafson is a
connoisseur of earth pigments*

152

Chapter 18 **PRECONTACT COLORS**

*Can the Ayoreo of Bolivia keep their ancient dyeing
and weaving techniques alive? Cheque Oitedie is
working for that to happen.*

162

Chapter 19 **EARTHY RAINBOW**

*Navajo dyer and weaver Irene Clark harvests rich col-
ors from gray lichens and other natural dye plants*

168

Chapter 20 **LIKE A PRAYER**

*Rupa Trivedi extracts vivid yellows from the marigold
petals left as offerings at Mumbai's renowned
Siddhivinayak Temple*

184

Chapter 21 **GOLDEN GIRLS**

*Audrey Louise Reynolds challenges fashion orthodoxy
with turmeric and other natural dyes*

188

Chapter 22 **PRECISE YELLOWS**

*Dyer, weaver, and artist Catherine Ellis embraces exac-
titude with weld and other garden-grown
natural dyestuffs*

194

Chapter 23 **INVASIVE COLOR**

*The Avani organization turns an invasive weed called
"forest killer" into beautiful, non-toxic yellow and
green dyes, crayons, and watercolors*

204

Chapter 24 **FRESH GREENS**

*Nilda Callañaupa Alvarez and the Center for Tradi-
tional Textiles of Cusco extract rare natural greens
from two local plants*

210

Chapter 25 **MINERAL SIGNATURES**

*Atelier NL turns sand collected from beaches all over
the world into place-specific greens*

216

Chapter 26 **BACK TO THE GARDEN**

*Sasha Duerr deepens her students' attachment to the
environment by using "natural color as a
gateway drug"*

234 NOTES
236 BIBLIOGRAPHY
238 INDEX
241 PHOTOGRAPHY CREDITS

A scarf dyed by the
author during a workshop
with India Flint

ENGAGING with COLOR

an introduction

As a child, I was convinced that Crayola had made a mistake: magenta should have been spelled "magneta" in recognition of the radiant, magnetic powers it deploys to penetrate the eye and reach deep into the brain. It was one of many colors that spoke to me in their own voices about their own meanings, carrying their own smells and flavors and sounds. Chrome yellows burst forward like a trumpet call, with brassy notes of optimism and (over)confidence. You danced to their tune at some peril. Dark forest greens sounded like oboes, wise but rather shy as they quietly revealed what was hiding in the shadows. You could trust them, but you had to listen very closely. Chartreuse tasted sharp, like an exotic citrus, and talked fast with the trickster voice of the violin's uppermost notes. Blood reds were salty and metallic like blood itself, intoning sensuality and warning in the inexorable voice of the piano's lowest octave—a motif throbbing constantly in the background like a living pulse.

A few years later, my first reading of writers like Nathaniel Hawthorne reassured me that I wasn't entirely alone in my immersive experience of color. The purples of "Rappaccini's Daughter" were every bit as hypnotic as magenta, telegraphing love and lust and otherness. The pink ribbon mentioned in the last moments of "Young Goodman Brown" whispered about attraction and danger, while *The Scarlet Letter* broadcast that message at full volume. Add to these the *roué* blacks of Baudelaire, the innocent whites of Shakespeare, the earthy, bawdy browns of Chaucer, not to mention the loyal blues of Vermeer, the sexy madders of Rossetti, the cynical bottle greens of Lempicka. Inevitably, I concluded that color is narrative: every shade has a specific story to deliver.

Color narratives expanded into communally experienced phenomena when my career put me in retail merchandising offices in New York and San Francisco and into artisan business development projects in the towns and villages of New Mexico, Kentucky, and a few dozen countries on five continents. Certain colors persuaded and tempted on the selling floor, and sometimes they spoke to issues of desire, comfort, and even healing. Sometimes color changes its meaning with surprising speed. As we've seen recently, the playful hot pink of Barbie accoutrements can suddenly turn, with provocation, into the protest statement of the Pussy Hat.

Some colors, rooted deeply in community traditions, spoke of shared meanings dear specifically to the people who lived there. In Luang Prabang (and elsewhere in Southeast Asia), the orange of a novice Theravada Buddhist monk's robe means one thing, whereas it means another in the marigolds of Oaxaca's Day of the Dead celebrations. A sense of context is vital to understanding color, and sometimes one's questions are not easily resolved, even with context. For example, does virtuous blue belong to the Catholic church's Virgin Mary or to left-of-center Liberals whose positions do not always jibe well with the traditional ideals of Vatican City? Because color and human experience move hand in hand, its stories are as complex as we are.

Eventually I found myself in the role of color forecaster for US-based Pantone and UK-based WGSN, as well as for individual commercial clients. This work required me to dig into the symbolism and meaning of color across time and social context, and to shape what I found into narratives that would be relevant two and three years into the future. What emotional, social, spiritual, and psychological needs would we experience in the years ahead, and what colors would satisfy us? Looking forward in time, would we crave safety or thrills, amusement or activism, tradition or rebellion . . . or some unforeseen combination of all of the above? What colors would we hunger for as we pursued these ideas?

Futuristic hungers bring me to why I had to write a book about natural color. Recent news reports warn us that we humans have few decades left to change our ways before we reach a point of no return, after which our environment's health can only decline. Few would dispute that we need to change our ways, but agreeing on which ways and how to change them is, of course, the subject of virulent debate. How do we align the interests of both people and planet in ways that make sense for the future?

The fashion and home industries contribute heavily to world pollution today, with harmful and wasteful habits in growing and sourcing materials, in manufacturing and waste disposal, in packaging, and in shipping goods all over the world. There is much room for improvement across the board. Color, so integral to our consumer choices, has a role to play in addressing our environmental challenges both through better practices and through more satisfying narratives. Embracing natural, sustainable, well-managed sources of color is an essential aspect of reforming not just fashion but consumer goods in general. Harnessing color narratives that create deeper relationships between us and our belongings can reduce consumption without sacrificing satisfaction.

Reminding one another of positive stories about our relationships to our fellow humans and our home planet is just as essential. One of the most valuable places to look for solutions to future problems is among communities with long and venerable pasts. Unfortunately, traditional cultures are often romanticized, abused, or ignored in proportion to their distance from modern life. Yet traditional peoples, such as the Mixtecs of Mexico or the Ayoreo of Bolivia who appear in this book, offer inspiring knowledge and know-how. Ancient approaches to the sustainable management of natural resources have much to teach us. Traditional comingling of botanically sourced color and botanical medicines suggests some interesting ways to revise our thoughts about what we wear and why we wear it. Traditional creators of color know much about finding mordants in leaves rather than mine shafts, and their impact on their surroundings remains admirably gentle. Just as we see an ongoing revolution in food, with the slow food and farm-to-table movements improving our awareness of not just quality but of variety, sourcing, and environmental and social impact, it's time for us to deepen our exploration of colors, fibers, and ways of making, and to evolve our consuming habits around clothing and home goods.

Embracing some older, thriftier habits even as we forge new ideas about sustainability will necessitate some aesthetic changes in our consumer decisions. But since it is high time we made those changes, they may present themselves as exactly what we're hungry for. As design groups like Buro Belén show (see page 74), the ideal of uniformity promulgated by over a century of mass manufacturing might need to give way to a more humanistic embrace of intriguing irregularity and individual character. Living like chilly unseeing machines with mountains of chilly machine-made stuff hasn't done us or our Earth much good.

I was a home merchandising director at Saks Fifth Avenue when I was introduced to weaver and natural dye expert Michele Wipplinger at some networking event or other. At our first meeting, she quite confidently proclaimed that she could make any Pantone color I would ever desire with natural dyes. I'm sure I nodded politely and changed the subject. Nevertheless, she persisted. When she eventually came to my office and opened her several cases of yarn samples, all skepticism vanished.

She had indeed mastered every color I would ever want with various combinations of the natural dye extracts she gathered from all over the world and sold through her Seattle-based studio, Earthues. Her first exposure to natural dyes happened in the early 1970s when, as a weaver, she saw that the complexity and nuance of natural color was vastly superior to synthetics. She trained with Jean Dufour, who shared his experience as a restorer and maker of tapestries at the Gobelins atelier in Paris. Later, she worked with Michel Garcia, another French expert in natural dyeing, who specializes in printing methods and diverse mordants.

In 1979, she began to offer workshops and has trained close to 500 people worldwide. If you include the audiences who attended her lectures, the number exceeds 10,000. Textile historian Mary Dusenbury credits Michele with shifting the palette of fiber artists in the Pacific Northwest with her stock of natural dye extracts and her teaching. The two workshops I took with her, one in Hanoi and one in New Harmony, Indiana, certainly deepened my own experience of color in profound ways. I still cherish a few articles of clothing I threw into her indigo vat on the last day.

When I began *HAND/EYE Magazine* in 2004 as a way to share the extraordinary creativity (and dedication to cultural preservation and social responsibility) of artisans, artists, and designers producing handmade works, Australian natural dyer India Flint reached out to me, and I had a second color revolution. Her natural color practice, featured in a chapter in this book (see page 130), challenged me with its ominous, unpredictable (except maybe to her!) beauty. A workshop I took with her in Arizona remains vivid in my mind, and I have boiled up bundles of paper and textile with weeds, windfall leaves, and garden perennials ever since.

After that, the floodgates of the world of natural color opened, and I have been fortunate to be able to know the work of extraordinary people like Aboubakar Fofana, Porfirio Gutiérrez, Juana Gutiérrez Contreras, Aviva Leigh, Rupa Trivedi, and Sasha Duerr. Working on this book has brought me into contact with still others. Their wise words, passed down to me through long conversations, emails, and phone calls, appear throughout the text alongside my own observations.

In addition to offering up the beauty of their colors, all have opened windows into their culture and their lives. I now experience certain colors not with the voices of musical instruments, but with the voices of these friends who have welcomed me into their worlds. I feel so lucky to be able to introduce readers to them now. May they enrich your world as they have enriched mine.

KEITH RECKER
March 2019

It's time for us to deepen our exploration of colors, fibers, and ways of making, and to evolve our consuming habits around clothing and home goods.

Chapter 1

Birgitta deVOS

A once-colorful Moroccan carpet whitewashed by Birgitta de Vos OPPOSITE: Birgitta de Vos, photographer, author, designer, and educator

A POINT of SILENCE

At the very beginning of the cosmos, there was darkness—
timeless, unfathomable, black. Then there was light—the
penetrating white that pierces the darkness. The white
that ignites time itself, as the book of Genesis suggests, by balanc-
ing the dark into a constant cycle of day and night. Linguists recognize black and white as the first colors to appear in all languages of
the world. Artist, photographer, and writer Birgitta de Vos engages
with primal white for both its imperturbable quiet as well as its
subtle engagement with every other color of the spectrum.

Birgitta de Vos began her career in the studio of Li Edelkoort, world-renowned trend and color forecaster, and went from there to founding her own clothing line—not just one but, over time, several. She also spent ten years at the Design Academy Eindhoven, eventually as head of its craft- and sustainability-centered Man and Humanity Master Program. Now Birgitta brings her decades of inquiry, experimentation, and careful observation to creating books and artwork that speak quietly, yet deeply, and frequently in a vocabulary of whites.

Why white? For Birgitta, white became a refuge from the ". . . never-ending story of things to do. Of lists that never seem to end. Of running faster and faster, doing more and more, without finding an end in sight and with the frustration of still running behind . . . I wasn't able to see things as they are anymore. I saw in each encounter a 'more-to-do' instead of an opportunity to enjoy what was offered."[1] Across 2012, she created a white composition each day of the year.

What did she find at the end of that yearlong commitment? "Each moment has its ending and a new beginning. With the color white, I enter a point of silence; a moment of newness. A 'just being,'" she says. A half-dozen years later, white still holds an important place in Birgitta's perception of color and the world, and in the iconography she uses to communicate both: "There is only now, and white is now. It has not been tinted by our individual perception of the past. It is not yet filled with dreams-come-true in the future. It is the crossing point. It is the void where all life sprouts from. It is in between breathing in and breathing out. It is in between the lines. It is there where something ends and something else begins."

Birgitta's artistic practice calls upon all manner of white materials: antique and vintage linens and apparel fabrics decommissioned from European convents, other natural textiles both old and new, gesso, chalk, limestone, and more. What is already white is framed, and dematerialized, with layers of other natural whites. What starts off more colorfully is abstracted and hushed with coatings and dustings and shieldings of white. Is she erasing differences and distinctions with her whitenings? Perhaps, but only in order to come to a spiritual understanding of self. "We are the universe and there are as many worlds as there are people. White shows me my own projection of the world around me.

"In my daily life, however, I like my white to be surrounded by a spectrum of skin tones and bare natural materials like undyed flax, the beige and brown tones of wood, rusted metals, a drop of black creating grays and a touch of dark black to turn on the light. White needs other colors to star and shine," Birgitta comments when coaxed to explain the meeting point between her physical world and her inner world. "In the 'real' world there is no such thing as just only white. Even if there would be only white, there would still be different shades of white depending on the materials used. Forms will be visible and their shadows will create shades of gray, depending on the surroundings, the moment of the day, and the light."

Birgitta's embrace of the noncolor of white frees her to see subtleties and nuances that might otherwise remain hidden. "In a world shouting for attention, in white I find this space."

> **"I like my white to be surrounded by a spectrum of skin tones and bare natural materials like undyed flax, the beige and brown tones of wood, rusted metals, a drop of black creating grays and a touch of dark black to turn on the light."**

Raw materials of
cotton gauze, linen
thread, gypsum,
and wax ready for
a new project

Chapter 2

Boubacar DOUMBIA

Contemporary mudcloth made at the Ndomo workshop in Ségou, Mali   OPPOSITE: Boubacar Doumbia, founder of Ndomo

TRADITION and PROGRESS

Amid growing social unrest in Bamako, Mali, during the mid-1970s, a group of art students became impatient with a heavily European academic curriculum that deliberately ignored just about anything African and Malian. Instead, they longed for a path forward into art and creativity that would reflect their own culture in ways that belonged to *them*. Six of these students banded together to create Groupe Bogolan Kasobane. The name means "prison is finished, we are free,"[1] a rallying cry for their exploration of Malian heritage. Mudcloth was their chosen medium.

As Boubacar Doumbia, one of Kasobane's founders, says, "We were the pioneers who explored mudcloth as a means of expression in the form of contemporary art. We saw mudcloth as the portal for everyone who wanted to learn." While the group's work embraced the earthy colors of mudcloth, it expanded the visual language from geometric symbols to scenes of nature and village life. In their hands, mudcloth became a school of painting.

Mudcloth in Bambara, one of the major languages of Mali, is called *bogolanfini*, a joining of the words for "mud," "made with," and "cloth." Mudcloth is indeed made with mud, but not just any mud. The process starts with dark, iron-rich silt dredged from the Niger River. Some say that March is the best time of year to send boatmen out to the middle of the river

to gather buckets of fresh sediment carried by spring torrents from the highlands of neighboring Guinea into Mali. Others, perhaps less poetically, gather it from the muck at the bottom of ponds.

Either way, the silt is decanted into large clay vessels, covered in a layer of water, and left to ferment for a year. These giant pots of mysterious dark goo are a common sight behind the homes or workshops of textile makers in Mali. They're often set three or four in a row, planted in the ground or in a low adobe *banco* to insulate the brew from extreme temperature changes. What's left at the end of the fermenting and settling process is a smooth, liquid clay slip that handles like paint.

Before the advent of machine-made goods, the slip was used to dye soft, lofty handspun cotton fab-

A sampling of contemporary patterns
OPPOSITE: A group of Ndomo student artists

ric, woven in strips about as wide as a human hand and sewn together to create blankets or panels for clothing. Strip-woven cotton is still sometimes used, though lately it has largely been replaced by a less august cotton cloth somewhat akin to light cotton duck. Cotton must be mordanted in a tannin-rich bath for the mud to do its dyeing work. The leaves of the *nglama* tree are often used, turning the cloth a bright ochre-yellow color that hardly mellows as it dries against the dry, red earth.

Traditional Bambara artisans then trace ancient ideograms onto the vivid yellow cloth, recalling a time almost out of memory when a sacred bogolan-fini garment telegraphed messages about its wearer. A double line of opposing zigzags means "the brave man's belt." A single tooth-like line of connected triangles means "the jealous husband's teeth." An hourglass shape represents the drum used to call warriors to battle. Women wore mudcloth, too, and some ideograms relate to female roles. A dot within a circle describes a traditional round house and the family living within it. A group of four circumflexes declares the wearer to be a woman of leisure.

In older mudcloth from the area around Bamako, these ideograms appeared against a dark, mud-dyed background, requiring a bogolanfini maker to brush mud over the surface of the cloth, meticulously avoiding the geometric shapes of the ideograms. As many as four coats of mud were required to create deep black tones. In some rural communities, browns were prized over blacks, because brown provided better camouflage for hunters. This meant more layers of nglama and other tannin-based pigments and less coverage of mud. Once the tinting and washing process was complete, the mudcloth maker whitened the ideograms by brushing them with mild bleaching agents.

Today, creativity around mudcloth has exploded, thanks to the influence of the Kasobane pioneers, as well as to the expansion of tourist and international markets. The black of mud, the browns and yellows of nglama, and the white of cotton have been joined by indigo blues, olive greens, and a host of other colors. Traditional ideograms still appear, but often in a context of freehand geometry and figural elements— the personal vision of each innovative artist.

OPPOSITE (top row): Nglama leaves mordant the fabric and dye it yellow ochre   OPPOSITE-MIDDLE AND BOTTOM ROWS: Whitening pattern elements, followed by an application of mud   HERE: The final application of mud creates a tone-on-tone effect

Forty years after founding Kasobane, the legendary Boubacar Doumbia is still focused on mudcloth, not only as an art form but also as a way to address the serious need for education and employment among young people. More than 50 percent of Mali's population is under the age of eighteen. The education system is weak, and there is little social safety net. In 2004, Boubacar founded an organization called Ndomo, based in his hometown of Ségou, which provides essential entrepreneurial training (including literacy, numeracy, and basic financial skills) and workshops in the art of mudcloth. Ndomo's two-year apprenticeship program features incentives to complete the course, encourages personal savings, and emphasizes a sense of community and collaboration. Boubacar's model development program has been successful enough to be replicated in other communities in Mali, and to bring Boubacar a well-earned reputation as a social entrepreneur.

At the Ndomo facility, young men and women are usually working side by side in the large, open workshop. With long-necked squeeze bottles in hand, they apply fine lines of mud dye or bleaching agent to yellow, brown, and blue cloth. Some artists still use brushes to cover large areas in mud, but most seem to value the background colors they've dyed, and their overlaid pattern work doesn't obscure them. The old ideograms pop up here and there, but so do assemblages of contemporary pattern, animal figures, and depictions of daily life unfolding outside the atelier. In some cases, stencils are used to create crisp black motifs on white backgrounds—a reversal of the tradition of white symbols on black.

Whatever the look of the work at Ndomo, the young people make the decisions, which means the art form is alive. Creativity is in the air and so is a hopeful feeling of purpose and self-determination; mudcloth is both an ancient art and a modern agent of social change.

LEFT: The inner courtyard
of the Ndomo center in
Ségou, Mali
HERE: A bleaching agent
creates pattern on a
vegetable-dyed background

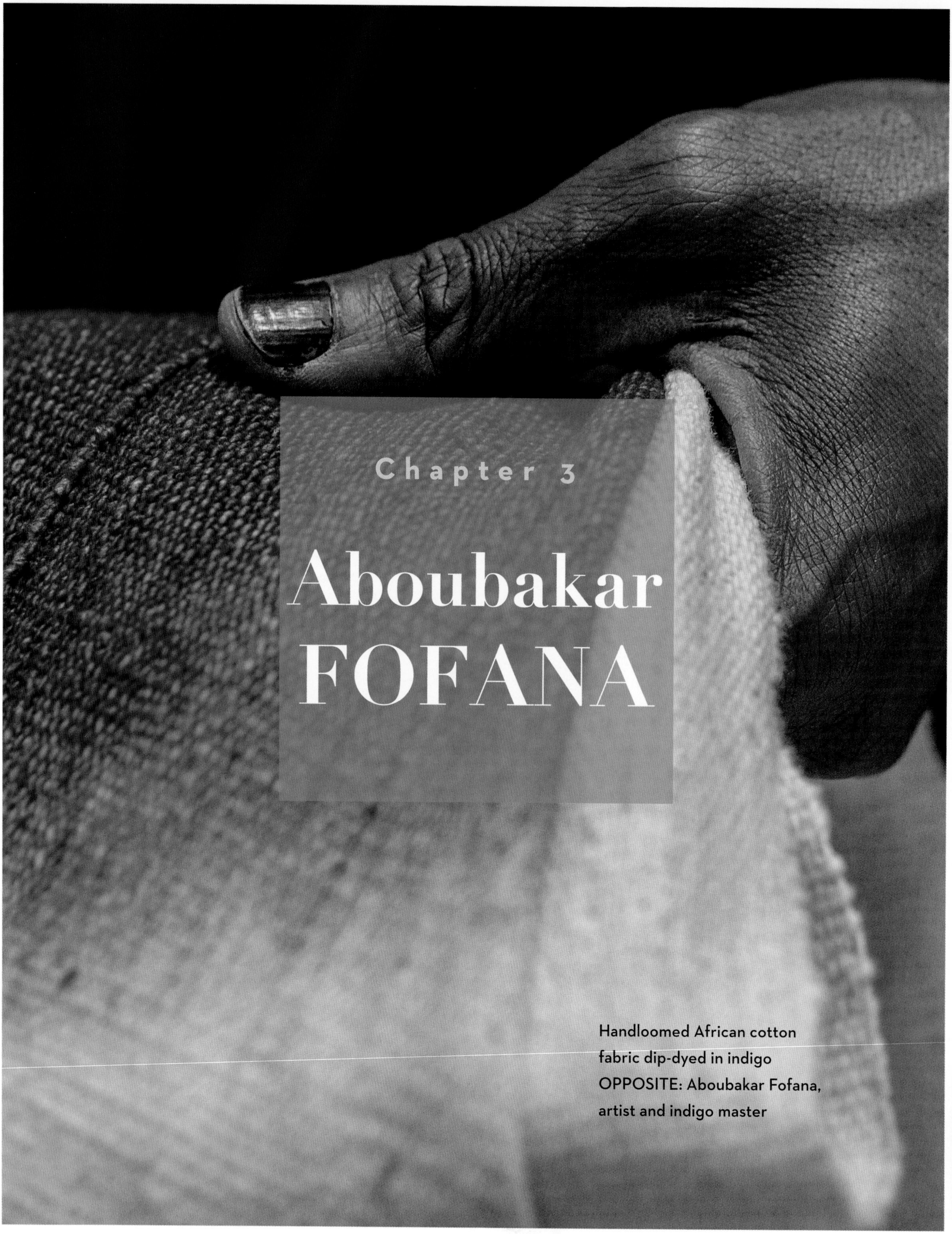

Chapter 3

Aboubakar FOFANA

Handloomed African cotton fabric dip-dyed in indigo
OPPOSITE: Aboubakar Fofana, artist and indigo master

BACK to BLUE and Beyond

A boy walks deep in a West African forest with his cousins, hearing the dark green leaves of the trees stir in the breeze, aware of the subtle movements of birds and animals, and the even subtler presence of the ancient spirits of these woods and meadows, unconcerned about a group of children walking in their midst.

Perhaps they will make their way to the river that flows nearby, stopping to swim at one of several waterfalls. But first, they need to find the plants their grandmother has asked them to gather. A respected elder known for her healing work, she has begun to teach her grandchildren about medicinal plants in Koniagui, her mother tongue. She has asked them to gather wild turmeric root, used in a variety of ways; a sort of basil she calls *soukolan*, for funeral preparations; and *gala*, a legume used as an antiseptic and anti-inflammatory.

One afternoon, when seven-year-old Aboubakar Fofana returned home to deliver the harvest to his grandmother, a woman in her household told him to crush the leaves of a gala tendril between his fingers. Its sap turned his fingers blue—a surprise that rooted itself within him.

"It stayed in my mind from when I first saw it," he recalls. "I realized that plants could give both

Knowing that plants could give colors really grabbed my mind and made me think about the potential that exists inside natural beings. It was also a link to my first home . . . Indigo has such a long history and strong presence in West Africa that, for me, it was symbolic of what I had lost and needed to find."

healing and color."

Not long after this idyllic moment, Aboubakar's world changed dramatically. He went from the villages and forests near the border between Mali and Guinea, from a life of nature and family, to a bleak *banlieue* on the outskirts of Paris where he was sent to live with an uncle he barely knew. "Everything I knew was gone in an instant," he says. "There was no comparison to Africa. This was a completely different place. It wouldn't be too much to say that I was completely lost for a long time."

But Aboubakar Fofana did not stay lost. "Growing up in a concrete jungle, through an adolescence untethered from everything I knew, I was full of energy and also full of anger. I was starting to really get in trouble. At a critical point, I found myself in a calligraphy exhibit in London, and there I met a woman named Sue Cavendish. She began talking to me about how, in order to create these beautiful scripts I was looking at, I would need to be in control of myself with extreme attention and awareness. I started

LEFT: Freshly gathered leaves of Yoruba indigo from Aboubakar's indigo farm
HERE: Crushed *Lonchocarpus cyanescens* turns fingers blue

to think that maybe I could do this. And quite rapidly, it became an obsession, because it did begin to give me discipline. I found myself through the medium of calligraphy."

Aboubakar's transition from ink to indigo was an organic process. "I was always thinking about what I had seen when I was very young, eventually reading about it. It was a logical progression when I returned to Africa, fully committed to my art. Knowing that plants could give colors really grabbed my mind and made me think about the potential that exists inside natural beings. It was also a link to my first home. During my time in France, I knew I was missing something, that I had started to learn about nature and wasn't finished. In a way, I was fundamentally incomplete. Indigo has such a long history and strong presence in West Africa that, for me, it was symbolic of what I had lost and needed to find."

BLUE ORIGINS

Present in Egypt for more than 4,400 years, indigo's history in West Africa dates back at least to the eleventh century, based on textile remnants documented by archaeologists in the 1960s and 1970s in a long range of 500-meter-high sandstone cliffs called the Bandiagara Escarpment. The Tellem people, so named by the Dogon, the next group to inhabit the area, buried their dead alongside clothing and textiles in natural openings high in the cliffs above their remarkably beautiful pueblo-like settlements. By sealing the burial chambers with clay, the Tellem protected them from the elements. Hundreds of surviving textile fragments show accomplished use of both cottons and animal fibers, as well as several natural dyes. Foremost among those dyes is indigo, used in plain and weft-faced fabrics, as well as in other, more elaborate weaving techniques.[1]

How indigo came to be used in West Africa remains an open question. Did it travel westward from Egypt or southward from the Maghreb? The great Sahara has all but erased the tracks of the dyers, weavers, and traders who may have brought indigo to this part of the world and made it part of the culture. Or is it possible that the complex process of extracting blue dye from green leaves developed, as it seems to have done in many parts of the world, from the imagination and invention of the people who lived here? The climates of sub-Saharan Africa are notoriously hard on textiles, and the archaeological record is nearly nonexistent. We may never know the full story.

Jenny Balfour-Paul's extremely thorough and readable 2011 book on indigo relates an origin myth from Liberia that says, "post-menopausal women gained from the High God the secret of dyeing with indigo thanks to a seeress who broke off a piece of

OPPOSITE: Pounded *Lonchocarpus cyanescens* is shaped into little balls, which, after drying, will be pulverized and added to a dye vat HERE: The foamy "flower" that forms atop a healthy indigo vat

Aboubakar Fofana's guinea fowl pattern, made with indigo and mud dye in a tie-dyeing technique

the blue sky to eat." During a visit in 2008 to a group of women indigo dyers not far from Cotonou, Benin, I heard a similar myth from the dyer in charge. When she finished her tale, one of her colleagues merrily put a less mystical spin on things: "The truth is that they gave it to us old women because it smells so bad no one else would do it."

MEANINGS, MEDICINES, AND METHODS

Humor aside, over more than a millennium in West Africa, indigo has gathered deep social and spiritual significance. In Bambara, Mali's most commonly spoken language, the name for the deepest shade of vat-dyed indigo—an interstellar blue-black—is *lomassa*. It means divine blue, a reference to the infinite night sky, to the primeval darkness from which every life emerges and to which it returns. Lomas-

sa's dark color is still a symbol of high status among many West African ethnic groups—in part a spiritual association and in part a reflection of the time, expense, and skill required to create it.

Among the Dogon, whose most accomplished dyers still use a traditional language of gorgeous tie-dye patterns laden with meaning, indigo dyeing is considered risky business. Traditionally, dyers belong to a "caste of artisans who work with substances that have a high, though potentially destructive, spiritual energy."[2] In several parts of the world, the failure of an indigo vat signaled death or other troubles on the horizon.

But when the indigo vat succeeds, beautifully positive associations emerge along with the beautiful color. Nigerian-born *adire* artist Gasali Adeyemo uses indigo extensively in his work. He describes indigo blue as a "color of love," often worn at weddings and naming ceremonies in his home community. "People in a happy relationship wear indigo clothing to show their love for each other. Also, when someone dies, we use indigo cloth to show how much the person is going to be missed. The husband or wife, whichever is still living, wears indigo for at least eight days after the death."[3]

Saharan Tuareg groups are traditionally identified by their dark blue head wraps, *tagelmousts*, whose deep color is sometimes enhanced by beating additional indigo pigment into the fibers with a wooden mallet. The highly valued cloth finished in this way rubs blue onto the skin of the wearer, perhaps useful as an antiseptic and a sunscreen, and gives the Tuareg their nickname, the Blue Men of the Desert.

As Aboubakar's grandmother knew, indigo-bearing plants are not only potent with aesthetic potential, they are also healing botanicals, used topically to disinfect wounds and to ease the symptoms of leprosy and other skin diseases as well as arthritis. She also used indigo-dyed textiles to assist in healing simply by coming into contact with their wearer's skin. Gasali describes how healers in his village would gather leaves from exhausted dye vats for use in pastilles swallowed to assuage stomach upset or dysentery. Modern scientific research is also uncovering interesting potential for Yoruba indigo in the treatment of psychotic disorders, an investigation suggested by the use of indigo in Nigerian folk medicine.[4]

Yoruba indigo (*Lonchocarpus cyanescens*), an indigenous legume, is the indigo-bearing plant most often used in West Africa. The plant's concentration of indigotin is highest in the rainy season, just before

His intensely artisanal approach, from seed to scarf, cannot be scaled up. Each plant needs its season to grow. The time and skill and fiber and dye required to make one scarf does not change just because the customer is willing to buy fifty items.

flowering. Leaves and stems are harvested and pounded with massive wooden mortars and pestles. The resulting pulp is shaped into palm-sized balls and dried in the sun for a few days. As many as 150 of these balls might be used in a dye bath to produce the darkest shades of indigo blue.[5]

When a vat of indigo is fresh and young, a glossy blue foam (referred to as a "flower") rises atop the dark greenish-amber liquid. An unmordanted cloth will color quickly with just a brief dip into this dye. The cloth emerges tinged with green and only gradually turns blue through exposure to oxygen. Each pass in the vat imparts a bit more colorant, with indigo's darker shades requiring at least eight immersions and sometimes two dozen, depending on the dyer, the dyestuff, and the vat.

How do green leaves produce a blue dye? Macerating indigo leaves releases indican, a water-soluble derivative of tryptophan, into a dye vat. Fermentation, fueled by living microorganisms, reduces the amount of oxygen in the vat, which breaks indican into sugars and indoxyl, a colorless substance sometimes called "white indigo." Indoxyl will coat most fibers immersed in the vat and then oxidize into blue when removed and exposed to air. The process may sound simple, but vast amounts of skill and experience are required to realize fermented indigo's full beauty with any consistency. An accomplished indigo dyer knows how to prepare the yarns or textiles that will be dyed, as well as how to set up the vat for successful fermentation. Throughout the lifetime of a dye vat, he or she must monitor temperature, alkalinity, circulation within the vat, and much more.[6]

THE MAKING of a MASTER

Aboubakar's status as highly skilled master dyer came slowly. "I succeeded in making a vat through lots of experimentation, based partly on what I had learned through old French Colonial–era texts I found in libraries. But making the vat was not the hardest thing at all. The hardest thing was to keep the vat alive. I must have killed so many vats, maybe more than a hundred, trying to keep the bacteria alive long enough to force the reduction of oxygen and produce luminous blues."

His path toward unlocking the potential of indigo-bearing plants was made more difficult by the dearth of African colleagues. "There was no one to teach me in Africa. I traveled so much to gather information, but in all of the places I traveled to, [fermented] indigo was already lost. Synthetic dyes had already taken over, and people were talking to me about things their grandmothers or great-grandparents had done." While Aboubakar did learn about many traditional West African textile details—the elaborate fringing of Soninke shawls called *dissa*, for example—he became an indigo dyer with all of the optimism, as well as the obstacles, of an autodidact.

Eventually, thanks to a 2001 grant from Villa Medicis Hors les Murs, Aboubakar spent six months in Japan with indigo master Masazuku Akiyama. "The only language we had in common was that of indigo, and we exchanged through that medium a shared passion. This was not a teacher-pupil exchange, this was a genuine sharing between two people from two different cultures who had so much in common." The self-taught Malian master found, alongside someone from halfway around the world, a chance to reinforce and refine what he already knew, and to fully engage with the ancient but still living ways of indigo dyeing.

In the wake of this collaboration, Aboubakar's work, with its complex layers of African, European, and Japanese exposure, garnered much attention in France and elsewhere. Because of his growing reputation, Aboubakar's artistic practice now reaches customers around the world and also touches the of lives of his entire community.

Starting usually with *Lonchocarpus cyanescens*, the plant that turned his fingers blue as a boy, Aboubakar brings teeming life to his 350-liter clay dye vats. He now knows well the habits of the strains of bacteria active in the process (likely *Alkalibacillus, Amphibacillus,* and *Oceanobacillus*)[7] and monitors the health of each vat by what he sees, what he smells, and sometimes by the taste of a finger dipped into the liquid. Like all living organisms, the bacteria require nourishment, and the glucose-rich foods they thrive on are delicious—porridge, honey, and crushed date powder among them. A respectful rhythm of nourishment, resting time, and dye activity keeps his vats vibrantly alive for up to fourteen months, throughout which Aboubakar brings into being twelve distinct shades of indigo blues, from pale and ethereal *baga fu* to dark and mysterious *lomassa.*

"Each of my blues has its own emotion," he affirms. Delicate baga fu, the blue of nothingness, speaks in whispers about pale dawns and misty twilights, of quiet beginnings and peaceful denouements. *Baga kènè*, lively blue, engages the eye with a playful,

OPPOSITE: Swatches of indigo-dyed fabric from a
workshop offered by Aboubakar Fofana
HERE: *Baga fu,* the pale "blue of nothingness"

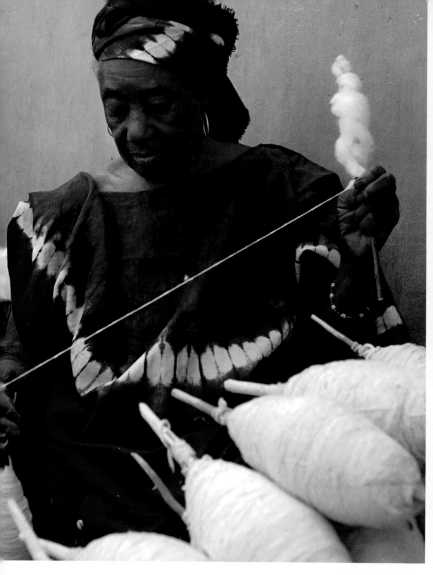

youthful energy. Mighty lomassa, of course, connects us to the great, deep Unknown, with its promise of ultimate wisdom and understanding. The depth of meaning in Aboubakar's work reflects his own spirituality as well as his heritage as the grandson of a healer: "When I make a textile, I am putting all my belief into that textile because it is an extension of my spiritual practice. The textiles contain healing and protective properties as well."

HEAVEN AND EARTH

In Aboubakar's atelier, located outside of Bamako, the capital of Mali, the extent of his metaphysical and aesthetic intentions is not hard to see. Aboubakar farms his own indigo plants. At first, growing his own supply of indigo seemed merely a smart move; it spared him from making a time- and resource-consuming 2,000-kilometer round-trip in a truck to source his raw material in the forests of Guinea. In short order, the increased quality of the homegrown dyestuff showed itself in the clarity and intensity of the resultant blues. And a deeper involvement in the growing cycle of his source of blue enhanced Aboubakar's sense of his own work. "It's very visceral, my connection to this raw material, from seeds to plants. The whole life cycle of this living thing is very important to me."

Growing indigo soon extended into growing cotton. Aside from some imported linens and cashmeres, Aboubakar has achieved vertical integration of his supply chain in Mali. He follows fiber and dye plant from sowing to harvest, and all the way through to finished textile. In the process, he himself is growing, too. "It's not at all the easiest thing, but I am learning such a lot, not only about plants but about all the skills that are needed on our farm. It brings me into contact with people I might not otherwise have met

LEFT to RIGHT: Hand spinning African cotton yarn. Drop spindles are used. Cotton enters the dye vat.

in such intimate circumstances, and it's greatly enriched my life." This intimacy explains the farm's recent cultivation of carrots, onions, zucchini, cabbage, and other vegetables to feed members of the atelier and their extended families. The work cannot be done with one pair of hands alone, and all involved must flourish for it to be done well and with dignity.

REMAKING WHAT WAS LOST

In conversation with Aboubakar, the definition of "all involved" quickly expands beyond himself and his story to the dozens of people who work with him in his atelier, to the community working on his farms, to the entire country of Mali, and to all of West Africa.

On a personal level, his art and his farm have re-created what he lost when he was taken to Paris as a young boy. The sense of community and the intimacy with nature he longed for in his urban life are now

his again. Because he built them himself, they can't be taken away, and this sense of stability, of groundedness, is palpable in both the work and the man.

Not content with recapturing what he lost as a person, this earthly foundation serves Aboubakar as a stable base from which to imagine repairing some of the post-Colonial ills of his home country. He sees the way he grows and makes indigo in twenty-first-century Mali as inherently political—an essential ingredient to, and an example of, a healthy, dignified future for his society.

"In the work that I do, in the textiles I produce, there is something quite political there, about being able to trace the whole supply chain that goes into these products. Since indigo completely left this area of West Africa many decades ago, we've been sold shoddy replacements for the beautiful fabrics and clothing we used to produce ourselves. Mali is a dumping ground for the discarded clothing of Western countries, and so we end up wearing the third-rate castoffs of people from other countries. Even local people no longer know what real indigo looks like. Being able to trace my work right back to its source, an indigenous plant that was cultivated for thousands of years, is a way of saying 'No, this is what we are really capable of, this is our true history, not what is dumped on us, or what has been assigned to us.' In having control over every step of my process, I want to tangibly demonstrate a truth of something innately African."

His passionate argument for African sourcing and African production intensifies in his thinking about cotton. "Cotton is and always has been present in Malian culture. Mali used to be the single biggest producer of cotton in Africa. In our cosmology, a celestial bird brought all the seeds that humans needed to raise for food, and with those seeds, the bird also brought the seeds of cotton. Mali used to have an astounding range of beautiful indigenous cottons, in many differ-

OPPOSITE: A simplified, fringed
dissa made by Aboubakar Fofana
HERE: Aboubakar's indigo
shibori on linen

ent colors and qualities, but when the French came, they wanted to control the production and privatize it for profit, and they broke the intimate relationships of farmers, spinners, weavers, dyers, traders, and in breaking this, they broke something very fundamental in Malian society. More than 90 percent of our cotton crops are exported for transformation because there is not a single cotton gin or mill in Mali. We have an astounding need here for work, for infrastructure, and yet the rupture that colonialism introduced sees one of our biggest resources, something we have done spectacularly well, taken entirely out of our hands. We see none of the benefits from our crops in Mali. We just get the used clothes made from it dumped on us at the end of their life cycle."

Aboubakar's activist energy extends beyond farm and atelier and into the way he sells his product, with a refusal to sit at the bottom of a supply chain just because his work is made by hand in Mali. He will not sell to traditional retailers, whose need for markup creates intense downward price pressure on all sources, including Aboubakar. His sense of responsibility to meet the needs of all the families who are part of his process is simply too great to shortchange his community.

In practical terms, he may be very wise to refuse. His intensely artisanal approach, from seed to scarf, cannot be scaled up. Each plant needs its season to grow. The time and skill and fiber and dye required to make one scarf does not change just because the customer is willing to buy fifty items. He may be giving up the chance to expand his operation more quickly, but he also sidesteps the sacrifices of quality, time, and creativity that often come with expansion. Instead, he sells directly to collectors and small boutique owners who are drawn to Aboubakar's gorgeous work.

These connoisseurs are a loyal and encouraging market. Some of them understand Aboubakar's reasons for vertical integration, as well as his search for

fairness in the global economy, and see their purchases not only as a way to support him but also as a chance to step away from the consumer habits that compromise the dignity of both maker and market. As the artist notes, "You don't need a lot of clothing, you just need the right clothing, and it should be made properly by people who are paid properly, who are respected for their skills and artisanship."

His aesthetic sense, joined with his sense of purpose, has brought him to the attention of the international art world. In 2016 and 2018, Aboubakar participated in Documenta 14 in Kassel, Germany, and Athens, Greece, with work that addresses the African diaspora as well as the culture, depth, and diversity of natural indigo itself. Inclusion in shows at prestigious galleries such as Sean Kelly New York has followed. When asked if his growing role as a contemporary artist changes his view of himself or his work, he answers thoughtfully: "Everything I do is really the same work, just different stages of expressions of it. No matter where it appears, I want my work to carry its principles and reasons for creation and stories with it, and for people to exchange with me, to learn a different way of interacting with value."

That answer sounds like something the spirits of the forests of his boyhood would notice. And appreciate.

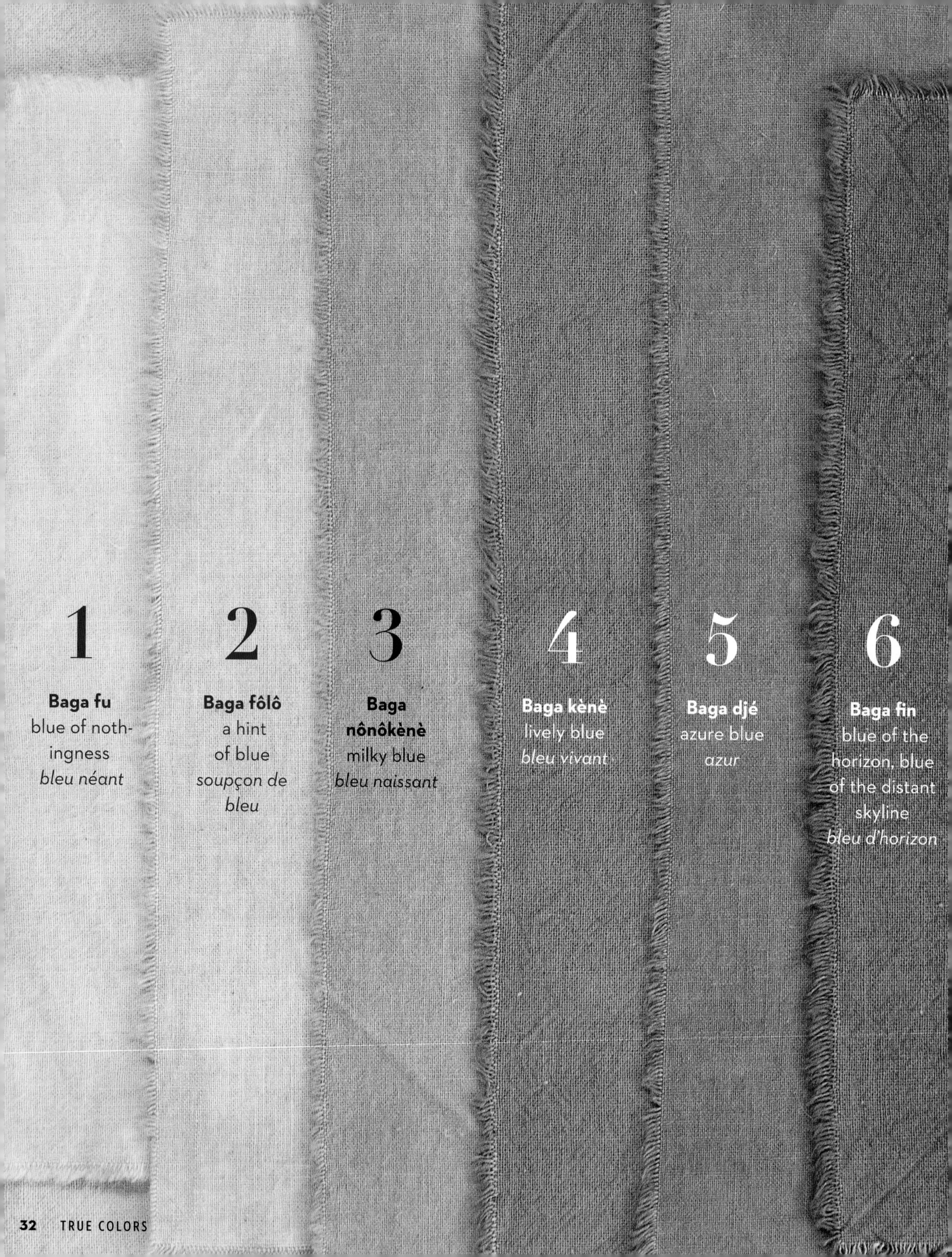

1

Baga fu
blue of noth-
ingness
bleu néant

2

Baga fôlô
a hint
of blue
*soupçon de
bleu*

3

**Baga
nônôkènè**
milky blue
bleu naissant

4

Baga kènè
lively blue
bleu vivant

5

Baga djé
azure blue
azur

6

Baga fin
blue of the
horizon, blue
of the distant
skyline
bleu d'horizon

The Twelve Shades of Indigo

7

Baga kalé
ltramarine
u outremer

8

Baga djalan
assertive
blue
bleu absolu

9

Lomassa
divine blue
bleu divin

10

Lomassa djè
light divine sky
ciel divin clair

11

Lomassa dun
deep divine sky
ciel divin foncé

12

Lomassa fin
profound
divine sky
ciel divin profond

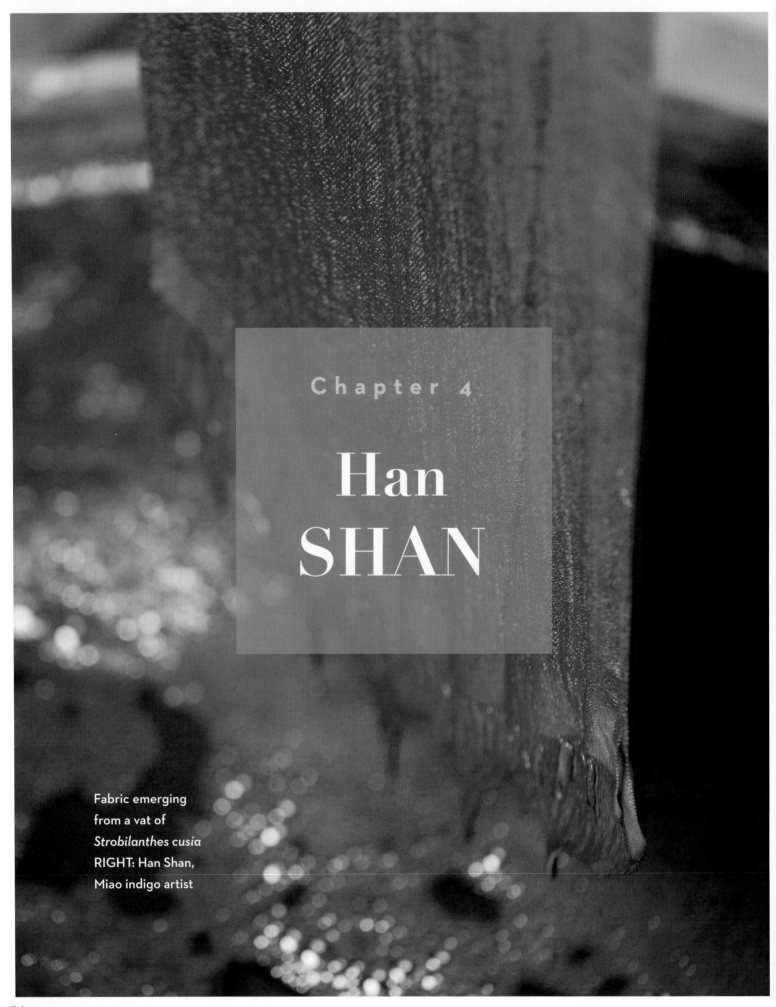

Chapter 4

Han
SHAN

Fabric emerging
from a vat of
Strobilanthes cusia
RIGHT: Han Shan,
Miao indigo artist

WANDERING into the BLUE

The third century and the twenty-first century meld poetically together in the elfin form of Han Shan. Once part of the massive migration from rural to urban China, Shan was a city dweller for a time. He survived the separation from grass, earth, plants, flowers, and family, and the grinding repetition of factory work, for about a year. He walked away one day and kept walking for fifteen years until he settled down for a while in the village of Mingyue near Chengdu to practice his singularly artistic version of traditional Miao indigo dyeing.

His mother, skilled in the indigo traditions of her Miao foremothers, taught Shan what she knew. Starting with *Strobilanthes cusia*, a purple-flowering perennial Shan calls "the blue herb," Miao dyers compost and ferment this indigo-bearing plant in much the same way as woad in Europe and *Polygonum tinctorium* in Japan. Intricate Miao indigo and white patterns made with a beeswax-resist batik technique date from at least the early third century CE, and possibly as early as the beginning of the Han dynasty in 206 BCE. In the absence of a written language, batiks—and song—keep alive the tales of the Miao, who, with 5,000 years of history, are one of China's oldest peoples.

Shan's fifteen-year "urban detox," carried out on foot across Tibet, Xinjiang, Gansu, Ningxia, and Yunnan, helped him refocus on his heritage without losing his own voice. His blues are often not the near-blacks of traditional Miao textiles. Instead, he plays with cobalt and cerulean and powdery sky blues. His patterns are not ancient, intricate geometries signaling old stories. Shan deals more in autobiographies of sweeping, gestural clouds and mountains, with one deer and one man sharing the view. It's not hard to imagine this solitary man crooning "Country Roads" as he strolls: Shan is a John Denver fan, and he sings as he works.

Han Shan recently disappeared from his beautiful studio. Tea and halvah are no longer served there. No bamboo flute notes waft down the stone terraces to the river. No gorgeous blues are being made there today. Shan is possibly detoxing from his popularity with the urban tourists visiting his studio. "In these hasty times, I just want to do something slow," he said. Certainly, Shan is gathering new textile stories to tell when he settles down again.

HERE: Han Shan's freehand batik flowers RIGHT: Bringing a bundled fabric out of the vat

HERE: A fringed silk scarf
dip-dyed in indigo
OPPOSITE: (top) Han
Shan's hands are perennially
blue (bottom) Drying fabric
after dyeing

living BLUE

Shibori dyeing and running stitch are frequently paired at Living Blue OPPOSITE: Masud Rana, Soptomi Rani, and Mohammad Enamul, members of the Living Blue dyeing team

BLUE REVIVAL

N*ilpharmari*, a word coined by the British for the growing of *Indigofera tinctoria*, means "the cultivation of blue." Bangladeshi social enterprise Living Blue farms gorgeous indigo whose aesthetic worth is matched by the community assets it creates on the way from farm fields to an international marketplace thirsty for authenticity and high quality.

The history of indigo cultivation on the subcontinent goes back many millennia to the Bronze Age Indus Valley civilization of Mohenjo Daro, where archaeologists have found evidence of indigo dyes. Starting in 1777, when Britain no longer had access to the slave plantations of the United States as a source of indigo, indigo crops from what was known as East Bengal became incredibly valuable for export. A vicious system of high-interest loans luring farmers into purchasing necessary farming supplies created an inescapable cycle of debt, poverty, terrible working conditions, and exhaustion of farmland. This combination created the Indigo Revolt of 1859–1860, viewed by some as the first nonviolent protest on the subcontinent's long road to independence. Nonviolence notwithstanding, reprisals from local and colonial authorities were brutal.

Shortly afterward, synthetic dyes swept the globe, and indigo cultivation at any scale disappeared in what is now Bangladesh because of the lack of economic reward as well as the lingering memory of abhorrent conditions and labor practices. Just over ten years ago, however, indigo regained a foothold here. "Living Blue restarted indigo dye production in 2006, and ever since, we have grown by leaps and bounds. Living Blue is currently the only producer of *Indigofera tinctoria* and the leading practitioner of true Bengal natural indigo dye in Bangladesh," says Mishael Aziz Ahmad, CEO of Living Blue and instrumental in its founding.

The farm-to-textile process at Living Blue is entirely local. Starting with high-quality homegrown seeds planted in late February or early March to take advantage of rain-soaked soil, mature plants are har-

HERE: Stitched and folded fabric goes for a dip in the indigo vat. OPPOSITE: Flakes of Living Blue's organic indigo pigment

vested by small, independent growers. Chopped and loaded into large tanks within two hours of harvest, plant material macerates in warm water for several days. The sludge that settles at the bottom is then shifted to oxidation tanks, where, mixed with water, it is circulated through pipes and sprinkler heads and stirred with bamboo sticks to maintain oxygenation. The sludge is again left to settle, excess water is drained off, and the beautiful blue indigo slurry at the bottom of the tanks is boiled in small batches to remove moisture. The resulting thick slurry is strained and spread out in shallow trays to dry in the sun. Flakes of dried pigment, known as indigo lake, are ground into fine powder ready to place in a fermentation vat.

Living Blue reserves about 300 kilos of indigo pigment a year for its own dyeing production and sells over a ton to other dyers and sellers of fine dyestuffs globally.

BEAUTIFUL BLUES

Indigo is more than a natural dyestuff. *Indigofera tinctoria*, a legume that enriches the soil with nitrogen, is used in crop rotation with grains and vegetables. The plants do not require anything other than monsoon rains to flourish, making indigo a fairly undemanding crop as well.

After the harvesting of the leaves, stems provide fuel for cooking fires at home. Even post-fermentation/post-dyeing effluent is released into the fields as a substitute for man-made nitrogen fertilizers.

CHANGING LIVES

Living Blue is co-owned by CARE Social Ventures (CSV), an affiliate of the global nonprofit organization CARE International, and by Nijera Cottage and Village Industries (NCVI), which represents 3,000 local farmers and more than 200 artisans and dyers. "The management team consists mostly of people

from the community. All proceeds from the business go back to the community, for their welfare and for expansion of the business," says Mishael. "Many of our artisans who have been with the company for several years now have saved and bought lands, constructed homes, sent children to school, and are having a decent and dignified life."

Living Blue artisans can apply for zero-interest loans, receive maternity and health benefits, and are paid punctually every month. The organization also conducts regular free health camps for artisans and their family members. These services are important in the Rangpur area of Bangladesh, which is mostly rural and remote.

Living Blue artisan Sona Rani Roy is a master quilter from Dinajpur. One of her white-on-white quilts was selected as one of twenty-six finalists out of 3,951 applicants for the Loewe Craft Prize 2017. Sona's involvement with Living Blue has changed her life:

> I had no work, and my husband had little income back in 2006. One day I came to know people from CARE Bangladesh who were visiting our villages. I expressed my interest in being associated with them. Then I was given training as a "natural leader," and later on, training in quilting skills. I could always quilt, which I learned from my mother and grandmother, but never before put it to commercial use. I had no idea I possessed a great skill. Now I am a cluster leader of some thirty artisans. With the newfound income, I slowly built my dream, which is my family. I bought lands, reconstructed our house, sent my kids to school.

OPPOSITE: (top) Finishing the edges of *kantha* patchwork. (bottom) Preparing indigo shibori for shipment to customers
HERE: Precise shibori patterns are created by wrapping fabric around a tube and tying it tightly with string

1. Harvesting and weighing organic, small-holder-grown *Indigofera tinctoria*   2 The indigo goes into deep tanks for maceration until sediment forms   3 Sediment and water circulate constantly in a second holding tank   4 The resultant sludge is boiled in small batches   5 Boiled indigo is spread out to dry in shallow trays   6 Flakes of pigment form

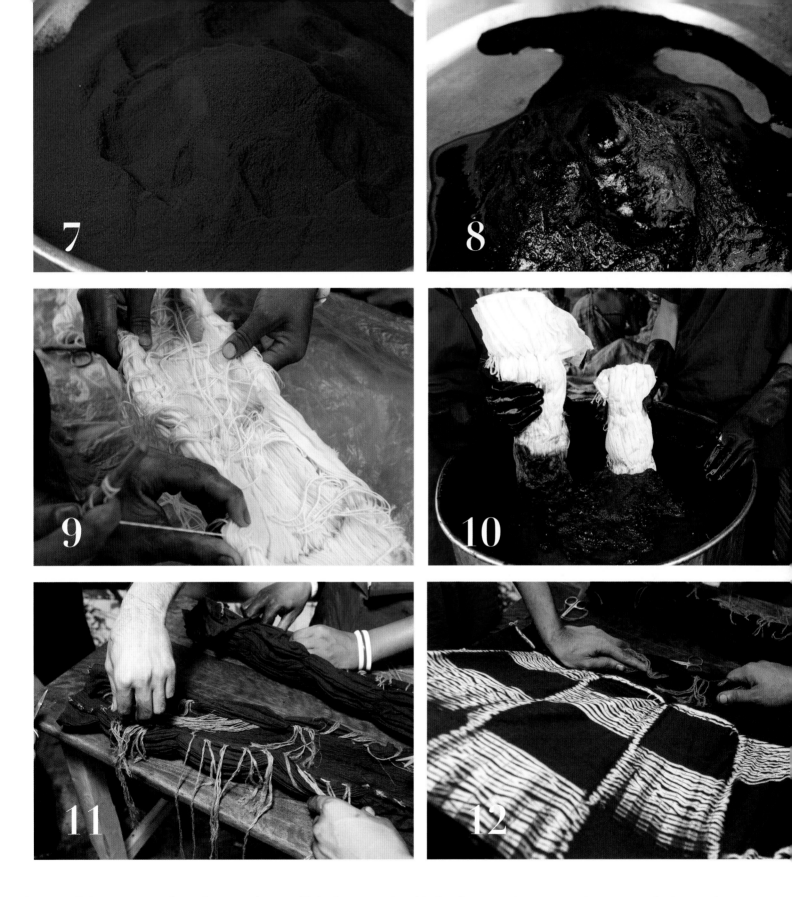

7 Pigment flakes are ground into fine powder   8 Slaked pigment is added to fermentation vats on the way to a dyeing session
9 A length of fabric folded and stitched for shibori dyeing   10 A dip in the indigo vat   11 After drying, shibori threads are pulled and the fabric dries   12 Squares of solid indigo and shibori alternate

GLOBAL REACH

Both ethics and truly sublime artisan skills are integral to Living Blue's successful entry into the global marketplace. Running-stitch techniques, known as *kantha* in this part of the world, come into play, of course. But other techniques are also layered into Living Blue textiles. Japanese *shibori* techniques (where tie-dye patterns are formed by stitching and gathering fabric prior to dyeing) are deployed to make undulating, wave-like patterns called *mokume* (a Japanese term, borrowed from metalwork, referring to a wood-grain-like texture), which are prized for their supple graphic movement. Kantha stitching joins layers of sheer cotton mokume with an old sewing technique called *dheu*, a gently gathered running stitch whose rolling puckers also resemble the movement of water. The combination of mokume and dheu on indigo is surreally beautiful, like deep blue streams running through your hands.

Living Blue works with designers and buyers from a dozen countries in Asia, the Middle East, Africa, Europe, North America, and Australia, with some of the world's most prestigious brands among them. Mishael explains that their global business is quite diverse. "There are retailers who buy our collection and retail it under the Living Blue label. There are design houses who collaborate with Living Blue by providing their design and patterns, which we make for them. Many of these buyers are repeat customers who look for and appreciate high-quality craftsmanship. We have gained their confidence."

The fact that this confidence extends all the way from farmer, dyer, and embroiderer to the rest of the world makes the blues of Living Blue altogether unique.

OPPOSITE: (top) White running stitch on indigo shibori (bottom) Shiuli Rani, Living Blue team member   HERE: An example of Living Blue's *kheta-kume* style, which blends *kheta* (*kantha*) stitching and the *mokume* effect of shibori pleat dyeing

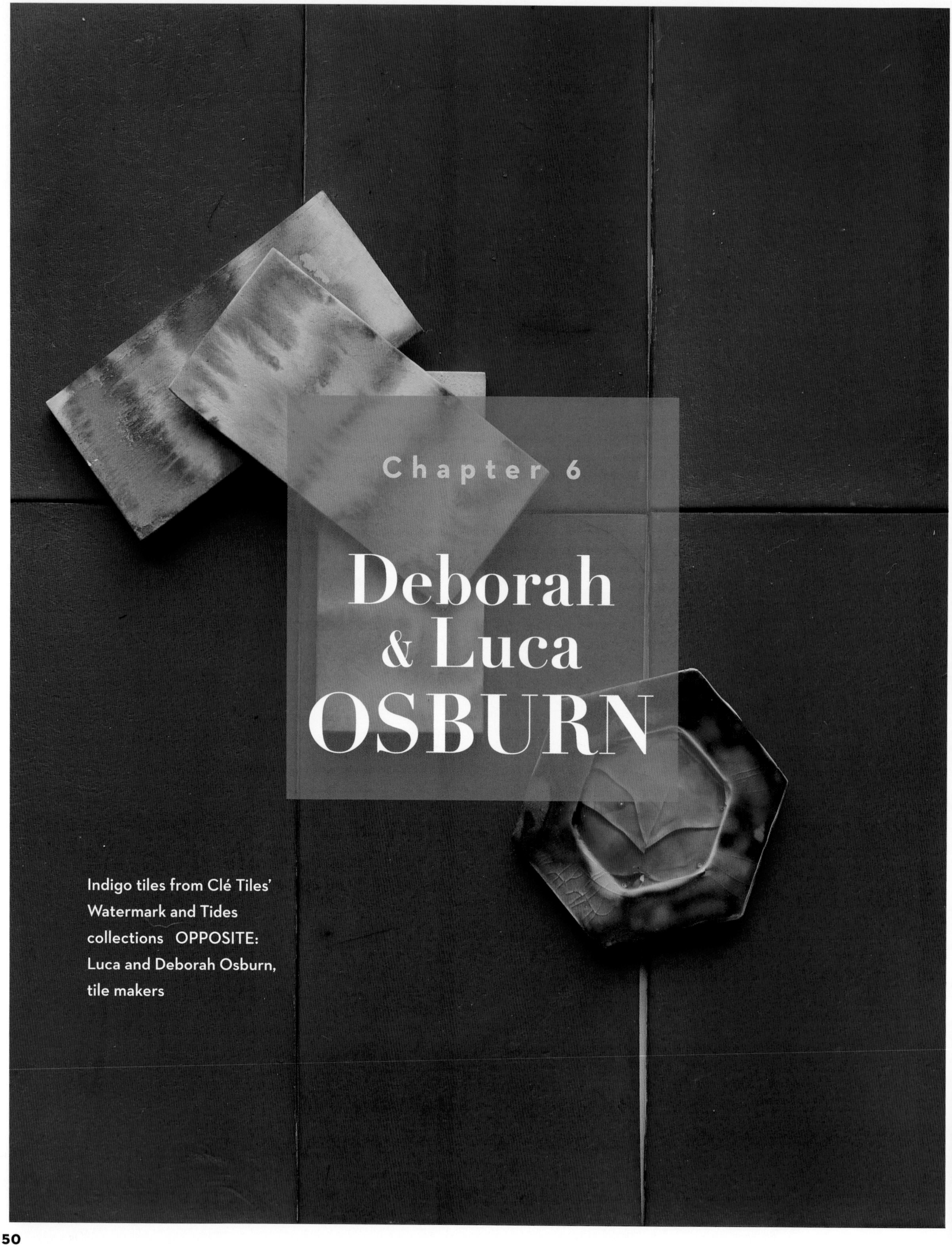

Chapter 6

Deborah & Luca OSBURN

Indigo tiles from Clé Tiles' Watermark and Tides collections OPPOSITE: Luca and Deborah Osburn, tile makers

INDIGO GENIE

Given the current fascination with indigo, it's no surprise to see it flourishing beyond textiles. Surprise did, however, play a role in Deborah Osburn's invention of indigo-infused tiles, now made and expanded upon by her son, artist and surfer Luca Osburn.

As Deborah tells it, the idea began not with indigo but with porcelain. "Twenty years ago, I visited a studio populated by former Heath Studio ceramists in the Point Reyes area. Very hippie, very much a part of the UC Davis/Peter Voulkos moment in Northern California ceramics. One of the two clay bodies they were using in tilemaking was a robust, gritty porcelain. I fell in love with the hand-hewn look they were achieving with it and picked up a few samples. Since I just knew it would stain, which isn't good for floor tiles, I put it out of my mind."

Around the same time, Deborah became interested in Japanese indigo shibori, researching the stories of master dyers and their techniques and eventually buying some indigo to experiment with at home. "One day I popped a couple of pieces of the gritty porcelain tiles into a jar of indigo and forgot about them. When I stumbled across them a month later, they were magical. The indigo had wicked up the rough, porous surface in waves of blue. These tiles had become *art*."

The artful accident was discovered a few months later by a visiting interior designer who found it languishing in Deborah's studio and placed an order.

The challenge of replicating the indigo's feathered and watery penetration began. "Luca, at that time about fourteen years old, and my father and I laid out pan after pan of upright tiles standing in an indigo bath. We went through quite a few tiles before we realized that the indigo liked slightly underfired ones that hadn't completely vitrified in the kiln. They were still capable of absorption. We figured out how to seal them properly, and our Watermark collection was born."

When *Interior Design* magazine named Watermark "best tile of the year" in 2014, Deborah "charmed" Luca into helping her with production. As a budding artist, Luca found the Zen-like application of color on ceramic satisfying. But it was his passion for surfing that really got him hooked. He saw images of water, waves, and tides in the indigo's patterns.

Luca's recent tile collection, Tides, adds verdigris and metallics to the indigo vocabulary of Watermark. "I wanted to expand the colors so that they resonated with different spots where I surf, different colors of water, different weathers," says Luca. While his mother measures out pigments with an eyedropper, Luca takes a more intuitive approach. "Potters call happy accidents the work of the 'genie in the kiln.' I'm looking for the genie in the indigo."

OPPOSITE: Tiles from the Watermark collection   HERE: (top) Luca's brushes during an indigo session (right) Tiles from the Tides collection (left) Luca takes inspiration from the colors and textures he sees while surfing

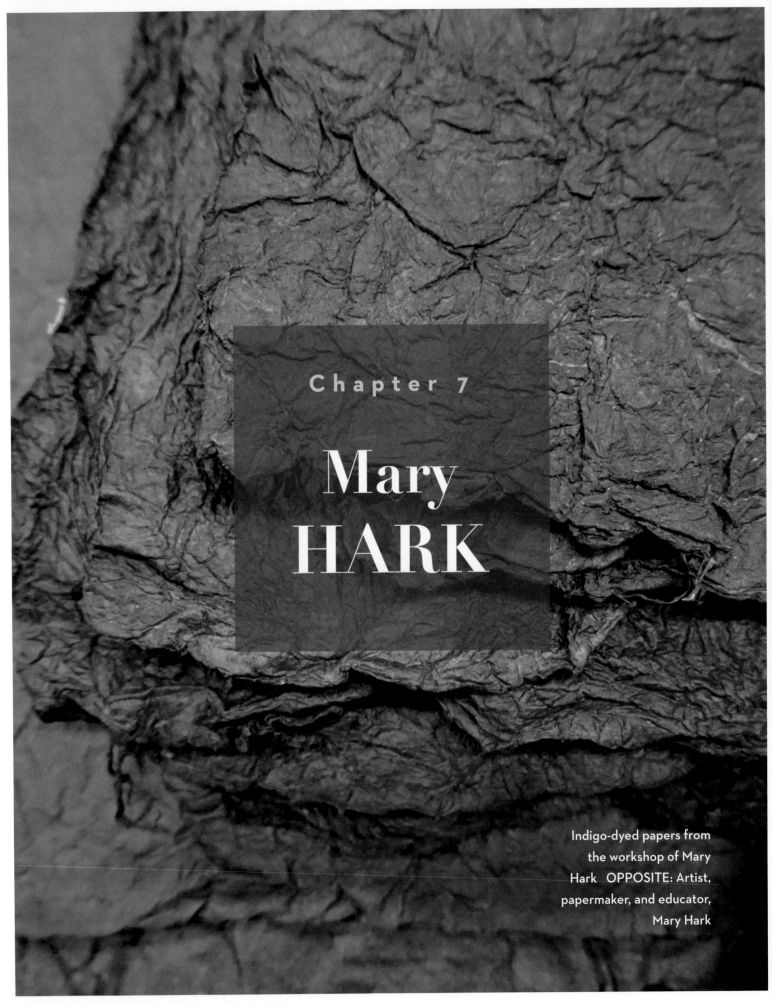

Chapter 7

Mary
HARK

Indigo-dyed papers from
the workshop of Mary
Hark OPPOSITE: Artist,
papermaker, and educator,
Mary Hark

LAYER upon LAYER

Mary Hark is always ready to take you for a swim—not in a lake or a pond but in a deep, complex sea of handmade paper. In her hands, paper is far from flat or rectangular or white. It roils and churns with curled-up edges. It ripples and flows with textures bubbling up from the fibers themselves. Among them are bast fibers, well known as sources of fine paper, juxtaposed or blended with fibers from local biomass as well as from recycled waste and upcycled fabrics. There's also pattern, delivered in pencil and paint, wax and dye, patchwork and collage and stitching. And, of course, there's color, most notably indigo.

Each sheet Mary makes is an entity in and of itself, but it's in the assembling and combining that her work blossoms. A sense of time and passion infuse what Mary calls "constructed paintings," as well as a stubborn commitment to stick with something until it is ripe and able to speak in its own voice. "It took me a long time to fully understand what it meant to be an artist," she admits. "It is much more than the facility to accurately draw a line."

Her artistic journey includes multiple degrees, single parenthood, and a long career as a teacher. Somehow all of these experiences blend in Mary's activism, taking papermaking and art out of the university context and into the community. Not long ago, she made 2,000 placemats out of local plant material and recycled waste for a sit-down dinner where the guests were neighborhood residents. About a decade ago, she helped to establish the first fine paper mill in Ghana.

Thanks to a 2006 Fulbright research award to work and study in a place where textiles are fully integrated into the culture, Mary learned about Adinkra clothmaking in the Ghanaian village of Ntonso. As she set up her own studio and searched for native plants to pulp into paper, she discovered that one of Asia's very finest sources of bast paper fiber, *kozo* or pulp-mulberry, grows rampant in Ghana. Since fourteen specimen plants were introduced there in 1969, kozo has become a damaging invasive species, interfering with local ecosystems and agriculture.

By 2009, Mary was making gorgeous fine papers by combining kozo with local plants and textile waste from Ghana's vibrant fashion sector. In partnership with Kwame Nkrumah University of Science and Technology (KNUST) and the support of the Forestry Commission of Ghana and Kumasi city officials, she launched a paper mill, the Ghana Paper Project. Some of the mill's paper was used by Take Time Press to create a publication now in the permanent collection at The Metropolitan Museum of Art.

Mary's first encounter with African indigo happened, paradoxically, in Iowa. At a museum exhibit there she fell in "love at first sight" with Tuareg veils whose glossy reddish-blue sheen was the result of both indigo dyeing as well as the beating of indigo pigment into the cloth with wooden mallets. Along

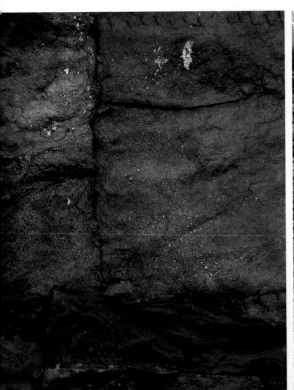

FAR LEFT: A work in progress
NEAR LEFT: Freshly dyed paper drying on a clothesline
ABOVE: Detail from Mary Hark's Driftless Reveries series

HERE: (top) Scraps of dyed papers in Mary's workshop (bottom) and OPPOSITE: Textures and color variations abound as a result of Mary's inventive processes

with the pigment, tiny pebbles and bits of dirt were occasionally embedded in the fabric, creating a deeper record of their making. After training with shibori artist Ana Lisa Hedstrom, Mary set off on her own indigo exploration, keeping those veils in the back of her mind.

"I quickly learned that I could approach the blue dye like a painter, building up color, spraying it away. And with paper, the intense color was only skin deep. I could peel away the top layer of the sheet, revealing undyed material," Mary recounts. "I could use a handwoven textile as a resist material over paper and end up with beautifully dyed cloth and corresponding papers that carried the marks of interlacement. I could embed the cloth in the paper, and overdye with indigo, then peel areas back to reveal all kinds of lovely complexities—sometimes astoundingly beautiful, sometimes earthbound, like rich, muddy dark soil."

Why has indigo maintained a presence in such an adventuresome art practice? Because it is, to Mary, unavoidable. "There is something elemental about the range of blues possible with an indigo vat, something universally understood. If I am looking up at the sky from my backyard in St. Paul or Madison or Kumasi, I am seeing the same blue as dyers in Japan, Indonesia, or Central America. Blue is the color of things that are essential to life no matter where or how that life is lived."

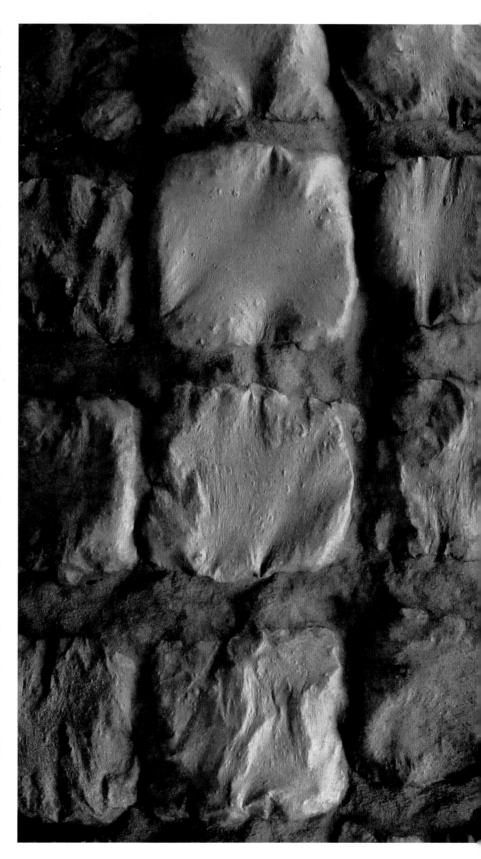

Chapter 8

Aviva
LEIGH

Local Norwich
yarns dyed
with woad
OPPOSITE:
Aviva Leigh,
artist and
teacher

Nevertheless, **W O A D** Persisted

Woad, a yellow-flowering member of the mustard family, has likely been part of humankind's library of dyestuffs for millennia. Seeds and seed husks of *Isatis tinctoria*, dyer's woad, have been discovered at several Stone Age excavation sites in France and Germany. Early Iron Age textiles found on the Sinai Peninsula show woad in use as far back as the thirteenth century BCE, which makes its later use in Egyptian court textiles no surprise.

A later Iron Age dig at Dragonby in the United Kingdom dates woad's use in Britain to the first century BC, around the time Julius Caesar's account of the Gallic Wars describes ancient Britons painting their bodies blue with it to frighten their enemies. The Iceni, ruled by Queen Boudicca, rose up against the Romans not long after Caesar's death, and they were said to be painted fearsomely blue as they marched to Londonium and burned it down.

Had they been asked, those ancient Romano-British Celts would probably not have cited intimidation as the reason for their blue skin; to them, woad was foremost a form of protection. It can be dissolved in fat, and a rubdown of blue-tinted lard would, at least, help keep these famously naked warriors warm. Woad also has antibacterial and antiviral properties, which might have helped quell infections among the wounded. It's also possible that specific designs drawn onto the skin with woad as a sort of temporary tattoo conveyed a sense of spiritual protection and communal belonging, helping to shore up confidence before a battle.

Woad itself is a botanical warrior, a tough biennial plant, probably originating in southeastern Europe or Central Asia. It was dispersed widely throughout Europe and northern Asia, by humans as a source of blue, as well as through its own deep and fast-growing root system, abundant seed yield, and lack of appeal to grazing livestock. Brought to California and Utah around 1900, probably mixed in with a shipment of Irish alfalfa seed, woad is officially an invasive species throughout the American West. Found in forty-four of the lower forty-eight states, it may be no coincidence that "weed" and "woad" are close etymological relatives.

THE WAYS OF WOAD

The process of turning woad into blue dye is not simple. In the plant's first year, when sown early and harvested during intense summer heat and sunlight, its leaves yield the most color. They are chopped and then milled into a paste, which traditionally is shaped into little balls and set in a dry place to cure thoroughly. When a dyer begins to prepare for a coloring session, the balls are crushed into a fine power, dampened, and left for a few days to compost. Add hot water and stale urine (or potash) and the vat is finally ready for thoroughly dampened cloth. As with vats of *Indigofera tinctoria*, cloth emerges a shade of yellowish green and oxidizes into blue. The blue color deepens with repeated dips in the vat.

But let's go back to the phrase "stale urine" for a moment. Its ammonia helps break down a colorless substance found in woad leaves (and in the leaves of indigo and a handful of other plants) called indican, and converts it into indoxyl, which binds to the fiber in the dyeing process. In the old days, the urine was sometimes collected in buckets set out near taverns and left to age. The smell was predictably terrible. Because of the stench, Queen Elizabeth I, in 1585, put constraints on how close dye-houses could be to her residences.

OPPOSITE: Woad leaves from
Aviva Leigh's studio garden
HERE: Woad-dyed yarns from
Aviva Leigh's dye vats

Handwoven woad blue scarf by Aviva Leigh
OPPOSITE: Test hanks recording a woad dyeing session in Aviva Leigh's studio

By that time, importing woad from France and Germany had become so expensive that English farmers and dyers, seizing an opportunity to cash in, had been planting the crop in such abundance that it threatened essential food production. In response, the queen limited the amount of land in her realm that could be devoted to growing woad. Fifteen years later, Elizabeth rescinded these laws when indigo pigment traded from the East began to make inroads into woad's economic importance. Indigo contained twenty to thirty times more colorant, and it was easier to work with. When synthetic dyes arrived in the nineteenth century to challenge mighty indigo, woad had mostly fallen out of cultivation. Some sources say that its survival as a dyestuff was due solely to its use as a "starter" for indigo fermentation,[1] though that seems a bit of an oversimplification, especially since the last woad mill in England continued to supply dark blue cloth for police and military uniforms until 1932.

A NORTHERN BLUE

Even after being eclipsed by indigo and again by synthetic dyes, woad persists into the twenty-first century. Among medical researchers, it is valued as a source of glucobrassicin, a compound with potential in the fight against cancer.

Among crafters and policy makers in search of authenticity or sustainability, it is again of interest as a natural-dye plant suitable for northern climates.

A European Union–funded project called SPIN-DIGO (Sustainable Production of Plant-derived Indigo) sponsored research of plant varieties, extraction methods, and best agricultural practices, with woad as a major focus. Simultaneously, the UK Ministry of Agriculture, Fisheries, and Food looked into woad as a sustainable source of blue colorant for inkjet printing.[2] More recently, two farming and retail operations, Bleu de Lectoure in southern France and Woad-inc, near Norfolk, UK, have attracted attention as sources of ready-to-use woad dyes and pigments.[3]

Some people are growing woad at home. Norwich-based textile artist and teacher Aviva Leigh has a generous patch of woad just outside her studio. She harvests enough to support about three dye vats a year and often sends her students home with a seedling to start their very own dye gardens.

Though she often consults Tudor-era recipes from the early seventeenth century, Aviva's modern-day exploration of woad does not involve stale urine. "Please emphasize that, if you don't mind," she requests. However, her experiments do bring slow cookers into play, along with a large mid-twentieth-century washing machine complete with mangle. Sometimes Aviva dyes existing clothes and home goods in need of a bit of a color refresh. And sometimes she dyes yarn and textiles for her artwork. "I must come across as a mad lady all in blue all the time. My 'fashionable' all-black wardrobe now sits unused."

What fascinates her about this somewhat anachronistic dye plant? "There's a softness in the blue. You can get really pale, delicate shades right up to some strong French Navy shades. Because it has much less indirubin, its colors are less red than *Indigofera* dyes. Treated properly at fairly low temperatures, woad

can keep a certain green quality—a hint of turquoise that reminds you of sky and sea.

"When my students see how alive the colors that woad can make really are, they're completely fascinated. They can't believe that the green plants outside the door make these beautiful blues." Indeed, student interest is palpable and keeps her motivated to continually refine and deepen her curriculum.

"Some people just love being together in the studio. On our 'Weaving Wednesdays' there's a great sharing of work and inspiration and sometimes some helpful problem solving." There's also the camaraderie of "textilians," whose love of fiber and natural dyestuff and technique are at the center of the conversation.

Woad has become integral to this exchange. As Aviva comments, "People here in the UK are interested because of the history and heritage it represents, and because they can grow it in their gardens from seed. Woad just feels like it belongs here."

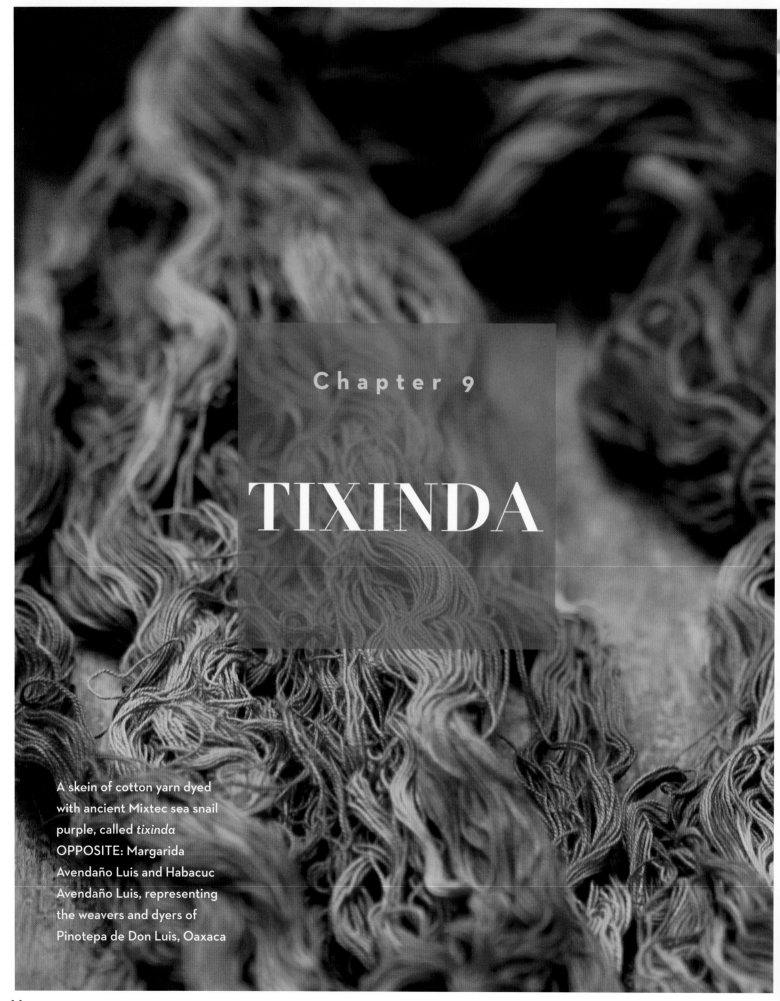

Chapter 9

TIXINDA

A skein of cotton yarn dyed
with ancient Mixtec sea snail
purple, called *tixinda*
OPPOSITE: Margarida
Avendaño Luis and Habacuc
Avendaño Luis, representing
the weavers and dyers of
Pinotepa de Don Luis, Oaxaca

The **LAST PURPLE**

At low tide, a few shirtless Mixtec men walk along the humid Pacific coast of central Oaxaca looking for sea snails. Dodging the waves, navigating wet, gray rocks with bare feet, they look for a particular kind of snail: *Purpura pansa* to scientists, *tixinda* to the Mixtec. After carefully prying one off the rocks, by hand or with a mango wood stick, they press just the right part of the snail's "foot" to encourage it to secrete a milky liquid. Left to their own devices, the snails deploy this liquid as a neurotoxin that paralyzes the smaller shellfish they consume.

To these seekers of tixinda, the secretion is a treasured and ancient dyestuff, and they apply it directly onto a skein of cotton yarn looped around a forearm. At first, the tixinda liquid stains the yarn a bruisy greenish color, but as the liquid oxidizes, it turns blue and eventually achieves a brilliant, colorfast, reddish-purple hue.

Once "milked," the snail is gently returned, unharmed, to its habitat to live another day. The dyers visit this cove only once per lunar cycle, to give the snails time to recover and recharge. Dyeing occurs from October to May so as not to interfere with the snails' breeding season.

"This is one of the most ancient dyeing methods still in practice today," notes Eric Mindling, an author, photographer, and tour organizer who has worked in Oaxaca for more than twenty years. "Mixtecs have lived on and near this coast for at least 1,500 years, and they revere this practice as integral to their heritage as a people. For about three hours a day, as long as the water level is low enough, a dyer might encounter about 400 snails, enough to dye a single 250-gram skein. That's 400 snails, lifted, milked, and settled carefully back onto the rocks one at a time over a few hours. It's the last place on earth this is still being done as an unbroken tradition. Traditional harvesting of the dye maintained this resource very well for a very long time. It's worth seeing."

The leader of these Mixtec dyers, Habacuc Avendaño, has made purple yarns this way for more than sixty years. One skein per low tide would have been a meager yield in the 1950s and 1960s when he learned his craft. "When I was little, there were many more snails back then, and larger ones," he says. "We would dye one sack of yarn [about forty skeins] during two weeks at the coast. Sometimes we would double- and triple-dye them to get very dark shades of purple." Across the entire 2017 harvest season, his group was able to color a mere fifteen skeins of single-dyed purple yarn.

Patrice Perillie, founder of Mexican Dreamweavers, a nonprofit whose sole mission is to support the Mixtec dyers and weavers of Habacuc's community of Pinotepa de Don Luis, underscores his words. "We're heading rapidly toward the disappearance of this art. Snails large enough to produce dyestuff are fewer and fewer. The problem is not necessarily coastal real estate development per se, or climate change. It's the pressure put on the snail population by more and more people living here and visiting here. Local fishermen gather the snails, as well as little *lapas* [a type of limpet], their favorite prey, and cut them up for ceviche." Foraging for food is so intense that she wonders how long Habacuc's group can continue dyeing.

The snail population has been under pressure before. It was nearly decimated in the early 1980s, thanks to a Japanese commercial operation whose dye harvesting practices were savage and wasteful. Marta Turok, a major figure in the world of Mexican folk art, describes the crisis:

> When the company called Imperial Purple began to overharvest coastal snails for their commercial purposes, a catastrophic plunge in snail populations was triggered. Beginning

"This is one of the most ancient dyeing methods still in practice today . . . Mixtecs have lived on and near this coast for at least 1,500 years, and they revere this practice as integral to their heritage as a people.

Detail of a traditional *posahuanco* woven with yarns dyed in indigo, cochineal, and tixinda

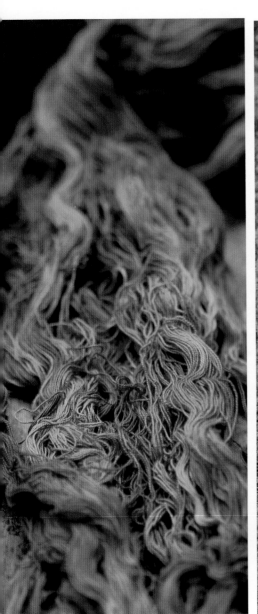

in 1983, I spearheaded what would become a lifelong project to preserve *Purpura* in Mexico. Over a five-year period, we conducted biological and ethnobiological studies coupled with a community development project whose results included Imperial Purple being denied any more permits. An accord signed among the Mexican Federal Ministries of Education, of the Environment, and of Fisheries regulated the use of the snail, based on Mixtec knowledge and sustainable techniques. For the first time, a natural resource was recognized as part of the nation's cultural and ecological heritage, granting exclusive rights to the groups who had made traditional use of it.[1]

Even so, snail numbers continue to decline, as do average snail size and dye yield.

The few skeins Habacuc's group can currently dye go directly to the women of a sixty-member weaving cooperative in Pinotepa, many of whom are related by marriage or blood to the dyers. Habacuc's wife, Teresita, is one of them. As an expert backstrap-loom weaver, she requires about three months to weave her

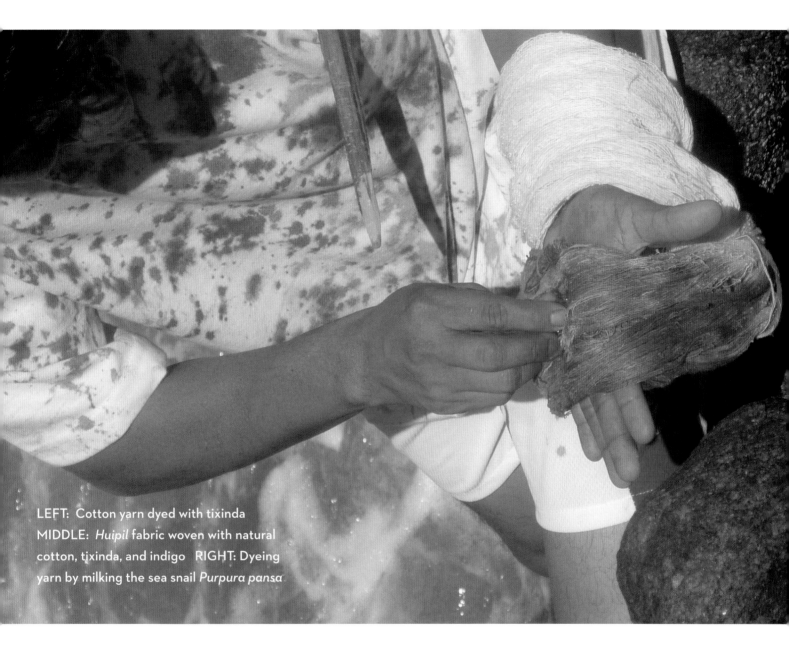

LEFT: Cotton yarn dyed with tixinda
MIDDLE: *Huipil* fabric woven with natural
cotton, tixinda, and indigo   RIGHT: Dyeing
yarn by milking the sea snail *Purpura pansa*

community's traditional long wraparound skirt, the *posahaunco*, which features bands of tixinda purple, cochineal red, and indigo blue.

Ancient motifs, rich with meaning to their Mixtec creators, bring certain of these bands vividly alive. In Pinotepa, there is still immense prestige associated with making and wearing posahuancos. "These clothes represent the way things were always done, up to just a decade or two ago," Eric Mindling says. "Since fewer than forty of these amazing garments can be made a year now—and maybe less than that—there is rarity and value to each and every one of them."

To Habacuc and Teresita, this sense of value goes beyond color and textile and deep into Mixtec culture. Both the snail and the purple color it makes are considered sacred. The color evokes associations with womanhood, the lunar cycle of human fertility, and blood. "The snails themselves are matriarchal in a way," Patrice Perillie observes. "The females are larger and produce more dye. They need a lunar cycle to recharge. Finding them is dependent on the tides, which are also influenced by the moon."

The community's very way of life was shaped around the making of purple. For example, the long

Habacuc milking a snail and applying the liquid to yarn
OPPOSITE: Harvesting purple in a
beautiful Pacific cove

trek from inland Pinotepa to the Pacific coast to dye yarns used to be a major event in the community's calendar. A group of dyers would walk eight days to the shore. "It was a real journey," says Eric, "involving several river crossings—at least one of which involved paying a ferryman to board a dugout canoe. The men, along with a few young apprentices, would carry their own food, and when their tortillas, beans, and coffee ran out, they would work at local farms to be paid in food. Once they reached their campsite on the coast, a place with a freshwater spring called El Jicaral, abundant seafood was available to supplement their basic supplies. They'd stay for about three months before heading back to Pinotepa."[2] Habacuc made his first journey in 1956, alongside an uncle.

Dirt roads of the 1970s and paved roads of the 1980s have reduced the journey to a short drive, and the stay along the coast to a few days. Somehow the decline of the snail population and the dwindling yield of dyed skeins to take back to Pinotepa give the abbreviation of the process an unfortunate logic.

"We're trying to educate local fishermen working the coves where the sea snail lives," says Patrice. "It's important that they not harvest them. But currently, we may have only five years or so left for this very important art to survive. The Coastal Mixtec are the last group of indigenous people in all of Mexico who grow their own cotton, handspin it, dye it with natural dyes, and weave it on backstrap looms. Unless we find ways to support this still-traditional craft, they will soon be buying their thread from salesmen, like other indigenous groups."

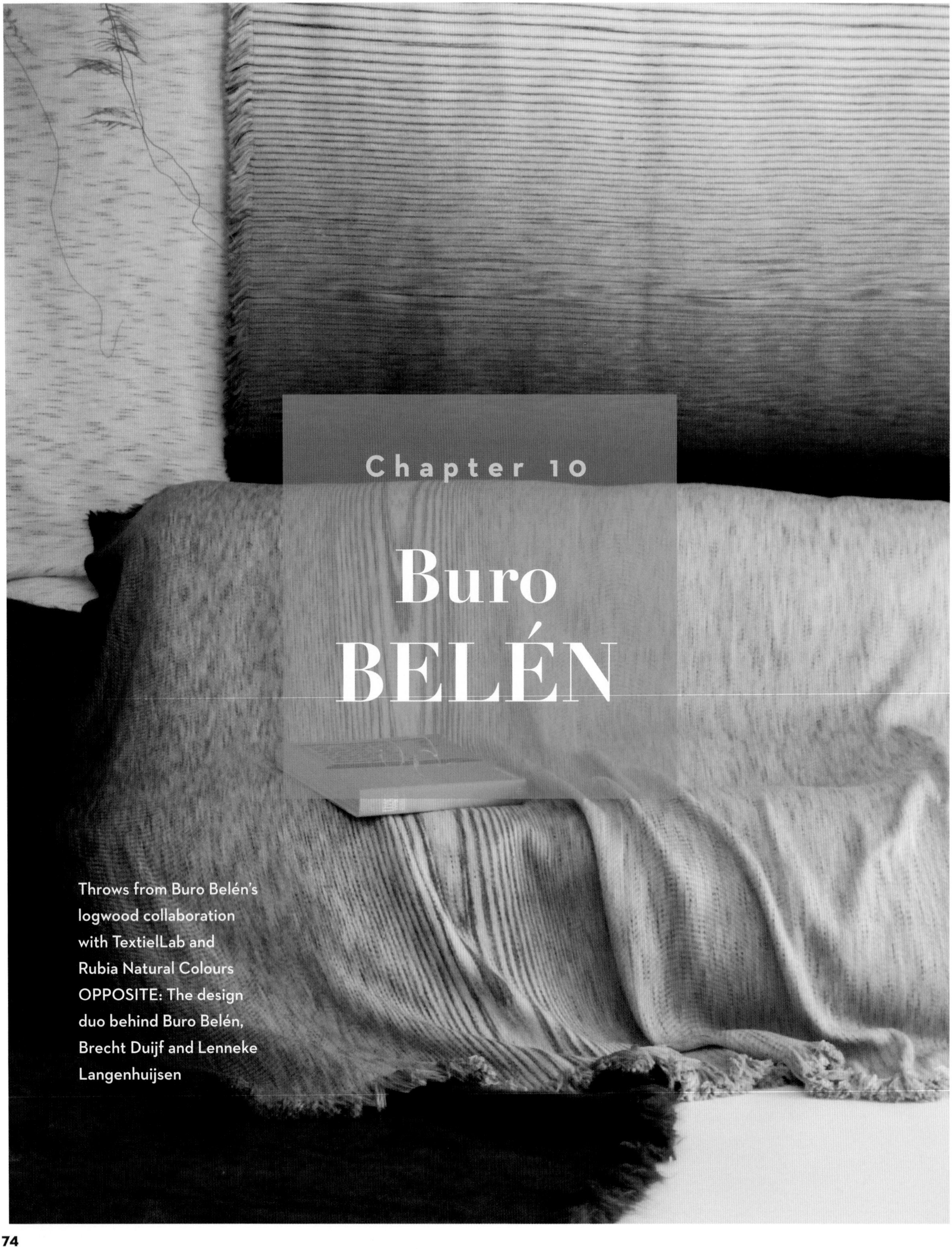

Chapter 10

Buro BELÉN

Throws from Buro Belén's logwood collaboration with TextielLab and Rubia Natural Colours OPPOSITE: The design duo behind Buro Belén, Brecht Duijf and Lenneke Langenhuijsen

SERIOUS SYMBOLS

Philip III, Duke of Burgundy, seems to have started it all in 1419 when he donned black from head to toe to mourn his assassinated father and never wore another color until his own death forty-eight years later. Never mind that his clothes were made of the finest silks and velvets, that he flaunted the large and lavish gold symbols of office that were de rigueur in his day, and that he had eighteen illegitimate children: Philip's all-black wardrobe brought him such a reputation for probity that his moniker was Philip the Good.

Shortly after his death, the powerful House of Hapsburg absorbed the Duchy of Burgundy by forcing the marriage of one of their own, Maximilian I, to Mary, Philip's granddaughter. Mary brought the Hapsburgs more than a wealthy realm. She also brought her family's predilection for black, which the Hapsburgs cultivated as a symbol of intellect, austerity, and Catholic piety.

Before Instagram, the noble classes were *the* style influencers, and Mary and Maximilian's grandson, Charles V, born in 1500, was in a unique position to define taste and fashion across his vast territories. His titles at various stages in his life included Holy Roman Emperor, King of Italy, King of Spain, Lord of the Netherlands, Duke of Burgundy, and Archduke of Austria, none of which explicitly acknowledge his dominion over Spanish and Dutch colonies in the Americas and Asia. He and his global courtiers were instrumental in defining black as a color of power, and it has remained as such in one form or another for centuries.

Old World recipes for black usually involved costly and complex overdyeing, such as finishing a very dark blue woad textile in a vat of concentrated madder. The results were lovely when new, but often fared poorly at the laundry. Nobles looking to telegraph status and power couldn't settle for dingy, crocked duds, and had to replace their clothing frequently. This sort of austerity was very expensive.

From the early six-teenth century on, the desire for a deep and durable black linked the courts of Europe with hard-bitten loggers working in terrible conditions in a backwater of the Spanish Empire. Far from the sophisticated capitals of Spain's New World territories along Mexico's hot, humid Yucatán coast, the logwood tree (*Haematoxylum campechianum*) flourished—along with crocodiles and mosquitoes. Swatting away bugs and beasts, loggers known as "baymen" chipped away pale sapwood in order to send logs or blocks of dye-bearing heartwood back to Europe.

Logwood dyestuff was so sought after that by 1600, a single ship of it could bring in more money than a year's worth of other goods.[1] British pirates interfered with Spanish shipments as often as possible until the English discovered their own cache of logwood in what would become British Honduras and later, the independent nation of Belize. The flag of modern-day Belize features a pair of loggers flanking a Honduran mahogany tree, which, in the nineteenth century, eclipsed logwood as a major export thanks mostly to the advent of synthetic dyes.

The reddish heartwood of the logwood tree is a powerful dyestuff. Soaking or boiling chips of logwood, and adding iron, can render rich, colorfast blacks. Adding potash instead of iron brings out logwood's purple values. Logwood is highly effective not just with textiles, but also with leathers, furs, inks, and artists' pigments. Interestingly, logwood is still used today in

OPPOSITE and HERE: Throws
from Buro Belén's logwood
collaboration with TextielLab
and Rubia Natural Colours

anatomical pathology laboratories around the world as an essential stain that defines the nuclei of cells, helping technicians evaluate growth patterns and identify cellular abnormalities.

For many of us today, centuries after Philip the Good, probity is expressed not necessarily by black, but by natural colors produced with sustainable methods. The variations and signs of wear traditionally seen as the downside of natural color are being reexplored as signs of authenticity. Buro Belén, founded by Dutch designers and educators Brecht Duijf and Lenneke Langenhuijsen, focuses on projects that bring natural color into play for aesthetic, sensory, and philosophical reasons. "For us, something that harms our world does not feel good," says Lenneke, referencing the company's commitment to environmental sustainability. "We're interested in designing things that look *and* feel good to us, so this is an important touchstone."

Their body of work explores wallpaper, paints, and spray coatings that combine natural colorants and natural materials to create interior finishes that are healthy and interesting, and that acknowledge time and light exposure as "design elements" rather than flaws. Depending on the frequency and intensity of light the materials receive, colors age and shift, often emphasizing the shadows cast by objects and furniture in unexpected ways and always providing an intimate, experiential dimension that unfolds across time.

While Buro Belén's blues and greens are relatively stable, their madder-based reds will often brighten and get a bit pinker, and their yellows will mellow into more golden shades. For the Living Colours line of paints, shifting values are documented in a "de-colourchart," which indexes Buro Belén's color library along each hue's unique path from fresh application to discoloration.

In 2016, Lenneke and Brecht explored logwood in a collaboration with TextielLab and Rubia Natural Colours. Intrigued by the complex purple tones produced by Rubia's sustainably farmed and processed logwood pigments in alkaline conditions, the duo looked at how the natural dyestuff behaved with wool yarns as well as at the machines used to dye and weave the yarns into blankets. As a hardwood-derived dyestuff, "logwood is not the most sustainable choice, so we had to work hard to reduce its impact," Lenneke explains.

To save energy, they left behind the idea that the yarn needed to emerge from the process with a uniform color, which meant that the circulating pumps in the dye machines designed to keep consistent amounts of dyestuff flowing around the yarn could be turned off. It also meant that the yarn itself did not need to be spooled and unspooled repeatedly in the dye bath. To save water, cleaning the machines between each dye bath was also eliminated, which meant that unpredictable amounts of residue carried forward into the next dye session. As Lenneke describes the energy and water saved by not striving for color uniformity, it becomes clear that one of the tenets of modern manufacturing and consumption—that each unit of production needs to be exactly the same as the unit before it and the unit after it—adds immensely to the resources consumed. Sameness looks efficient, but it is not.

Buro Belén's process simply involves placing the perforated plastic cones around which the yarn is coiled (for storage as well as for easy threading of machine looms) in a dye bath and leaving them alone. The yarn closest to the exterior of the coil absorbs the most color, of course: it becomes dark purple. But because the perforations of the cone expose the yarn intermittently to the dye, some of the yarn closest to the cone is dyed in a sort of Morse code dot-and-dash of dark and light. Whether the yarn is wound in a simple vertical spiral or in a pyramid of zigzag loops around the cone dictates which parts of the yarn turn dark purple, which parts retain their natural color, and how much yarn receives intermediate exposure to the dye. Skipping parts of the usual mechanical process "encourages all the colors within the dye to appear across the yarn. We often see hints of light blue, salmon, or beige as the dye moves along the yarn out of the areas of darkest saturation," Lenneke notes.

Two cones of yarn dyed in this way are machine woven to make a two-faced blanket, each side showing unpredictable resist-dye patterns—sort of a random ikat effect. No two blankets are alike, just as one side of a blanket is noticeably unlike its partner. They are sold in limited edition by Dutch design dealer and gallerist Thomas Eyck.

"Changing ideas about production takes a lot of imagination, and I often think that we are too far ahead of consumer tastes. Maybe in another ten years we will see a larger hunger for the nuances and shifts of natural substances," Lenneke says. "But we have to take these early steps now and hope that companies and consumers can follow later. That's something we really look forward to."

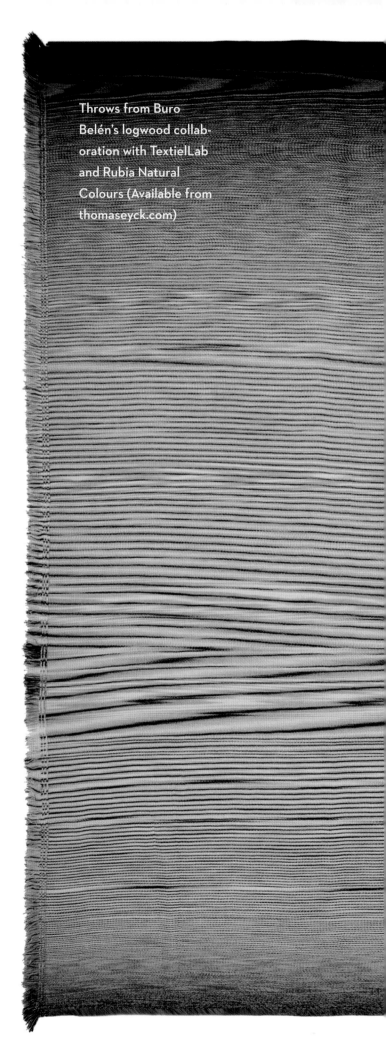

Throws from Buro Belén's logwood collaboration with TextielLab and Rubia Natural Colours (Available from thomaseyck.com)

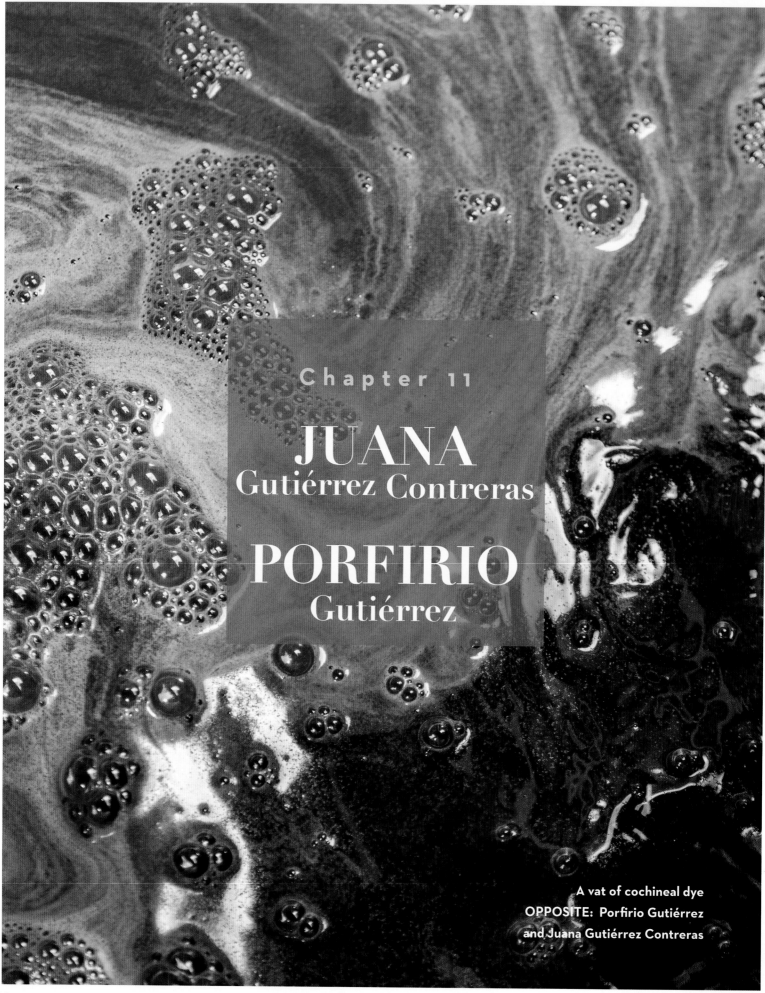

Chapter 11

JUANA
Gutiérrez Contreras

PORFIRIO
Gutiérrez

A vat of cochineal dye
OPPOSITE: Porfirio Gutiérrez
and Juana Gutiérrez Contreras

AUTHENTIC VOICES

Corn, beans, and squash grow profusely in the fields around Teotitlán del Valle, tended largely by hand by Zapotec farmers. Juana and Porfirio Gutiérrez's father is one of them. He sows the corn first. When the cornstalks stretch tall enough to act as trellises, he plants the beans. Not all at once, but a few at a time to stagger their eventual ripening. Squash planting comes last. The ground-hugging tendrils spread out to shade the soil and keep it moist. Most Oaxacans are farmers, and they've cultivated the "three sisters" of New World food this way since time out of mind.

of life in Teotitlán for over five centuries, along with shearing, carding, spinning, and dyeing their wool.

Most importantly, weaving remains a strong symbol of cultural continuity. In pre-Hispanic times, Zapotecs paid their taxes to the Aztecs in the form of colored and patterned cotton blankets woven on backstrap looms. Though examples of early textiles have not survived in Oaxaca to anywhere near the degree that they have, for example, in Peru, archaeologists find evidence of a rich and diverse repertoire of textile pattern in ancient murals, architectural carvings and statues, and ceramics. Clothing for men and women, particularly from the upper classes, was densely patterned, sometimes in designs similar to those on *huipils* and *quechquémitls* still worn today, though traditional garments are seen less and less as time goes on.[2]

Wool, now dominant, became part of the region's fiber vocabulary in the mid-sixteenth century, when Bishop Lopez de Zárate brought sheep to Teotitlán. He also brought upright treadle looms,[3] which displaced backstrap looms and turned weaving from a woman's craft to a male-dominated one, with women focused on carding, spinning, and dyeing. The tools and materials used in Teotitlán's weaving workshops today, as well as the gender roles, descend from this period.

While weaving and wool have maintained a certain primacy over many generations,[4] exactly what is woven has changed dramatically. Accounts from the late nineteenth century tell us that Teotitlán was well known for high-quality woolen *mantas*, which for centuries served as both blankets and cloaks. Teotico blankets sold well in the nearby markets of Oaxaca and Tlacolula, a business that broadened to other Oaxacan towns until machine-made competition entered in the 1930s. Cheaper competition notwithstanding, the skill of Teotitlán's weavers still

A few well-worn paths trace their way upward from the alluvial plain of Oaxaca's Central Valley into quiet foothills and rolling sheep pastures, and from there upward still to the peaks of the Sierra Madre. Looking away from the modest sprawl at the edge of this prosperous town, the dramatic landscape seems to have been like this forever. Tradition explains the sense of timelessness with the claim that Teotitlán was the first Zapotec settlement. Although archaeologists put the Monte Albán ruins at the beginning of the classic Zapotec era, at around 800 BCE, this has not disturbed Teoticos' deeply rooted identity as the original Zapotecs.[1]

Location and crops are hardly the only Zapotec touchstones of remembrance. The Zapotec language is a cherished link to the past for many Teoticos, as is ancient knowledge of wild medicine and dye plants, which sends townspeople upward along those mountain pathways to forage during the lush growing season. Grazing sheep have also been an integral part

OPPOSITE: Juana Gutiérrez
Contreras grinding cochineal
beetles on a stone *metate*
HERE: Juana's Gutiérrez Contreras's
hands during a long afternoon
of cochineal dyeing

earned customers in neighboring states through the 1950s and eventually in top-notch tourist shops in Mexico City and Acapulco. Tapestry orders from Europe and the United States took off in the 1960s and 1970s.[5] The 1980s craze for Southwest-style décor in the United States saw a marked uptick in rug making,[6] and it is tapestry-woven rugs that still occupy almost all Teotico looms today.

It is not only the type of weaving that has changed over the last century or so; Teotitlán's pattern vocabulary has evolved dramatically as well. Many motifs are seen by the weavers as traditional: the zigzag *montanitas* pattern, the *maguey* pattern based on abstracted agave shapes, and the more figural *ven veshee* design of a deity sitting cross-legged with a censer. But it's equally possible that these designs appeared not as a result of craft continuity but rather as the fruits of more recent archaeological study of motifs or other ancient sources—or at the requests of merchants, designers, tourists, or collectors. For example, many motifs commonly seen in Teotico weaving today derive from Navajo-inspired designs sought by US customers and first introduced in Oaxaca by US importers more than fifty years ago.

As is the case with many of Mexico's extant heritage crafts, liberal borrowing and adapting of patterns from many (sometimes global) traditions is part of Oaxaca's dynamic textile culture.[7] Protean visual experimentation is to be expected and highly valued. In a recent PBS *Craft in America* account of Oaxacan weaving, brilliant ethnobotanist and textile expert Alejandro de Ávila Blomberg commented that in the context of a "3,000-year record of how textiles have changed over time, people are doing finer tapestry than was ever done, and they're being much more experimental."[8]

While the hills and fields of Teotitlán may be timeless, its weavers and their work are energetic, dynamic, and deeply creative. Their weaving is rooted in the past, but each generation conjures up its own take on tradition, blending the need to earn a livelihood with fresh artistry and creativity.

FROM ONE GENERATION TO THE NEXT

Juana Gutiérrez walks the line between past and present in her own way. At fifty years old, her generation is perhaps the last in Teotitlán to wear traditional clothing on an everyday basis, though her style is not purely traditional. She dresses in a more comfortable 1960s update on the ancient blouse, skirt, and sash combination.

She and her husband, Antonio, live with the youngest of their children in their own home very near Juana's parents' house. Juana has been heard to say that she is not just a natural dyer, she is also a wife and mother, which means that her to-do list is always long. Upon waking early in the morning, she prays to the Virgin on her family's altar before cleaning up the dyeing workshop, which occupies most of the courtyard of her house. A deep portico provides shade and shelter from the elements, with tools and raw materials hung on the walls and dye vats in their own corner. Though it's mostly quiet outside, the sounds of the street reach through and around walls and gates. Juana sees her quiet ritual of praying and tidying as a positive start to each day.

After a quick visit to the market to buy ingredients for the family breakfast, she cooks. The whole family sits down to eat together. Afterward, the workday begins by washing a new batch of handspun yarns ready for dyeing or with careful preparation of a new

OPPOSITE: Juana grinds cochineal on a traditional stone metate
HERE: (top) Juana checks the color of cochineal dyed yarn before removing it from the vat. (below left) Various shades of cochineal-dyed yarn dry in the sun. (below right) One of Juana's vivid crimson shades comes from cochineal

FRONT: Juana and Porfirio's parents
BACK: (from left to right) Javier Contreras, Porfirio Guttiérez, Juana Gutiérrez Contreras and Antonio Contreras

valuable dye and medicinal plants, examined their leaves and flowers and roots, repeated their names, told their stories, and shared their uses. This oral tradition extends back far beyond Juana's parents, grandparents, and even great-grandparents. Plant knowledge is part of Zapotec heritage, integral to a life unfolding in rhythm with the seasons, with the life cycle of both wild and domesticated plants delineated by daily rituals and punctuated by annual town festivals and religious observances.

As with anything learned in a context of family traditions, Juana's knowledge was proved and expanded as part of everyday life. She remembers her father testing her by sending her out to collect a kind of salvia used in the family's dyeing repertoire. "But I couldn't find any. Later that day, my mother and grandmother and I went down to the river to wash wool. As we did our work and enjoyed the cool river, I saw a plant with a pink flower on it, a kind of reed. I picked it, just to see if it might be useful, and the juice stained my hands. My mother thought we should take it home to see what color it might give us, and when we tried it out, it gave us a mustard color. We still use it when it's fresh, picked during the wet season."

At the age of fifteen, Juana undertook her first solo dye journey, using the aforementioned salvia mixed with bark from a local oak tree to make a light-yellow yarn. She mastered about ten colors, thanks to her family's teachings. Almost thirty years later, she has mastered a dye vocabulary of 200 colors, from that first light yellow all the way through the spectrum to deep blacks and browns. Indigo makes blue. Tree moss makes warm beiges and golden tans, and pecan leaves and black *zapote* fruit make richer browns. *Maruush* leaves render a lovely olive green, while fermented pomegranate skins yield black. *Pericón* provides yellows, and the cochineal beetle a

vat of natural dye. Sometimes carding and spinning is on the agenda, though much of their yarn is made by family members and neighbors. On dyeing days, once the vats reach the right temperature and the yarn is soaking, Juana slows for a second or two to think about the work that must be done in the coming days. At noon, the family comes together for a snack, with conversation that keeps every member of this family enterprise informed of what's going on. That brief pause will be the only time Juana stops moving between kitchen and dye workshop all day long.

Toward dinnertime, five-year-old granddaughter Maria Luisa often comes for a visit, and Juana will repeat the names of the dye plants bundled and hung from the rafters to dry, passing on what Juana herself learned as a child. As a youngster, Juana and her eleven siblings would often make a pilgrimage into the hills around the town. Their parents pointed out

gorgeous range of reds. Deployed with a few mordant options, an intimate understanding of how much dyestuff to use, and the right times and temperatures, Juana's color vocabulary is rich.

"My eyes were hungry for more colors. I saw how our family's colors worked well with the natural colors of sheep's wool, but I wanted to see brighter and richer colors, too. My first experiment was with tree moss, a hairy lichen that grows on tree branches up in the mountains. The first try gave me a pale, warm beige, a color we still use in the workshop. I added a lot more tree moss to the next batch, and I got a brown color we already had. The next time, I cut back on the moss, switched to a stainless steel vessel, and I got a rich golden beige like toast. It's still a color that I like and that we use."

In addition to loving the work that she does, Juana values the connection to nature it gives her. "When you work with nature with respect, you do no harm. You don't need damaging chemicals. You don't need to harvest in ways that destroy. You don't hurt the environment and the world. I think this is what positive change is about: working with the gifts my parents and God gave me, working in harmony with nature, and working in ways that we can teach to the young people so that they can earn a living and keep our world healthy. I think I put those thoughts into all the colors and rugs we make, and into all the pieces of my life." The respect with which the twenty people in the Gutiérrez family business treat Juana show that they agree.

As with anything learned in a context of family traditions, Juana's knowledge was proved and expanded as part of everyday life. She remembers her father testing her by sending her out to collect a kind of salvia used in the family's dyeing

THERE ARE NO ZAPOTEC DYEING MANUALS

The quiet and assured way Juana goes about it lends her dye work a kind of magic. Her wordless process depends on her ability to read the vat: How hot is hot enough, how much of a particular dyestuff needs to be added to achieve a particular color, how much time will get her to the end she desires?

A dye session is preceded by even more silent assessment: When is the right season to pick which plants, and are they best used fresh, dried, fermented, or some combination thereof? Do they grow in the garden, in the foothills, or high up in the mountains? How much of any plant must be harvested or purchased during the right season to get the family workshop through the production cycle in front of her? Because there are no Zapotec dyeing manuals, all of the answers to these questions live in Juana's mind, supported by a single little notebook and a few yarn swatches.

Color is only the tip of the proverbial iceberg: some of the dyestuffs in Juana's practice have deep histories and other uses. Pericón, for example, known in English as Mexican mint marigold and botanically as *Tagetes lucida*, is a plant with ancient New World history. The Aztecs are said to have used it in combination with other plants as a hallucinogen effective in treating lightning strike and shock, as well as a tranquilizer for people about to be sacrificed. Scientific analysis shows pericón to contain compounds similar to some well-documented psychotropics, which probably accounts for its current use in Huichol and other shamanic traditions.[9]

In Oaxaca, pericón is considered "merely" medicinal, given as a tisane to help with cramps and stomach upset. Some studies suggest that the plant may have antimicrobial and antifungal properties, which perhaps explains its effectiveness. In a different form of "medicine," Juana's husband, Antonio, adds pericón and other herbs to locally distilled mescal— sometimes along with scorpions and worms.

As a natural dye, pericón produces radiant yellows, from a pale, warm, buttery tone to a glowing mustard. Using the leaves of the *lengua de vaca* tree, a tannin-rich species of *Buddleia*, as a mordant, Juana coaxes out paler, subtler tones. When she uses alum instead, the colors head into richer zones. She also uses the pericón vat as a step toward warm reds, oranges, and corals (overdyed with varying intensities of cochineal) as well as teals and greens (overdyed in the indigo vat). Across an afternoon, she can make as many as ten variations on a color. Hung together to dry in the workshop, the harmonies she creates sing even before they eventually make their way to the loom.

Juana values the many dimensions of her relationship with plants. "We use certain plants by drinking them, healing with them, dyeing with them, decorating with them," she says. "They are important to our health. Because they connect us to Mother Earth, they are a deep part of our body and our wellbeing."

A COLOR OF HISTORY AND FAITH

Juana's favorite color is the deep, deep burgundy she coaxes out of vats of cochineal, an amazing dye source that can also produce soft pinks, vivid pinks, various reds and oranges, and a deeply satisfying rainbow of burgundies and purples.

LEFT: Weighing cochineal on its way to the vat RIGHT: Juana Gutiérrez Contreras tending the fires. The green leaves are *maruush*, which will yield green color on wool yarn.

The dye itself is carminic acid, which comes from the bodies of the female *Dactylopius coccus*, a parasitic scale insect that feeds on *Opuntia cacti* (*nopales* in Spanish). Carminic acid makes up approximately 25 percent of the body weight of the domesticated cochineal insect, about double the ratio of several species of wild cousins. Domesticated cochineal also lacks some of the woolly protective "coat" of wild strains[10] that is composed of lipid proteins that can interfere with dye absorption.

Juana, like most Zapotec dyers and weavers, sees cochineal as integral to the cultural patrimony of Oaxaca. Archaeologists date Oaxacan textile fragments dyed with cochineal to approximately 1000 CE, and very detailed descriptions of cochineal farming and dyeing survive from codices and missives dating to the early Spanish Colonial era. The Spanish, who eventually exported cochineal to Europe in great quantities, considered this vivid, beautiful red dyestuff "one of the great treasures of the New World,"[11] along with gold and silver. Much has been written about cochineal's lucrative and prestigious role in the European textile trade across the centuries prior to the invention of synthetic dyes. But the origins of the cochineal insect and cochineal dye practice are not exactly a matter around which there is universal agreement.

Some posit Peru as cochineal's point of origin. The Peruvian textile record of cochineal stretches back 400 to 600 years earlier than Mexico's, with subsequent increased use among the Inca, where red was a symbol of kingship.[12] Observers point out that Mexico's more humid conditions generally destroy ancient textiles and call into question conclusions reached only by citing Peru's well-preserved textile remains; just because evidence does not survive in Mexico doesn't mean it didn't happen there first.

Recent mitochondrial DNA studies of domesticated *Dactylopius* populations in Mexico, Peru, and Madeira (the latter population introduced from Mexico) show more genetic diversity in Mexico, a strong indication that the species originated there.[13] Others refer to Mexico's greater diversity of predators feeding on cochineal as a sign that "Mexican cochineal and its predators have been coevolving for a much longer time than their Peruvian equivalents."[14]

By way of explaining the ancient domestication of cochineal, Juana and her family refer to the domestication of corn. "People in this area took a simple grass and turned it into our most important food, so they knew something about breeding," she says, clearly not much interested in discussing Mexican versus Peruvian cochineal. She's more engrossed in the colors she makes with it. "I *feel* the colors I get from cochineal, especially dark burgundy, because I relate it to my faith. Long ago in church I saw the red blood of Jesus, and cochineal brings me back to the fact that He died for us. It's emotional. It's powerful. It's alive," she says. "I feel its magic."

Juana and Antonio produce a few kilos of cochineal themselves—less than a fifth of what they use each year—mainly to show visitors to the workshop the full story of cochineal dyeing. There are always several dozen paddle-shaped leaves of nopal hanging in their courtyard, protected from rain, heat, and birds that might eat the beetles. Every three months in warm weather and every four months in cold weather, each mature beetle is brushed by hand from the cactus into a bowl with a tiny flat stick. Smaller beetles are left on the cactus for another week or two to grow. When the insects are harvested, the nopal is composted to make room in the courtyard for new cactus leaves.

Bowlfuls of harvested beetles are tossed into a sieve, which is tapped gently over fresh nopal leaves laid flat on the floor of the courtyard. Tiny young beetles pass through the sieve and onto their new homes. It only takes a few hours for the beetles to bite into the nopal and begin feeding. Once the little ones choose a place to feed, they don't budge, and the nopal leaves are hung undisturbed until the next harvest time comes around.

The harvested beetles are dried and then ground on a stone *metate* prior to a dyeing session. The luscious purple-red powder is first dissolved and then filtered through cloth as it enters the dye vat, eventually producing an equally luscious range of pinks, reds, oranges, and purples, depending on what is added to the vat or how the yarn is treated beforehand.

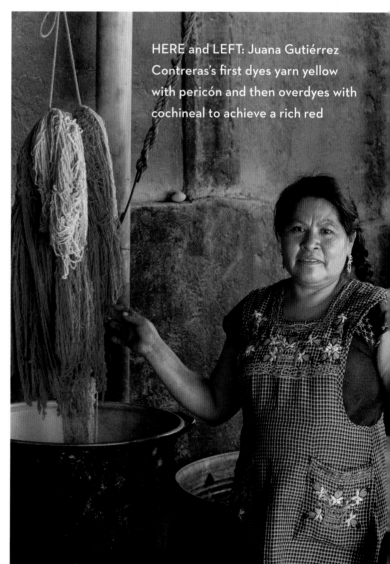

HERE and LEFT: Juana Gutiérrez Contreras's first dyes yarn yellow with pericón and then overdyes with cochineal to achieve a rich red

CLOCKWISE from top left: Paddles of nopal cactus thick with cochineal beetles at bottom and fresh paddles newly infested on the top. Beetles are removed by hand, one at a time. Tiny young beetles slip through a sieve before biting into and feeding on cactus.

CLOCKWISE: Grinding dried beetles on a stone metate. Ground cochineal is first slaked and then strained through a cloth as it enters the vat. To make this rich aubergine color, yarn is first dyed yellow with pericón, then overdyed with cochineal, and finished in an iron-rich bath of pomegranate skins.

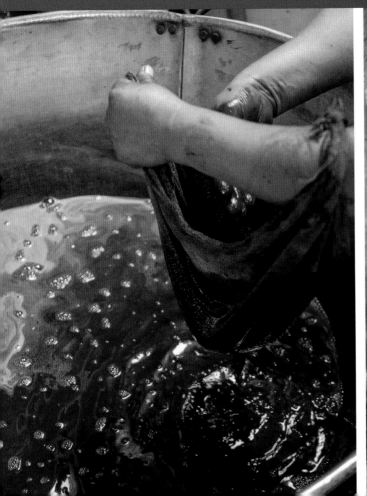

When Juana mordants yarn with lengua de vaca leaves, she can create pink cochineal shades that darken to dusty violet in an iron vat, or fully saturated purples when overdyed with indigo. Mordanting with alum pushes cochineal toward the reds. An iron vat will darken these tones toward burgundy. She achieves still other colors by using yarn already dyed with pericón that, when overdyed with cochineal, turns coral, orange, or warm red. The most delicious, rich aubergine emerges when these warm reds are immersed in a vat of pomegranate.

NATURAL COLOR REVIVAL

Juana says that her commitment to natural dyes took root when, as a girl, she witnessed a young neighbor badly burn himself on the stomach with sulfuric acid used in synthetic dying. Whatever the motive, her study of natural color began during a time when some influential Teotico elders had begun to embrace botanical dyes as a matter not just of safety but of culture and heritage.

Weaver Juan Isaac Vázquez worked with internationally renowned artist Rufino Tamayo, and later with Francisco Toledo, to weave tapestries they designed. Tamayo's search for cultural and artistic authenticity, in contrast to his highly academic training and early professional life, led him back to his home state of Oaxaca to study major Zapotec ruins like Monte Albán and to work with Oaxacan artisans to realize his projects. These collaborations undoubtedly played a role in elevating Teotitlán's current reputation as a weaving center. For twenty-two years, Vázquez and Tamayo explored tapestry together, with the idea of reestablishing a pre-synthetic vocabulary of color as part of their collaboration. Many credit Vázquez with the revival of natural dyes. Although they have not entirely supplanted synthetic methods, they do have important proponents, the

Gutiérrez family among them.

Famed Zapotec artist and teacher Francisco Toledo continues to work with highly skilled weavers like Roman Gutiérrez to push the discipline forward at the Centro de las Artes de San Agustín.

Elena Phipps, former chief textile conservator at The Metropolitan Museum in New York, sees the impetus behind the relatively recent reexploration of natural dyes as coming from outside Central and South American weaving communities. "It's tourist driven," she says. "While it's great that people are re-learning natural dye processes, it's complicated culturally because it derives from the American do-it-yourself movement and other impulses." Author, educator, and expert observer of Teotitlán's weaving scene, Lynn Stephen supports Phipps's observation: "For consumers, buying the 'old ways,' the traditional culture, is often as important as buying the products themselves."[15]

Whether the revival of natural dyes originated in a search for artistic authenticity and cultural heritage, like the collaboration of Rufino Tamayo and Juan Isaac Vázquez, or in a quest to meet the demands of external markets, Teotico natural dyeing is defined as a point of pride, a competitive distinction in workshops that pursue it, and as a responsible path in environmental terms. The Vasquez and Gutiérrez families, along with other skilled Teotico practitioners, are in the best position to weigh the personal and communal merits of going natural.

ROOTLESSNESS AND ROOTS

As a teenager, Porfirio, one of Juana's younger siblings, left Teotitlán for the United States to work in restaurants. Although English was his third language (after Zapotec at home and Spanish in grade school), he quickly worked his way up to earning a decent living, eventually as manager of a cement-making facility. He spent over a decade away from his family and his birthplace. During that time, Porfirio became completely at home in the newness and noise of life in California, the world's fifth-largest economy. "I really left Oaxaca," he says. "I became Mexican-American."

Eventually he returned to Teotitlán. It was a shock. "I wasn't a tourist. I was home. But the simplicity of it all hit me really hard—the dirt floors, the reed fences, the outhouses. Everything felt harsh."

He found respite in standing by his father's loom, talking to him while he worked, watching a process he had mostly ignored as a child. He found himself watching his mother prepare meals in the kitchen, moved by her combination of skill and spirituality. "I intuitively understood the sign language, the movement of her hands grabbing the blessings from the sky and bringing them to the food, bringing a sense of greater Being down from above into what she was making for us, her family." An undoable knot of associations, part individual biography and part collective heritage, tightened in Porfirio. "I said to myself, 'This is where my deepest roots are. My people have been here for hundreds, maybe thousands of years.' In the face of so much rootlessness in the world, I had roots."

After his long absence, Porfirio saw his home with new eyes. His vivid reconnection to his native culture took shape in three ways. First was an ancestral sense of belonging to the land. "Our whole culture starts with people living off of this land: food and plants from the land, water from the land, cotton and wool for clothes from the land, clay from the land. My food, my life, my nurturing happened on this land," he says, still energized by his simultaneously new and ancient sense of place.

Second came a deep appreciation for the rituals of Zapotec life. Beginning with his mother's ritual blessing of the family's food, Porfirio started to ask questions about deeply ingrained everyday habits. "As I began to see how spiritual Zapotec people really are, I wanted to learn more. I turned into 'the headache kid' at home, always asking questions: What is that? Why do you do it that way? Where did that come from? My

Cochineal and lemon juice make warmer reds

mom sometimes answered with her stories and sometimes just said, 'This is just what we do and how we live. These things don't have to be explained!'"

One of his lines of inquiry focused on *petates*, mats handwoven of dried palm leaves. During his childhood, Porfirio paid no attention to these humble

A rug designed and woven by Porfirio Gutiérrez, based on his exploration of traditional woven palm mats called *petates*
OPPOSITE: Porfirio Gutiérrez, weaver, entrepreneur, and keeper of Zapotec culture

floor coverings, but a returnee's fresh sense of discovery helped him see how ubiquitous they are in Teotitlán. "I have eyes now for what passed unnoticed every day. I see now that when a woman gives birth at home, it happens on a petate. When newlyweds come to the altar to say their vows, they stand on a petate. When someone dies, the casket is placed on a petate during the funeral and is usually covered by one. In the days before coffins, petates did that work, too. In the old days in church, women and children would sit on long petate runners while men and priests would use chairs or benches. We're grounded by these simple petates throughout our lives." Very recently, he has extended his interest in natural fiber crafts to include palm leaves, agave fiber, and jute in his weaving work. "I want to understand the reasons for the old arts, to listen to my elders, and remember their stories."

The third element of Porfirio's reconnection to home and family came as a surprise. "I discovered a passion for weaving that I didn't even know I had," he says, a bit of astonishment still coloring his voice. Yes, he had woven his own backpack as a child. But no, he had no intention of becoming a weaver. Nevertheless, that remarkable Teotico touchstone of weaving reached out and grabbed him. The only way to explain Porfirio's sudden focus on weaving is that he found in it a way to express the depth and beauty he was seeing with his part-American, part-Zapotec, part-Mexican eyes. "I can tell the story of our *reality*," he exclaims. "I know our way of life and our beliefs and our heritage, and I see them with a self that comes from here. But I also come from there," he explains, pointing north. "I bring this complex story now to what I make. I grab all the tools available to me, including my cultural DNA and my own individual experience, and I weave."

Starting with Juana's naturally dyed yarns, Porfirio's first weaving was mostly olive green, from maruush leaves, and included traditional Zapotec design elements like the zigzag pattern called montanitas. "Yes, they can look like mountains. But I also saw in them the shape of rivers flowing back and forth across valleys, carrying the water that makes the difference between life and death. The back and forth looked to me like contact between this living world and the next, between now and history, between who I was and who I am, and even who I might be one day."

The emotional and spiritual tendencies that Porfirio was uncovering and expressing through weaving eventually joined with his interest in petate mats. He found himself weaving wool tapestries of enlarged petate patterns, sometimes emphasizing the over-and-under rhythm of their simple patterns, sometimes contrasting broad bands of light and dark. In this new body of work, Porfirio wove himself a metaphorical mat upon which to stand during his period of spiritual and cultural reentry into his homeland. He continues to weave, among other things, interpretations of petates to ground him in his burgeoning identity as a weaver.

Porfirio's exploration of ancient palm mats was entirely new to the tapestry weaving traditions of Teotitlán. His creative extension of the heritage craft of Zapotec weaving occurs in a visual language that is at once personal and traditional. Because the great craft forms of Mexico have always appropriated what seemed beautiful from other traditions—whether they came from Spain, from Pacific trade with Asia, or from neighboring peoples—Porfirio's work clearly rests comfortably on the contemporary end of a millennia-old Zapotec weaving continuum.

BECAUSE I MADE IT

Not everyone sees it this way. Porfirio is sometimes criticized on both sides of the Mexican-American border for pushing the boundaries of Zapotec weaving away from familiar motifs and compositions and into new territory. As the artist himself says when countering these occasional judgments, "If I have no say in what I'm making, then I am not an artist." Ancient traditions, as precious and valuable as they are, can't become straitjackets in which artists are expected to live out their creative lives.

"Evolution has always happened. If a craft community is deeply rooted in the craft technique, the tradition, and daily experience, it will have changes," Porfirio points out. If an art form is alive, its creators engage with it and channel it into expressions of what is beautiful and important to them through their choices of material, color, and technique. They "discuss" issues that weigh on them or lift them up to the light using their motifs and patterns. They reveal themselves, sometimes unconsciously, as artists always have, in symbolism.

As the forces of culture and tradition pass through the individual creator, they are not just expressed, they are transformed. They are used and they are added to, and it is this very tension that keeps a tradition alive and viable.

Porfirio's response to criticism of his adventuresome work is very clear. "My work is authentic because *I* made it! Artists are also inventors. We change the course of life and history, the way of living and seeing, the sense of what's useful and important. If you want to talk about authenticity, let's talk. Tell me who you are. Ask me who I am. Let's be authentic together."

Yarn emerging
from the cochineal
dye pot

A Family of Reds

A family of reds, from purples and violets to deep reds, pinks, corals, and oranges, is created with different amounts of cochineal, different mordants and modifiers, and various overdyes of cochineal and other natural dyestuffs. These are among the most splendid of Juana Gutiérrez Contreras's 200 colors.

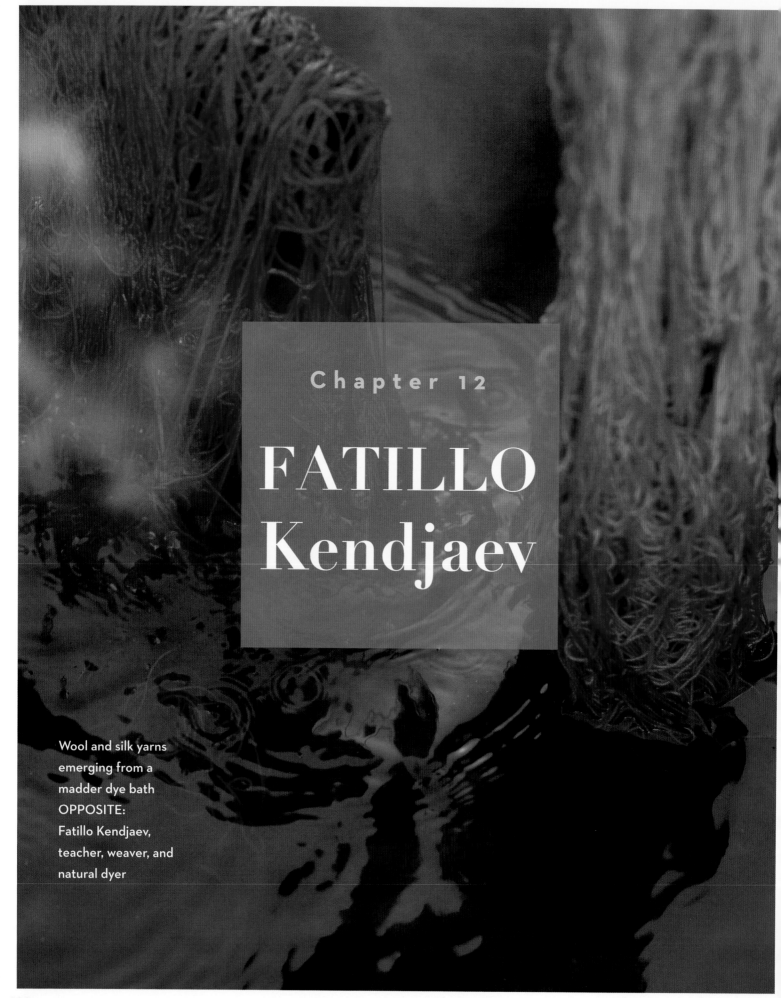

Chapter 12

FATILLO Kendjaev

Wool and silk yarns
emerging from a
madder dye bath
OPPOSITE:
Fatillo Kendjaev,
teacher, weaver, and
natural dyer

BUKHARA RED

In 1997, when Fatillo Kendjaev decided to revive the ancient carpets of his native Bukhara, he had his work cut out for him. During the seventy years of Soviet rule that ended in 1991, renowned traditional crafts like Uzbek ikat had been outlawed. Like ikat, the carpets represented old ethnic identities that the Communist Party wanted to replace with their monolithic ideal, the Universal Soviet Man. Uzbek ikat weavers sometimes suffered stays in prison for making their textiles undercover in basements and hidden workshops.

ABOVE: *Suzani* embroidered with several shades of madder-dyed thread (and other natural colors) by Fatillo's daughter, Zarina
RIGHT: Yarn emerging from the madder bath

The suppression of traditional native crafts, coupled with the broad industrialization of the twentieth century, led to a serious decline of Uzbek handmade traditions. While carpets remained important gifts and essential elements of décor in Uzbek culture, machine-made goods were very much in ascendance.

Fatillo was motivated to take on the craft challenge by a post-Soviet wave of interest in Uzbek identity. What had been outlawed was celebrated once again by this newly independent people. Trained in both fine art and teaching, Fatillo first taught private students the furrier skills he learned from his father, eventually transitioning to natural dyeing and Bukharan carpet making in 1997. UNESCO funded a carpet-making school in 2001, with Fatillo as its leader, and his talented wife, Firuza, and daughter Zarina as teachers. Together they trained more than 250 apprentices, some of whom have gone on to start their own businesses.

Fatillo's carpets give voice to centuries of Uzbek heritage. His meticulous research into textiles depicted in miniature paintings of the fourteenth and fifteenth centuries, as well as museum collections of eighteenth- and nineteenth-century nomadic and urban carpets, opened up an entire world of pattern, much of it little known to twenty-first-century weavers.

Naturally dyed yarns deepen the authenticity of every carpet Fatillo and his family make. All yarns, wool and silk alike, are dyed in copper pots with alum as mordant. Walnut hulls from mountain farmers create deep browns. Onion skins from local vegetable markets make yellow, as do apple, grape, and mulberry leaves. Pomegranate skins create a

beautiful bronze green. Indigo comes from India, and cochineal from Peru. Madder root, essential to the spectacular reds, oranges, and chocolate browns of Central Asian textiles, is imported from Uzbekistan's neighbor to the south, Afghanistan.

One of Fatillo's most popular designs originally came from Turkmenistan, whose border with Uzbekistan runs along the Amu Darya River. Madder variations, from orange-umber to dark red, smolder against each other. What is called a Bukhara Red carpet grew out of the textile traditions of the Tekke people, whose repeated geometric medallions were generally rendered in white, black, and russet against a deep madder-red background. The patterns within the medallions revealed which nomadic Tekke clan made each carpet. So many of these were traded through Bukhara, the city nearest to the Tekke lands, that the patterns took on its name.

The reds of madder run deep in this part of the world. Fragments of an exquisitely worked leather quiver made in Mesopotamia (and dyed madder red)

CLOCKWISE: (from top left) Ground madder root on its way to the dye pot   Fatillo Kendjaev tends
the pot. Zarina and Fatillo at work Yarn takes on a brilliant madder red   OPPOSITE: Bukhara Red
rug designs, rich in madder tones, come from the Tekke people of Turkmenistan. They are called
"Bukhara Red" because they were traded through the city for centuries.

were found in an Egyptian tomb dating from around 2000 BCE, roughly the same time as the earliest evidence of settlement in Bukhara. Bukhara would have been an outpost in the Bronze Age trade in luxury goods, which stretched westward to the Mediterranean and eastward to China. The Silk Road grew out

of these early routes, and Bukhara, because of its location, prospered as trading center and caravanserai. Skilled artisans, dyers included, played an important role in creating products whose beauty commanded a price that justified the long and sometimes perilous journeys of traders and merchants.

The perils facing merchants today stem largely from internet behemoth Amazon rather than roadside bandits, but Fatillo is insulated from the worst of this competition. Much of his sales come from tourists looking for an authentic memento of their visit to Bukhara or from visitors to the annual International Folk Art Market in Santa Fe, New Mexico. Fatillo and his family are regulars there, carrying their Silk Road heritage and their madder reds to the United States.

LEFT: Fatillo Kendjaev and his wife, Firuza, tend to their vats. HERE: Daughter Zarina's suzani hanging in the courtyard of the Bukhara School of Carpet Making and Natural Dyes

Chapter 13

Institute for KHMER Traditional Textiles

HERE: Traditional Cambodian *samphot hol* ikat featuring the reds of lac

OPPOSITE: The late Kikuo Morimoto, founder of IKTT

RED RISES AGAIN

The late Kyoto-born textile artist Kikuo Morimoto arrived at the Thai-Cambodian border in 1994 to help people displaced in the aftermath of nearly twenty-five years of civil war. From 1970 to 1993, the entire country was shaken to the core by political and social upheaval, culminating in the brutal Khmer Rouge regime, under whose policies up to 25 percent of the population perished. Among the groups hardest hit were minorities, intellectuals, and artists. Cultural preservation group Cambodian Living Arts estimates that 90 percent of Cambodian artists were lost. After the conflict, traditional arts, textiles included, lived on only in the minds of elderly survivors.

In 1995, Kikuo received UNESCO funding to survey the state of sericulture and silk weaving in thirty-six villages across eight provinces, some of them still in sensitive areas not fully reclaimed from the Khmer Rouge. "In 1994 a third of the country was still fighting, so there were many areas, called the pink (or danger) zones that we should not enter, but it was in one of the villages there that I found three grandmothers who possessed magnificent skills,"[1] Kikuo commented some years ago. All in all, his research revealed a scant handful of women in their seventies and eighties who still knew the old ways of dyeing and weaving.[2] Inspired by these "silk grandmothers," Kikuo founded the Institute for Khmer Traditional Textiles (IKTT) in 1996 to revive Cambodia's ancient arts of sericulture, dyeing, and weaving.

The first Khmer kingdom rose in the seventh century and expanded to its greatest breadth during the reign of revered ruler Jayavarman VII in the twelfth century. Three hundred years later, the empire collapsed, leaving behind centuries of glorious architecture. Most notable among the 1,400 surviving temples are Angkor Wat and the Bayon, just a few kilometers from the town of Siem Reap. Detailed bas-relief wall carvings indicate an elaborate vocabulary of pattern in classical-era textiles featuring natural motifs as well as geometric patterns thought to descend from Indian ikats called *patola*.[3] The skirts of dancing *apsara* spirits are especially lovely.

Kikuo saw a direct line between these carved patterns and the *chong kiet* (the Khmer term for ikat) still being made, though very rarely after a generation of conflict. He was especially impressed with the dense, small-scale ikat patterns of *samphot hol*, the hip wrappers or sarongs that were worn by both women and men. Traditionally woven of resist-dyed yarns in natural reds, yellows, blacks, greens, and blues, patterns varied beautifully among Cambodia's diverse ethnic groups.

The most prominent color in these textiles is lac red, ranging from saturated brick red to vibrant fuchsia tones. Lac is an ancient dye made from the insect *Laccifer lacca* (formerly *Coccus lacca*), which feeds on more than 160 tree varieties from northern India to Southeast Asia. Temperature sensitive, lac insects thrive best in the shade of a mature forest canopy. They secrete a resinous substance around living twigs

The most prominent color in these textiles is lac red, ranging from saturated brick red to vibrant fuchsia tones. Lac is an ancient dye made from the insect *Laccifer lacca* (formerly *Coccus lacca*) which feeds on more than 160 tree varieties from northern India to Southeast Asia.

OPPOSITE: Spools of carefully dyed silk yarns carry the patterns of these weft ikats
LEFT: Weaving on the loom ABOVE: By masking specific parts of the weft threads, patterns are dyed into them prior to weaving

Traditional, small-scale patterns require precision in both dyeing and weaving to render their patterns in the final cloth

Sticklac is ground with mortar
and pestle prior to dyeing
BELOW: Spools of space-dyed
threads ready to weave
RIGHT: Lac-dyed silk drying
in the sun

to form a cocoon called sticklac. The female insects lay their eggs within it. Natural shellac is made from the resin, while lac dyes come from the female insects whose cells are rich in laccaic acid, a natural red colorant.

When the sticklac is harvested, still populated with insects and eggs, it is pulverized and then decocted in a water bath for a few hours. Water treated with tamarind leaves, naturally heavy in aluminum, is added as a mordant. Skeins of silk are repeatedly soaked in the dye bath and then beaten as many as nine times to achieve a sumptuous red.

Until 1970, Cambodia was a major exporter of lac, but the time of upheaval, followed by rampant logging in the postwar period, ushered in a major decline in the shaded habitats suitable for the lac insect. Most lac is produced in India now.

In part as a reaction to the deforestation and loss

of natural habitat, Kikuo moved IKTT to a forest-ed 57-acre plot of land about 30 kilometers north of Siem Reap, which is now home to 250 textile artisans and their families. In addition to establishing homes and workshops, dye gardens and food gardens, the IKTT family has planted 10,000 mulberry trees to ensure food for the six or seven broods of Cambo-dian silkworms they tend each year. Carved at the entrance to the institute is a sign that reads: "If you don't care for the tool, you don't care for the work. If you don't care for the forest, you don't care for life."

A young student visitor, Antonia Beard, described the wooded realm of IKTT: "The forest is more than just a place of work. It is a place where working to-ward reviving lost traditions has meant the bringing together of a strong and caring community."[4] It is a place where more than 1,000 years of Cambodian textile tradition have been revived, from the growing of silkworms and dyestuffs to the weaving of sophis-ticated traditional ikat patterns.

Midori Iwamoto, who worked with Kikuo before his passing in 2017 and is still in a leadership role in IKTT, notes that lac continues to be important to the work of IKTT dyers and weavers, but at present, they need to import it. Reestablishing lac in Cambodia has been a slow process.

One of IKTT's most recent projects grows from the realization that some ancient Khmer ikats were woven on indigo-dyed warps, creating a spectacular dialogue between the rich red of lac and the haunt-ingly beautiful blues of indigo. IKTT artisans are currently working with Japanese experts to master indigo farming, processing, and dyeing.

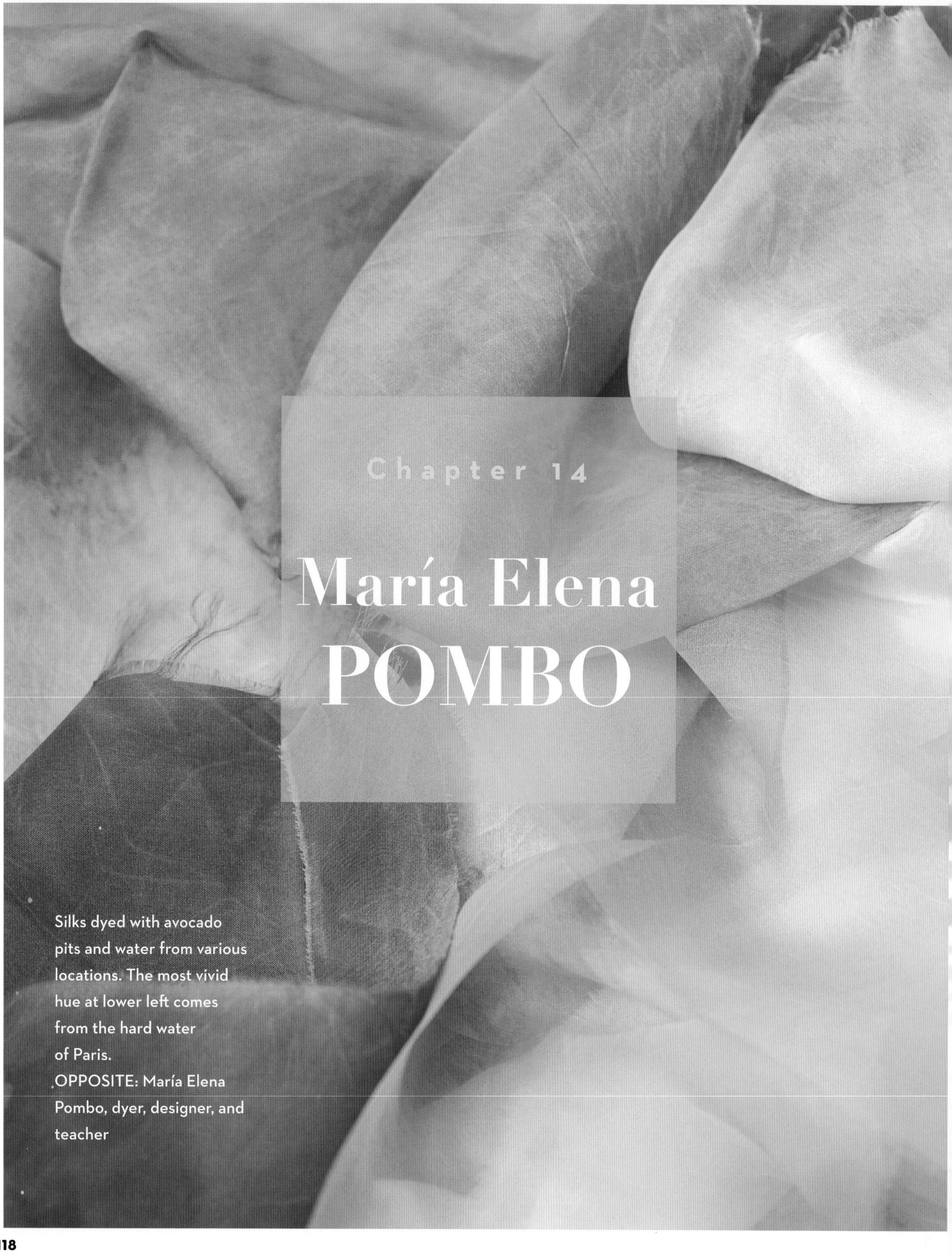

Chapter 14

María Elena POMBO

Silks dyed with avocado pits and water from various locations. The most vivid hue at lower left comes from the hard water of Paris.
OPPOSITE: María Elena Pombo, dyer, designer, and teacher

IN THE WATER

María Elena Pombo is clearly open to change. She moved from Venezuela to the United States and from engineering to fashion design, accruing the skills of a natural dyer and teacher along the way. These four occupations are expressed in her transformation of the seeds of an ancient fruit, relished as part of the human diet for more than 10,000 years,[1] into a range of blush and rose tones. In her hands, avocado pits yield fascinating colors, in part because because of her investigation of the mineral composition of waters from around the world.

As most readers of do-it-yourself books and online articles can tell you, it is not especially difficult to turn avocado pits into colors like the soothing, reassuring pastel-of-the-moment, Millennial Pink. Rich in tannin, the pits carry both mordant and color within them. "The process is like making tea," says María Elena (who goes by Mari). "You simmer the colorant out of the seeds and dye the fabric in the colored water. Colors and intensities vary with the amount of material you start with, the concentration of dyestuff in the water, and the fiber content of the fabric."

The color also depends, she discovered, on the water itself. During a teaching trip to Paris, Mari saw a marked difference between the colors she achieved with Parisian water and the colors she made with New York City tap water in her studio. Paris water brought out magenta and burgundy tones, while New York water reliably revealed a spectrum of blush hues. Because she brings an engineer's rigor to her design and dyeing work, it became Mari's mission to figure out why.

In her studio, which is a combination of laboratory and fashion atelier, Mari analyzed the chemical makeup of bottles of water delivered by friends living or traveling around the world. Relying on pH strips as well as available data on the mineral composition of various water supplies, she found that, yes, pH levels matter. "Acidic water will make avocado colors shift toward a yellow undertone, while alkaline water will intensify and redden the colors." But the minerals and metals in the water also make a difference. "Hard water, like Parisian water, will also help along the intensity of color."

Each water she has analyzed shows a different fingerprint. The geological conditions of the source of the water plus metals used in pipes and infrastructure to deliver the water plus local pollution will contribute something to the water. Iron, aluminum, and copper are all well-known natural-dye catalysts, each

LEFT: Avocado dye and two modifiers used by María Elena Pombo
HERE: Avocado pits are crushed prior to soaking in hot water to create the dye bath

of them shifting tones and intensities in their own way. Waters sourced from different locations contain these elements in divergent combinations, capable of influencing dye effects in interesting ways—effects that can be (almost) replicated through study of the properties of waters and the tones they evoke. Mari offers some basic examples: "Water is easily modified with acids like lemon or lime juice or alkalines like calcium carbonate or baking soda. You can adjust things to make the shades you are looking for," she suggests. Working with, and playing with, the qualities of local water has become a staple of her natural-dye workshops in North America and Europe.

The collections Mari designs for her own fashion line, Fragmentario, always put her discoveries to work. Recent seasons have incorporated her avocado alchemy in ethereal designs. Inventive use of ground avocado pits in a contact-dye context creates texture, and hints of other botanical dyestuffs such as turmeric and onion skins enhance and shift the avocado/NYC-water blushes that predominate. Should her work inspire a session of overdyeing or dyeing at home, she offers dye kits that make it easy to achieve some of her effects.

water origin
Colombia

water origin
Pari

Alkalinity

pH

Hardness

Iron

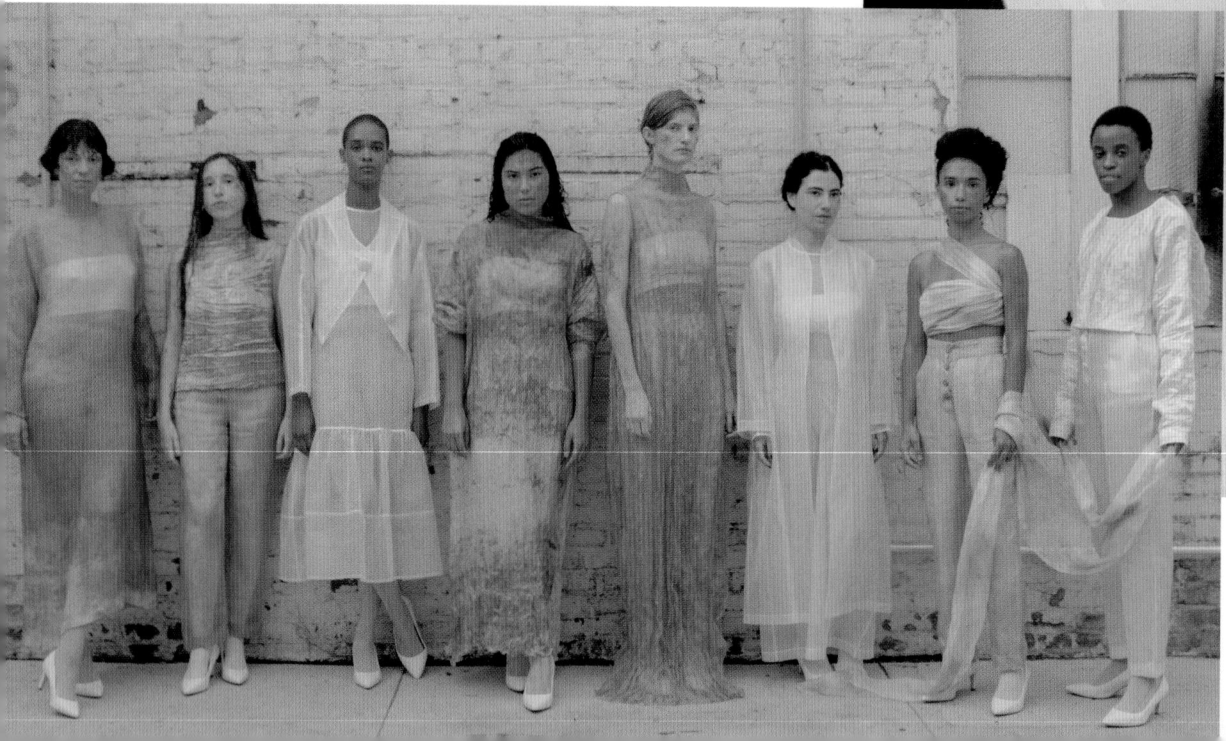

Cop

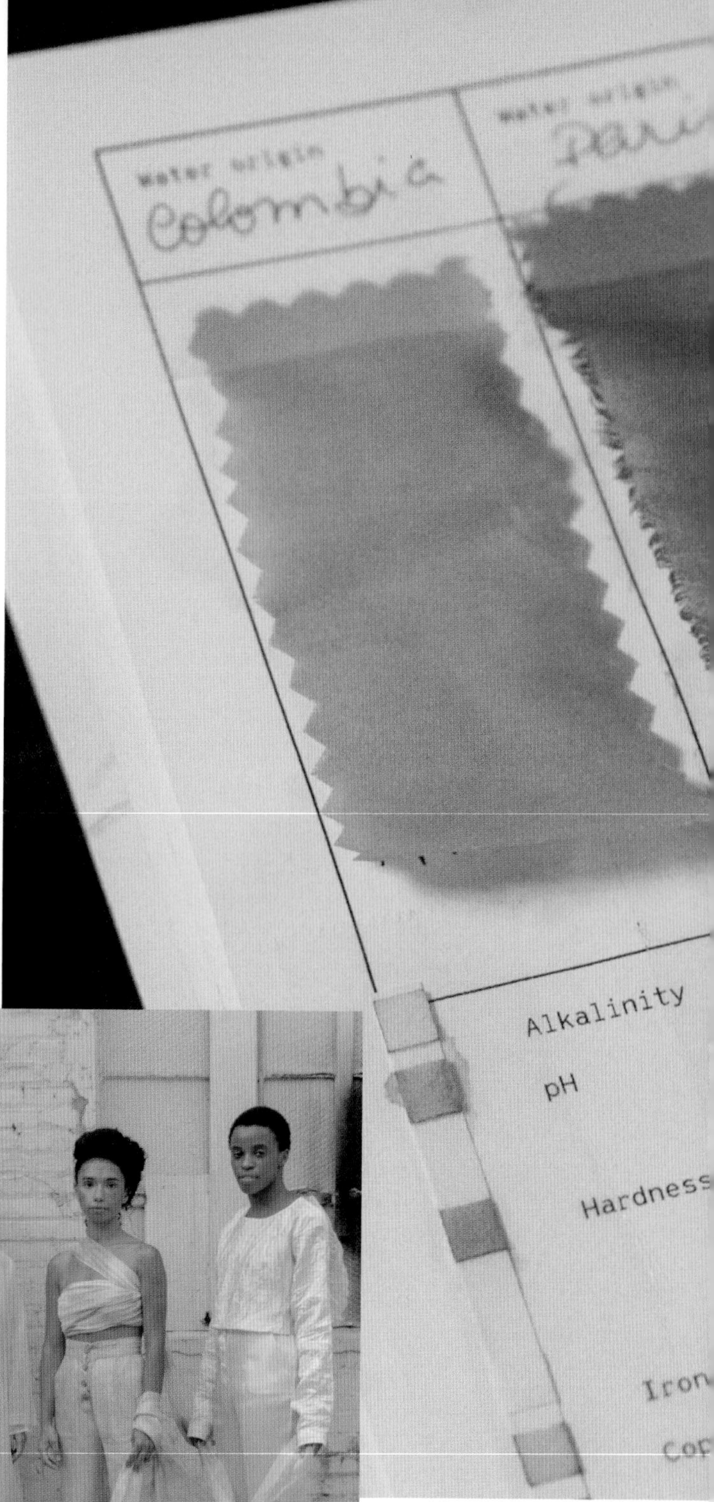

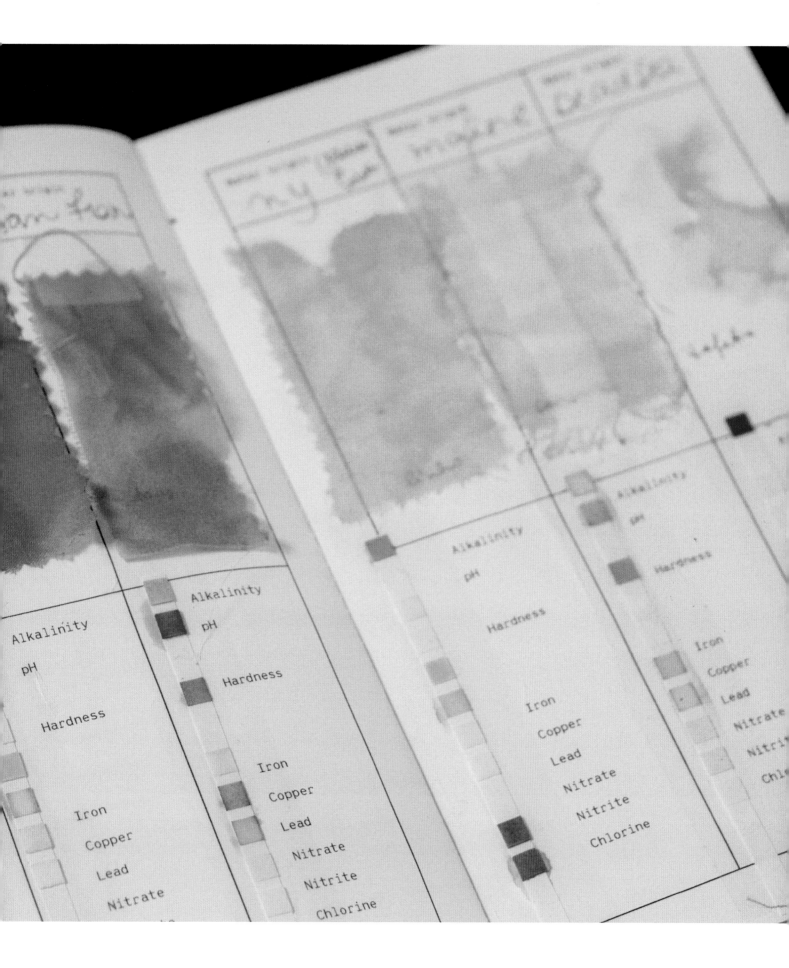

Alkalinity

pH

Hardness

Iron

Copper

Lead

Nitrate

Alkalinity

pH

Hardness

Iron

Copper

Lead

Nitrate

Nitrite

Chlorine

Alkalinity

pH

Hardness

Iron

Copper

Lead

Nitrate

Nitrite

Chlorine

Alkalinity

pH

Hardness

Iron

Copper

Lead

Nitrate

Nitrite

Chlorine

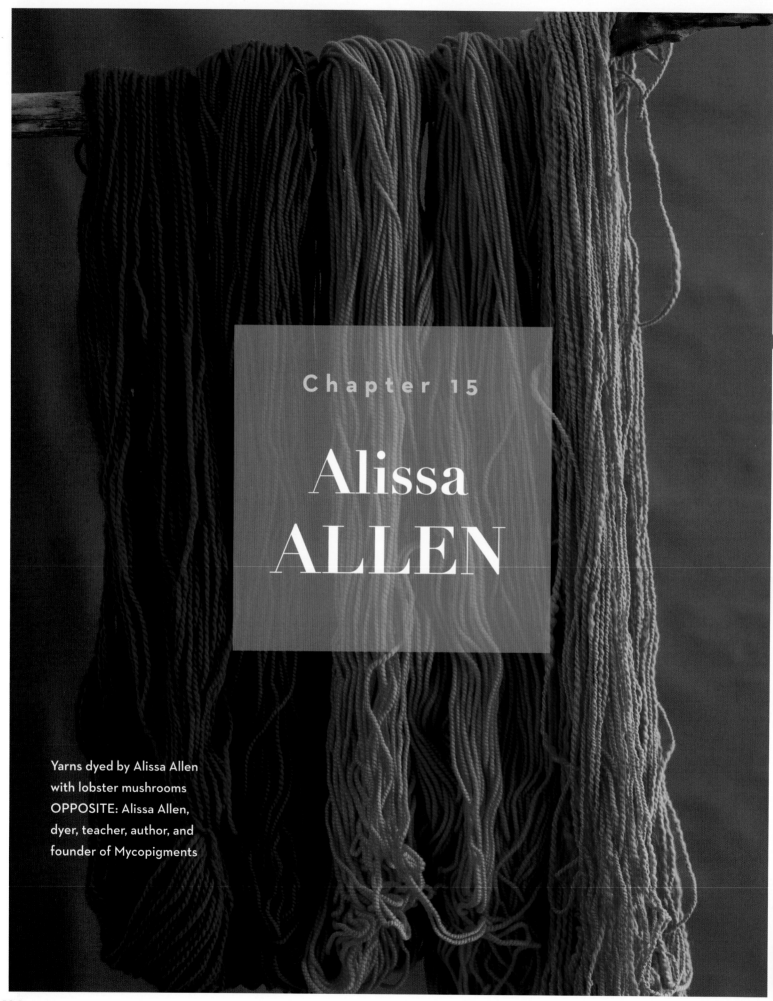

Chapter 15

Alissa
ALLEN

Yarns dyed by Alissa Allen
with lobster mushrooms
OPPOSITE: Alissa Allen,
dyer, teacher, author, and
founder of Mycopigments

Stalking
WILD COLOR

"Mom 'stalked the wild asparagus,'" Alissa Allen says, describing her childhood. "As a veteran food forager, she taught me to be comfortable looking at the ground for useful things." Only in her twenties did Alissa realize that many people she wasn't related to were interested in mushrooms, too, which prompted her to join the Puget Sound Mycological Society in 1998.

At the group's annual wild mushroom show, she noticed a fifteen-year-old poster board featuring yellowed feral specimens alongside a card of yarn samples. Their saturated reds, greens, and ochres gleamed against the faded background. As the text explained, the colors had been made with mushrooms. Fellow society member Sarah Clark, the dyer of the samples, offered Alissa a starter kit of mordanted yarn and other supplies. "I tried it at home," she says, "and it was love at first sight. "I really dove into mycology at that point. I was a sponge. I was hanging out with the identifiers, the taxonomists, memorized the names. I really came at color from a mycology perspective, not a fiber arts perspective."

FUNGAL ANTECEDENTS

Aside from Sarah, Alissa came into contact with few mushroom dyers. She read books by Miriam Rice and Arleen Bessette on the topic, building her technique through practice and experimentation.

Neither archaeology nor oral tradition suggests that mushrooms were historically used for color in any important way. It seems to be a late-twentieth-century phenomenon. Miriam Rice, considered the originator of mushroom dyeing in contemporary times, started her colorful work in Northern California in the 1970s, when there was no shortage of rain and mushrooms were plentiful. She began by throwing a foraged handful of sulphur-yellow *Naematoloma fasciculare* into a dye pot with some yarn,

There are several different avenues to travel if you're looking for some noticeable myco-dye colors. Oranges and reds, can be made with *Dermocyedes* from any region. If using fresh mushrooms, a one-to-one ratio of fiber to dyestuff will yield nice color on yarns mordanted with alum.

she expanded the natural color vocabulary of dyers in the United States and Scandinavia.[1] Miriam Rice passed away in 2010, but the International Mushroom Dye Institute continues her legacy.

A LIFE IN MUSHROOMS

As Alissa's mastery grew, she taught dye workshops for mushroom clubs and fiber groups in the Puget Sound area for a few years, transitioning gradually from emergency room medical assistant to full-time instructor of mushroom dyeing. Her sought-after sessions, offered in the US and abroad under her company's name, Mycopigments, are consistently sold out. She is currently writing a book about her discipline.

The colors possible in mushroom dyeing are, of course, dependent on particular species, with some in more sensitive ecological circumstances than others. Alissa's curriculum addresses many of the sensitivities around mushroom harvesting. "Mushrooms are the fruiting body of a much larger organism. When you pick a mushroom, you are only taking the sexual organs away; any fleshy mushroom has likely dropped its spores and played its role in the prop-

which, satisfyingly, turned lemon yellow. Working across many species and five mordants, which she eventually whittled down to just alum and iron, the range of colors she made was impressive, and her sample library of dyed wools, silks, and cottons was vast. Through her book, *Mushrooms for Color,* and her lectures,

Dyeing with mushrooms can deepen
our awareness of low-lying ecosystems
living along the forest floor

Lobster mushrooms yield earthy
shades of brick red and coral
OPPOSITE: Colorful parasitic mold
Hypomyces lactifluorum gives what
we call "lobster mushrooms" their
characteristics. Most mushrooms
can be colonized.

agation of the species already. Some mushrooms are so tremendously prolific that there's less worry. If, for example, you've been hunting for chanterelles or morels in North America, you know that you can't pick them all, even if you try.

"But if you're in areas of denser population, you do have to be careful. Specific groups of mushrooms with delicate mycelium structure, like those from the Thelephorales order, have declined in numbers recently. They produce blue or blue-green or gray, depending on how stringent your definition of blue is. *Hydnellum peckii* yield different colors based on where they grow. Specimens from the northeast US yield grayer colors, while their Alaskan relatives make a dark, almost teal shade. Nonetheless, I'm shifting the way I teach about these mushrooms. If you want blues, go for indigo or woad, less problematic sources."

Another aspect of mushroom ethics involves preserving the forests where most mushrooms thrive. "We must protect the forests we have left, and you're more likely to protect them if you have a connection to them. If you get out there and know the woods through mushroom harvesting, you're invested. It's all part of my secret ploy to get people engaged with their local ecosystem."

BRIGHT COLORS FROM SHADY PLACES

"There are several different avenues to travel if you're looking for some noticeable myco-dye colors. Oranges and reds, for example, can be made with *Dermocydes* from any region. If using fresh mushrooms, a one-to-one ratio of fiber to dyestuff will yield nice color on yarns mordanted with alum. If using dried, double the number of mushrooms. Adding vinegar will shift the color from red to orange," Alissa advises. "*Cortenaria cinnamomeus* works, too."

Particular favorites are lobster mushrooms, which are mushrooms infected with a parasitic mold that covers them with a thick coat of red-orange. "*Hypomyces lactifluorum* is a fungus that grows on a number of mushroom species all over the US, and it's a delicacy to eat. I often find them past their prime,

a little too slimy to eat. But they're perfect for the dye pot. Very pH sensitive, they will yield soft corals to brick reds on unmordanted yarns, which can be helped along with a little washing soda or ammonia. Alum mordant will intensify the colors. To get magentas, add more alkalinity."

To get the full rainbow of mushroom colors, taking a workshop with Alissa Allen somewhere in North America is a good idea.

Chapter 16

india
FLINT

A detail of one of India Flint's
contact-dye eucalyptus leaf
ecoprints   OPPOSITE: India Flint,
dyer, environmentalist, author,
and teacher

O L D Ways, N E W Techniques

Born to Latvian-German parents displaced in the Second World War, India Flint absorbed some old-fashioned ideas in her early years passing through Austria and Canada, later taking firm root in Australia. Thrift was part and parcel of life, with well-loved clothes dunked into dye pots to freshen them up, or made into aprons and tea towels, or cut into patches for mending. Thrift was part of the impetus behind the family garden of fruits, herbs, and vegetables, but not the only one. Grandmother's freesias, violets, and lilies brought beauty and instilled in young India an appreciation for the slowly unfolding nobility of plants as well as an attachment to the land under her feet.

The string that keeps
ecoprint bundles
together is art in itself
OPPOSITE: Eucalyptus
will color the water of
the dye pot

Folkways from the "old country" deepened all of this with a sense of heritage and belonging. "As a small girl I loved to sit on the front stoop with my grandmother, listening to her telling stories as the sun gradually set. My favorite was that of the princess who finds herself alone in the forest and must make her clothing from what she can find . . . leaves, grass, and wisps of fur caught on the bushes. I imagined the dress of leaves pinned together with thorns, bejeweled with luminous beetles and dewdrops. This . . . dream dress . . . featured heavily in the drawings that covered my schoolbooks,"[1] she writes.

FROM EASTER EGGS TO ECOPRINTS

Grandmother's Easter egg dyeing techniques also made a lasting impression on young India. Following Latvian tradition, together they would adhere tiny shoots and leaves of springtime herbs and garden plants to the shells of eggs, wrap their assemblage in onion skins, and secure them with embroidery thread. The heat of boiling, and the natural attraction between animal proteins and certain botanical dyestuffs, transferred colors and marbled textures onto the shells, except for the parts masked by the leaves. "My marvelous grandmother was endlessly patient and allowed me to help not just with eggs but when she was dyeing her clothes." As she admits in a recent interview, "I'm surprised that I didn't think of transposing the Easter-egg-dye method to cloth much earlier."

The eureka moment came in the late 1990s when India collected a clutch of eggs from the rain-sodden, eucalyptus-lined nest of a hen in her yard. The heat of the hen's body and the dampness of the nest had combined to approximate those childhood Easter egg dyeing sessions, leaving tinted leaf impressions on each eggshell. Already aware of the encyclopedic inquiry into eucalypt dyestuffs of Jean K. Carman's

1978 *Dyemaking with Eucalypts*, all of which required the use of metallic mordants, some of them toxic, India was encouraged by the hen and her nest to wonder whether mordants were necessary.

"I began to make up bundles of silk and wool cloth together with eucalyptus leaves and discovered to my absolute delight and astonishment that the intense heat of the boiling process was a catalyst to luminous dye color completely unrelated to the color of the leaf," she recalls. Only leaves, water, heat, and time were required—no mordants, and thus no toxic effluents with which to pollute the environment. The water left in the pot could be reused to enrich the next dyeing project or spilled into the garden after cooling. What remains of the plant material could be added to garden compost.

Over time, India's experiments with contact-dye techniques (or "ecoprinting," a word she coined more than two decades ago and that appears in her book *Eco Colour*) have shown her that a wide variety of plants will yield color and pattern. When foraging outdoors in town or countryside, she looks for windfall matter so as not to stress local ecosystems. Waste

OPPOSITE: Leaves will transfer color and texture to paper. These bundles are ready for the boiling pot.
HERE: India Flint often assembles small pieces of ecoprinted fabric into a greater composition

9 THINGS TO THINK ABOUT

by INDIA FLINT
(from *The Bundle Book*
[Mount Pleasant, South Australia: *Prophet of Bloom*, 2014];
reprinted with permission of the author)

KNOW YOUR PLANTS.
Identify them before harvesting or using and make sure you are aware of their properties.

ACQUAINT YOURSELF WITH THE LOCAL WEED LIST.
Reducing the local weed burden helps the environment.

USE DEDICATED DYE VESSELS—
never the family soup pot.

CHOOSE WINDFALLS OVER WILD HARVEST.

START IN YOUR OWN GARDEN
if you have one.

IF IT SMELLS BAD, THEN IT *IS* BAD.
Don't use it.

PLAY, IT'S THE BEST WAY TO LEARN.

USE SCRAP METAL MORDANTS
rather than metallic salts.

TIME IS YOUR FRIEND—
things improve when you are patient.

from florists or past-their-prime bouquets is fair game. Unless they're headed for the trash, she avoids edibles. No mordants are ever needed, though the metal content of dye pots or a bit of found scrap metal can be part of the color-making equation. These self-imposed limits in no way reduce the sorcery and magic of India's craft. "If a lesser amount of things were made, and better, we'd use fewer resources and they'd go a lot further. Do more with less and take better care of what you have. It's as simple as that."[2]

Often starting with used clothing and cloth, she coaxes brilliant reds and oranges from the leaves of her still-favorite plant, the eucalyptus, with especially beautiful effects on wools and cashmeres. In addition to imparting color to these fibers, their dramatic leaf shapes impress themselves into almost Art Nouveau patterns and textures. When purple plum trees shed their leaves, India transfers their graceful curves and shadowy hues onto cloth. Pollen-heavy anthers from faded store-bought or garden-grown lilies leave behind fragments of rusty orange. Strawberry hulls on their way to the kitchen bin mark cloth with gray-edged sunburst patterns. When India's tightly twined bundles of protein-based textiles emerge from the boiling process, the results are never entirely predictable—except for their consistently wild and unpredictable beauty.

BEYOND BOILING

"Natural dyes sit at the nexus between science and art," India observes, "conflating elements of ethnobotany, chemistry, physics, craft, medicine, history, even archaeology. It's all interrelated, and all fascinating,"

Like a scientist, India's sense of inquiry continues to push her into new territory. For example, since some flower colors are destroyed by heat, India experimented with freezing rather than boiling iris, violets,

A eucalyptus ecoprint cooling in nature

Sensuous and surprising reds and oranges and dusky pinks
seep out of eucalyptus leaves in the
heat of the dye pot

HERE: From different dye pots with different ingredients, eco-printed blouse and skirt complement each other OPPOSITE: (top) India Flint's materials and processes result in clothes with a sort of "Neolithic" glamour (bottom left) An ecoprint fabric from India Flint (bottom right) Windfall eucalyptus leaves and twigs en route to the dye pot

and other purple blossoms, and then dissolving their icy petals in warm water. The pale lavender blues that result are readily absorbed by silk fabrics. Because she lives in an arid part of the world, conserving water became a concern, as did putting carbon into the atmosphere by burning wood or gas to heat her dye vats. This resulted in a solar-powered technique of bundling dyestuffs and textiles into mason jars for long, sun-soaked séjours that use little water and no fuel. Textiles emerging from these jars have an out-of-focus beauty different from those produced by the ecoprint technique, but they are every bit as interesting.

"Really, what I do is driven by pragmatism," India comments. "I've lived most of my life in places where

I have had to actively harvest drinking water from the sky and store it somewhere clean. I gather wood for my fires. I have never lived with air conditioners or central heating. I mend my clothes as required and overdye them as necessary. I experiment, analyze results, and back up my hypotheses with science. It's how I was raised."

India takes the lessons of her upbringing and her hybrid artist-scientist sense of inquiry to students worldwide with artist residencies and workshops. Her students and followers take a page from her thrifty primer, look to the ground for dyestuffs and to their closets for textiles, and revel in the interesting and ecologically sound results.

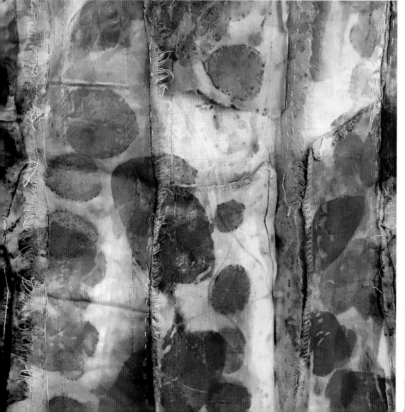

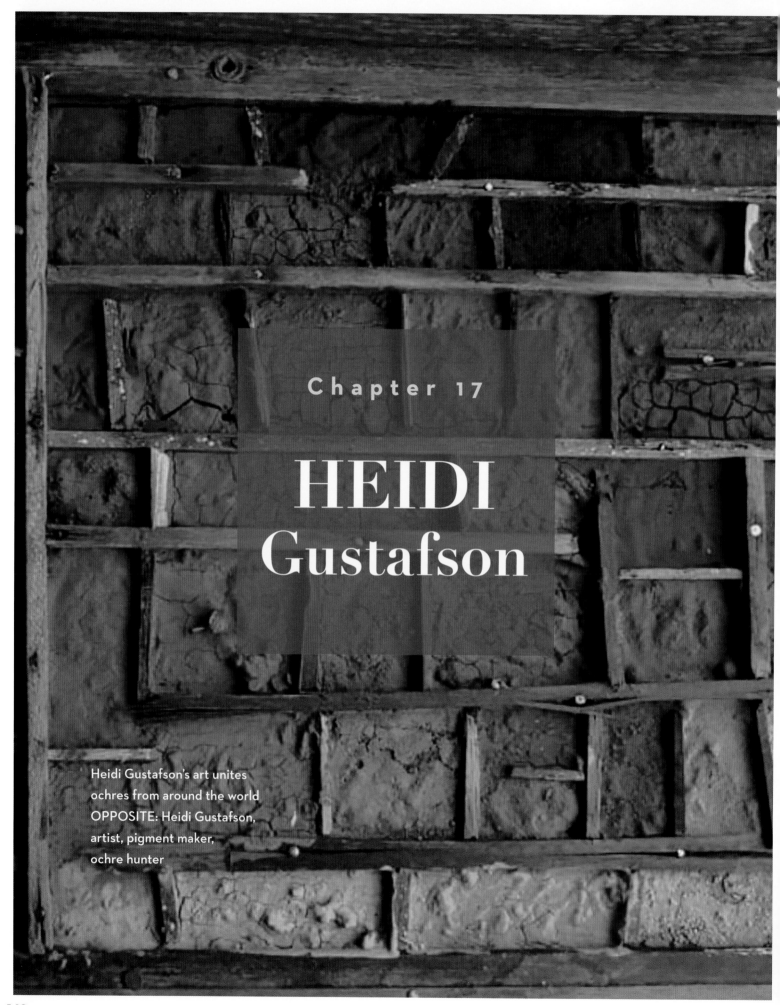

Chapter 17

HEIDI
Gustafson

Heidi Gustafson's art unites
ochres from around the world
OPPOSITE: Heidi Gustafson,
artist, pigment maker,
ochre hunter

IN THE BEGINNING

The name of Adam, the first human mentioned in the Bible, descends from ancient Hebrew words for *red earth*. Genesis tells us that he was made with the dust of the ground and the breath of life—a primeval joining of the terrestrial and the celestial, the physical and the spiritual. Whoever Adam was, and wherever he first drew breath, his name and story point us toward humankind's profound and ancient fascination with the most colorful earth, red ochre.

Archaeological evidence suggests that red ochre was in use by our Neanderthal cousins in Europe at least 300,000 years ago, 100 millennia before modern *Homo sapiens* fully occupied a branch on the humanoid family tree. The frequency of red ochre in archaeological excavations from the Middle Stone Age in Africa is evidence of *Homo sapiens'* passion for it. At nearly 200,000 years old, these findings coincide with early human signs of imagination and abstract thought. We have specific evidence of pigment and paint making as far back as 100,000 years ago, though extant cave paintings are only 40,000 years old.

The similarities between blood and red earth evidently sparked something visceral in our forebears. Artist and pigment maker Heidi Gustafson certainly sees it that way. "Ochre has an uncanny ability to resemble blood. Crush some red ochre stone into dust and add spit or fat or milk, and it really does taste, smell, look, and feel like blood," she exclaims. "It's also somehow emblematic of life on Earth. Consider what the Earth is made of: an inner core of solid iron wrapped in an outer core of liquid iron, with a little nickel, surrounded by our oxygen-rich atmosphere. Red

ochre is a meeting point of those elements.

"Consider, too," she continues, "the human organism. Our body's hearth—our heart, our central core—is designed to move iron-rich blood around so that it gathers oxygen in the lungs and delivers it to the rest of the body. Iron plus oxygen is the living red blood in our veins—a microcosm of Earth's composition circulating in our very bodies. It's easy to sense the connection between red ochre and our deep insides, but it also connects to our core creative expression, our aspirations. I am personally drawn to it because red ochre tells us something about *life force*—about how we make meaning, mystery, beauty."

Heidi's art practice is an ongoing dialogue with iron ochres. Her first encounter with them came in a dream about a wall of colored rocks. Not long afterward, "in some kind of post-dream divinatory hunch," she happened upon images on Google maps of a defunct mining area in the nearby Oakland hills of California. "I drove there, and as soon as I began to walk down the trail, I was reliving my dream. The rocks were exactly the same as I had seen them." This colorful spot was once an ancient indigenous ochre quarry. "Going to this

OPPOSITE: Each unit of this work on paper shows ochre from a different source
BELOW: A range of ochre pigments gathered in Santa Cruz, California

Heidi Gustafson in an old
Native American source of ochre
OPPOSITE: Natural ochres from
white to dark brown

particular meaning-saturated ochre landform to touch ochre stones, gather them, hold them, do rituals, set me off on a parallel path of learning geologic history, reading hundreds of research papers on ochre and iron oxides. That's when I made my connection to my life's work, which is a humbling, undetermined process."

Heidi's compositions allow color-yielding ochre stones from around the world "to hold council." Situated in wooden frames or in hand-placed arrangements in the studio, the rocks regain an ancient sense of sacredness. The eye perceives subtle differences in color and texture, each telling the story of their source. The variations build into a beautiful narrative of the home planet we share, of the colors of this Earth, and of an ancestral reverence, buried deep within us, of its unfathomable beauty.

Heidi defines this sensation as the result of her "subtle earth activism," a phrase she coined herself. "I think of subtle activism as a way of attempting to change habits and culture through subtle, *intimate* practices as opposed to more overt methods like protests, laws, rules, force, etc. This can be literal intimacy: talk, gazing, touching and carrying pebbles, making art in lived-in spaces, one-on-one compassionate presence with other people. Or, maybe more importantly, creating experiences that are felt intimately."

When Heidi helps other artists in the sourcing and preparation of ochre pigments, the same principles are in effect. "When I make pigments for and with another person, there is a deep consideration that we are sharing sensual, aesthetic intimacy, that we are touching each other on some level—and that the earth is touching us, is already within us, quietly teaching us how to be."

ABOVE: Poetic images by Alireza Memariani of the ancient ochre mine on Hormuz Island, Iran.
OPPOSITE: Workers at the ochre mine on Hormuz Island

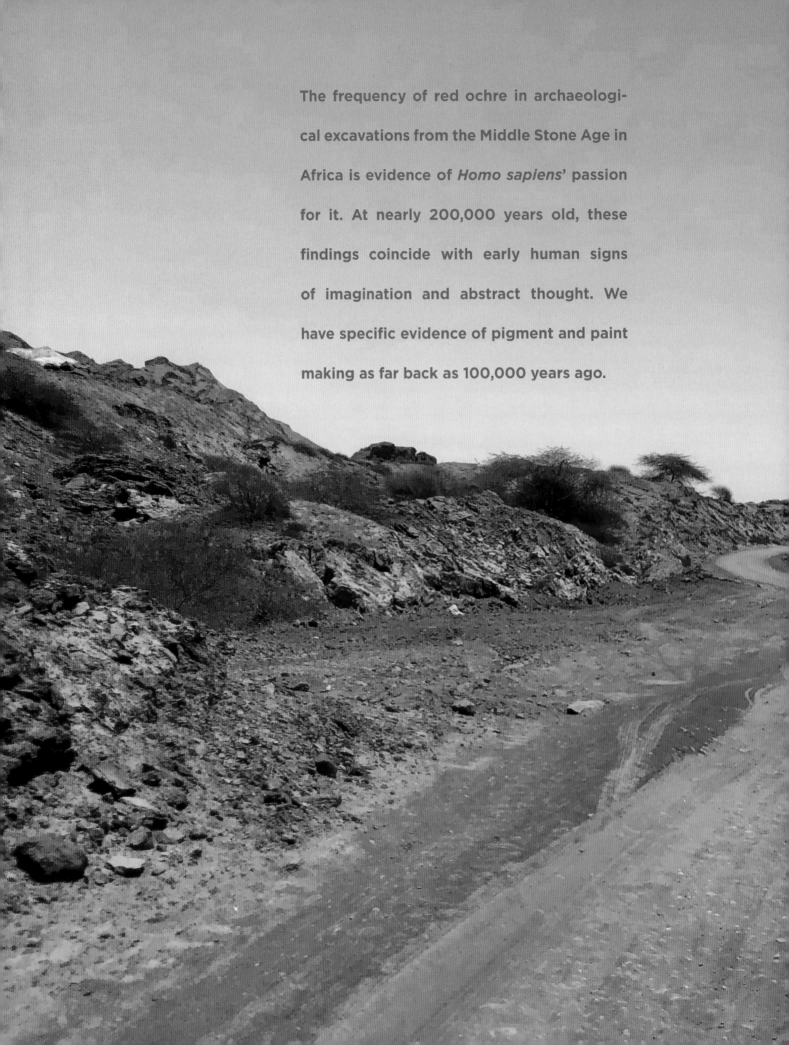

The frequency of red ochre in archaeological excavations from the Middle Stone Age in Africa is evidence of *Homo sapiens*' passion for it. At nearly 200,000 years old, these findings coincide with early human signs of imagination and abstract thought. We have specific evidence of pigment and paint making as far back as 100,000 years ago.

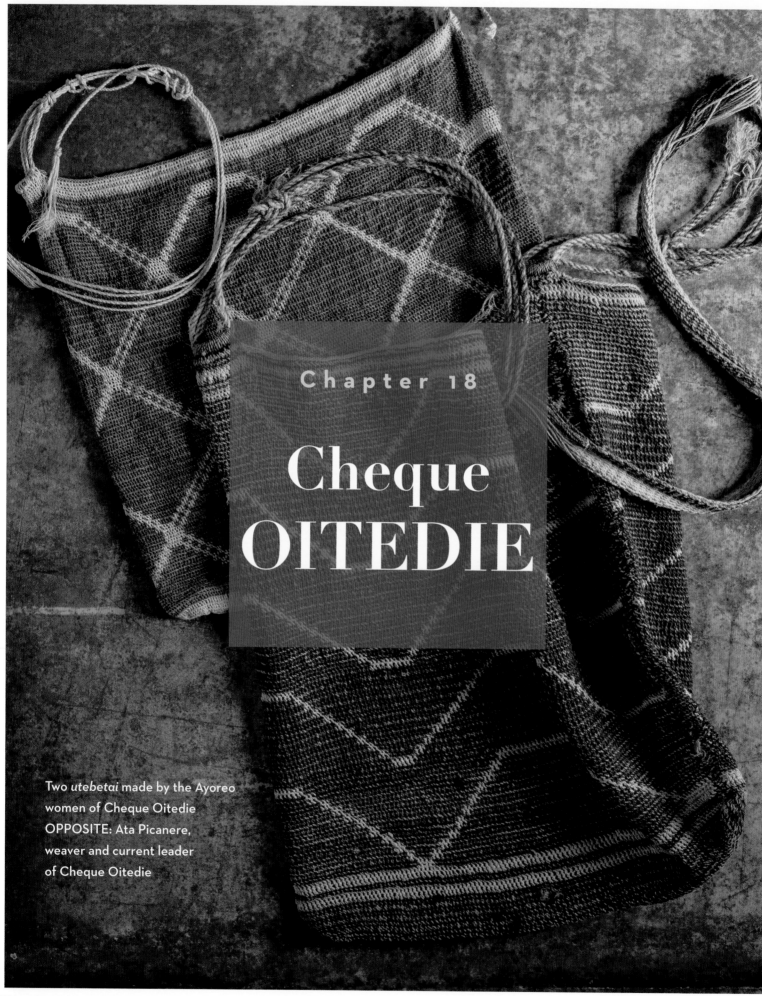

Chapter 18

Cheque OITEDIE

Two *utebetai* made by the Ayoreo
women of Cheque Oitedie
OPPOSITE: Ata Picanere,
weaver and current leader
of Cheque Oitedie

PRECONTACT COLORS

Ayoreo mothers have taught their daughters the art of traditional bag making since time out of mind. The ability to weave tough but pliable fibers harvested from ground-growing bromeliads is an essential part of Ayoreo identity. Women who weave baby carriers, hunting bags for men, gathering bags for women, and drawstring bags for carrying household items hold status and respect in this community that, between the 1970s and 1990s, gave up its nomadic life in the arid tropical forests of the Gran Chaco region spanning parts of Bolivia, Paraguay, and Argentina.

The women's way of passing on these ancient skills saves the first part of the process, the harvesting of the leaves of the *dajudie* plant (*Bromelia hieronymi*), for last. Because Ayoreo parents don't force their children to learn, letting them decide for themselves when and what interests them, this is a wise move. The spines along both edges of every dajudie leaf make their harvest a painful step. Often, after gathering plant material, weavers have to wait a day or two for the swelling of their hands to subside before they can continue the process—hardly a happy first experience for a novice.

When their hands have healed, the women remove all spines and scrape soft plant tissue away from the fibrous matter at the core of the dajudie leaves. The pale fibers are washed and then left to dry and bleach in the sun for a few days until they're ready to be made into twine. Pristine fibers are thigh-spun along the spinner's leg, using ash from burned termite mounds to smooth the fibers and to mordant them prior to dyeing. Because the weaving of a flat, medium-sized bag (called an *utebetai* in Ayoreo) requires more than 430 yards of fine twine, the spinning process alone may take fifteen to thirty days, working about two hours a day.

Gladys Dosape, a forty-year-old Ayoreo artisan, began her path to weaving when her friend Dara taught her to spin. "As soon as I started spinning, I loved working with dajudie," she says. "This work is like breathing. I will stop only when I die."

ABOVE LEFT: Bark-dyed twine made from *Bromeliad hieronymi* RIGHT: An utebetai takes shape with row after row of linked loops

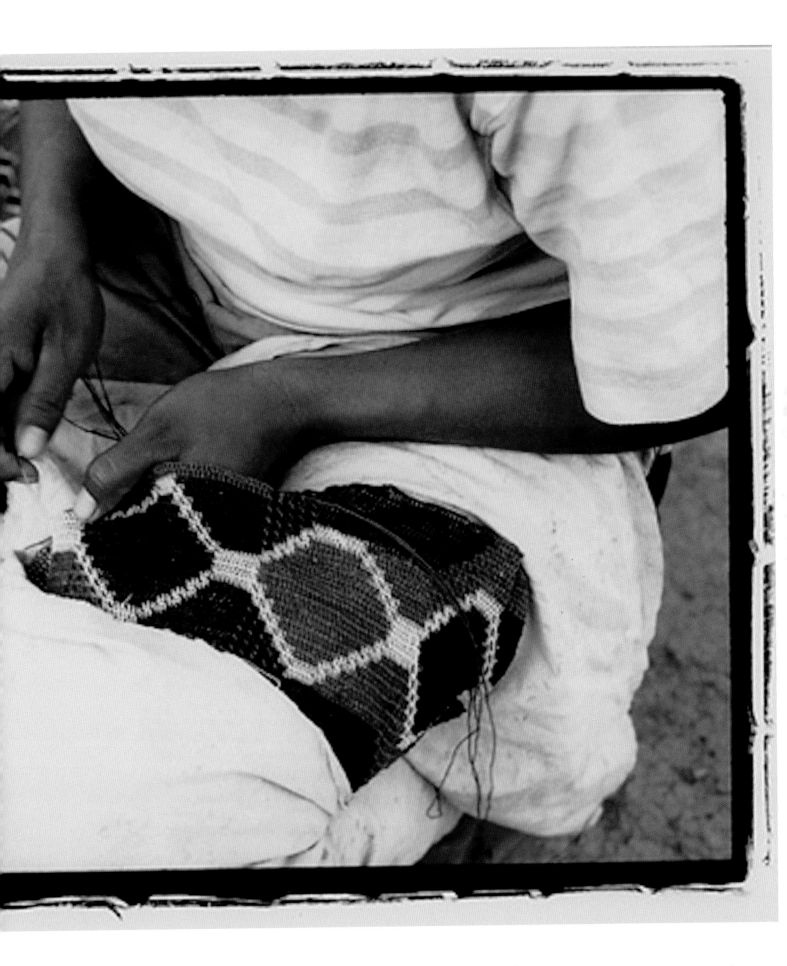

The utebetai is a prestige item for Ayoreo men and brings respect to the women who make them. Traditional patterns are associated with the seven clans of the Ayoreo people.

Traditionally, seven patterns ornament the bags, each associated with one of seven Ayoreo clans. In the past, a clan member could wear only the pattern of his or her clan, a sign of group identity in times of peace as well as conflict.

Once enough twine has been prepared, the dyeing process starts. Traditionally, only materials indigenous to the Gran Chaco forests are used: tree barks for browns and soft reds, resin-soaked barks and berries for darker browns and black. These days, some chemical colors are sourced in the nearby city of Santa Cruz. Ata Picanere, a seventy-five-year-old Ayoreo weaver, has been making bags since she was eight. Her favorite dyestuffs come from two leguminous trees, which she has planted in her yard for easy access. Bark and sapwood from the *ajunao* tree (*Pterogyne nitens*) make a mellow cinnamon-brown color, and resin-soaked bark from the cupesí tree (*Prosopis* cf. *alba*) makes a rich black-brown. Water and bark are boiled to release the color, and twine is added and boiled for an additional two or three hours.

The bags are constructed in loops done with dajudie fiber threaded onto a needle. Feet, knees, hands, and eyes all come into play as the rows of loops take shape. Traditionally, seven patterns ornament the bags, each associated with one of seven Ayoreo clans. In the past, a clan member could wear only the pattern of his or her clan, a sign of group identity in times of peace as well as conflict. Nowadays, clan designs are worn freely according to preference rather than identity. As it is, because of the effort involved, dajudie fiber bags are made for sale rather than local use or are given as gifts to important visitors.

CLANS and DESIGNS

CHIQUENONE
Fingers and toes

CUTAMURAJANE
Women's facial paintings

DOSAPOEDE
Footprint of the anteater

ETACORONE
Rattlesnake skin

JNURUMINONE
Clouds

PICANERANE
Vulture's tail

POSORAJNANE
Fawn's spots

Bark, shredded and boiled, tints *dajudie* fibers in black and browns

NEW CHALLENGES

Utebetai bags woven for daily use by Ayoreo people of Bolivia's Puesto Paz area are now crafted of wool. Dajudie fiber bags, difficult to produce and held in high esteem, are primarily made for collectors and discerning travelers. With the earnings, women buy school supplies, medicine, and food. The income is vital to family wellbeing. For the post-nomadic Ayoreo, chronic unemployment and low wages combine in dire ways. Until 2006, prostitution was the main source of income for young women.

Ayoreo families try to make ends meet through a combination of weaving, urban migration in search of work, renting land at low rates to external farming operations, and agricultural labor in the soybean fields taking the place of the forests, which cover less and less of their home of barely two generations.

The expansion of agriculture mounts even more pressure on the Ayoreo. Their customary hunt for meat, honey, wild fruits, and vegetables becomes harder to pursue with every acre of deforestation. During the rainy season, the elderly continue to cultivate small plots of watermelon, squash, corn, and beans, as they once had done in forest clearings. But the harvest does not fully feed their families, and it's not something younger people have taken up. Recently, bills for water and electricity have begun to arrive, adding to families' need for cash.

Going back to the old way of life is scarcely an option. Even though they inhabited the wilds of Gran Chaco for many centuries, Bolivia and Paraguay fail to recognize their claim to their ancestral lands. Only in 2007, with the advocacy of the Rainforest Fund and the Bolivian nonprofit organization Comunidad Viva, were Ayoreo granted legal title of their current zones in Puesto Paz, Zapocó, Rincón del Tigre, and Tobite. Land-driven conflict between nomad and settler is a familiar issue, as are long disputes over the notion of ownership. We have only to look at our own North American history for an equally tough example. Even with land rights, the Ayoreo are still searching for a way forward in the context of modern twenty-first-century life.

Forming a women's cooperative is one tentative solution. Ines Hinojosa, an ethnobotanist who has worked with the group since its inception, lists the

Traditional utebetai are vanishing and may disappear completely in another decade OPPOSITE: The late Ique Etacore, one of the founders of Cheque Oitedie

goals: "Cheque Oitedie, which means "best weavers" in Ayoreo, was founded to help eradicate prostitution, to recover and strengthen the cultural identity of Ayoreo women, to demonstrate to Western society that Ayoreo women of Puesto Paz are preserving their culture and that they are able to generate income." Yet the cooperative faces challenges. "We started with eighty-five and we are down to forty-five," she says. "Because they must do other work—some in the home for the family, some outside to earn money—the most accomplished weavers can make only six bags a year. Some can only make two. This is valuable supplemental income, but obviously there is more than interest in money here. The women also want to be respected in their society."

Ique Etacore, founding leader of the Cheque Oitedie Cooperative, confirms Ines's words: "We are proud to say that weaving with dajudie fiber is our job, our identity as Ayoreo women, and the legacy of our ancestors."

Nevertheless, Ines is concerned about the survival of this ancient craft. "In a time of intense and rapid communal change, it is impossible for me to predict the future. Currently, many Ayoreo women wear nontraditional purses or backpacks, but that's not the case with Ayoreo men. They always wear utebetai, usually of wool. In my opinion, the day that Ayoreo men stop carrying utebetai will be the day when this symbol of Ayoreo identity will be lost, along with the traditional knowledge of making and dyeing dajudie fiber. How close is that day? It will depend on the Ayoreo people." When pressed, Ines sees that day coming no more than ten years from now.

Chapter 19

Irene CLARK

Naturally dyed yarns in Irene Clark's weaving studio
OPPOSITE: Irene Clark, weaver and keeper of Navajo textile traditions

EARTHY RAINBOW

Drive north from Gallup to Sheep Springs, then southwest toward Crystal, New Mexico, population 311. Somewhere along State Highway 134 you'll see a turnoff with a cattle guard. You'll cross dry washes and a confusion of dusty pickup tracks. You'll see endless acres of sagebrush and, depending on the season, a splash of vivid scarlet globe mallow or gleaming yellow rabbitbrush. Eventually, you'll reach the Navajo hogan of Irene Hardy Clarke and her husband, Jimmy.

Step inside, and you feel that this hogan is larger inside than it is outside. There's the typical generous bed, the dining table, the woodstove—and the looms. Many looms. And baskets of yarn, singing with color. Irene is known for her warm, vivid vegetal dyes. Maybe it's those colors that create a sense of space, echoing the sunrise colors of the Chuska Mountains to the west.

Irene's colors come from the land. Dusky blue-grays from the blue corn in her fields; soft yellow or greenish gray from sagebrush (*Artemisia tridentata*); bright yellow from rabbitbrush (*Chrysothamnus* spp.); rich browns from walnut hulls (*Juglans major*) or canaigre, the tuber-like root of dock (*Rumex hymenosepalus*); remarkable rich rusts from the unassuming ground lichen (*Parmelia molluscula*)—and so many more. The thing about plants of the desert Southwest is that almost any will yield some color, with an em-

Irene learned to weave from her mother, Glenabah, but not in the typical way. As a child, she tended sheep. She didn't begin to spin, dye, and weave until she went away to Chilocco Indian School in Oklahoma and came home a married woman.

phasis on tan, pale yellow, or beige. In fact, almost any plant will yield a range of hues, depending on when it was gathered, how much was used in the dye bath, how long it was steeped or boiled, what else was added.

Take Irene's rusty-orange lichen dye, for instance. You have to be very attentive in collecting the stuff; ground lichen looks like nothing so much as scraps of grayish crust lying in the dirt. To dye a pound of wool to a medium shade, you'd need a pound of the papery-thin plant, gathered across many hours of walking the land and paying close attention. You'd need to simmer it in a large amount of water for at least an hour, and let it steep even longer for a deeper shade. Irene adds natural alum, harvested in the mountains near her home. The range of hues she achieves, from soft apricot to lusty orange to deep rust, is at the heart of her warm palette.

LEFT: Lichens yield a tawny orange to this yarn RIGHT: Freshly dyed skeins in various natural colors dry in the sun

TOP LEFT: Carpets woven by Irene Clark TOP RIGHT: The red rocks of the Southwest at sunset
BOTTOM: Irene at the loom

ABOVE: Irene gathers sage.
OPPOSITE: One of Irene's naturally dyed carpets, and some of her tools

The soft greenish yellow that complements her rusts and oranges might come from the sagebrush so abundant on her land, or she might have traveled across the Lukachukai Mountains into Arizona, where the sagebrush has larger leaves and might give a subtly different hue. For Irene, dyeing with nature's plants is less a science than something drawn from her acute sensitivity to the world around her.

Songs, prayers, and good thoughts are associated with every step of her weaving. "I thank Mother Earth for the plants that give color to my wool, for sky above me, the air I breathe, for Mother Earth for grounding me. All this gives me a good feeling to weave," she says.

Irene learned to weave from her mother, Glenabah, but not in the typical way. As a child, she tended sheep. She didn't begin to spin, dye, and weave until she went away to Chilocco Indian School in Oklahoma and came home a married woman. And even then, she learned by watching rather than by direct instruction.

Weaving is in her bones, though. She was born of the Water's Edge Clan, a clan noted for its many master weavers. As her son, Ferlin, says, "Every strand of naturally dyed yarn is interwoven with my family's clanship and our belonging to one another. The colors of a rug symbolize the array of colors depicted in the rainbow—the strength that protects and paves the path to beauty and harmony."

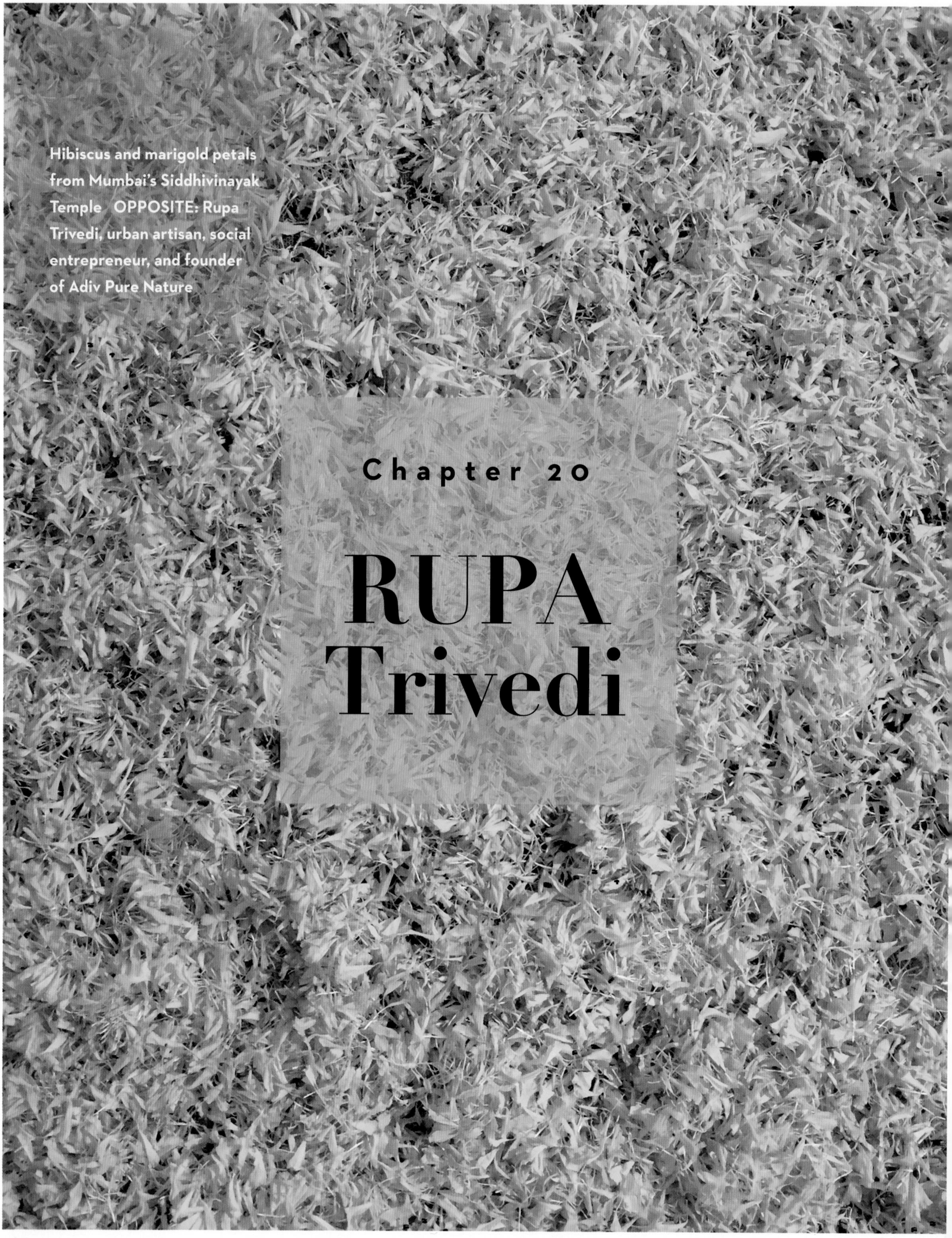

Hibiscus and marigold petals from Mumbai's Siddhivinayak Temple OPPOSITE: Rupa Trivedi, urban artisan, social entrepreneur, and founder of Adiv Pure Nature

Chapter 20

RUPA Trivedi

LIKE A PRAYER

Rupa Trivedi carries many titles. Some of them are traditional: daughter, wife, mother. Some are modern, like ultrasonic technician and entrepreneur. One title is entirely her own invention: "urban artisan," a moniker she shares with the thirty members of her Mumbai atelier, Adiv Pure Nature, where every color is natural, including the hues made from marigolds, hibiscus, roses, and coconut husks recycled from one of the city's most venerable Hindu temples.

Plucking petals prior to a dye session   OPPOSITE: Adiv Pure Nature uses up to 900 kilos of marigold petals a week in their natural dye workshop

In a blend of spirituality and social action, tradition and innovation, aesthetics and science, Rupa and her team are making more than textiles. They're inventing a sustainable, scalable approach to natural color. And creating social change while they're at it.

EARLY DAYS

"I was born and raised in Mumbai by an educated Hindu family. Visiting temples and seeking the blessings of many spiritual masters was very much a part of my childhood," says Rupa of her upbringing. "Some of my earliest memories are of visits with my parents to Ganeshpuri, a temple village and powerful energy center a few hours from home. I loved participating in temple rituals there and enjoyed the surrounding countryside, so rich in medicinal flora and fauna. It was so different from the city."

Ganeshpuri is known both as the home of twen-

tieth-century guru and Hindu saint Nityananda, whose temple complex is part of the city's religious life, and as the seat of a large Adivasi community. The name hints at their identity: *adi* means beginning, and *vasi* means dweller—in other words, "original inhabitant." Their presence in India predates the Indo-Aryans, who began their migration to northern India in 1500 BCE, bringing the Indo-European roots of Sanskrit with them, as well as their customs and beliefs. Acknowledgment and reevaluation of Adivasi heritage, begun in the last century, is still an ongoing process.

Ganeshpuri's rural surroundings, unique population, and traditional temple culture spoke to Rupa in unforgettable ways. "I deeply related to the idea that the human quest for inner peace could be fulfilled with nature's beauty and color and a sense of inclusive community."

The practice of *puja*, the fundamental act of religious devotion in several Indian religions, dating at least from Vedic times, is almost always carried out with a symbolic offering of flowers. The very term itself may have etymological roots in ancient Tamil words meaning "the flower act."

FLOWER POWER

Rupa's childhood fascination with nature was reinforced by Indian traditions and beliefs that have existed for millennia. The Vedas, written between 1700 and 1100 BCE, are laden with descriptions of forests and gardens and with the trees, plants, leaves, and flowers that grow in them. The practice of *puja*, the fundamental act of religious devotion in several Indian religions, dating at least from Vedic times, is almost always carried out with a symbolic offering of flowers. The very term itself may have etymological roots in ancient Tamil words meaning "the flower act," indicating an intrinsic connection between nature, in the form of flowers, and spirituality.

Whether honoring manifestations of the Divine in a temple, or at home, welcoming guests or celebrating life's milestones, flowers and leaves—within easy

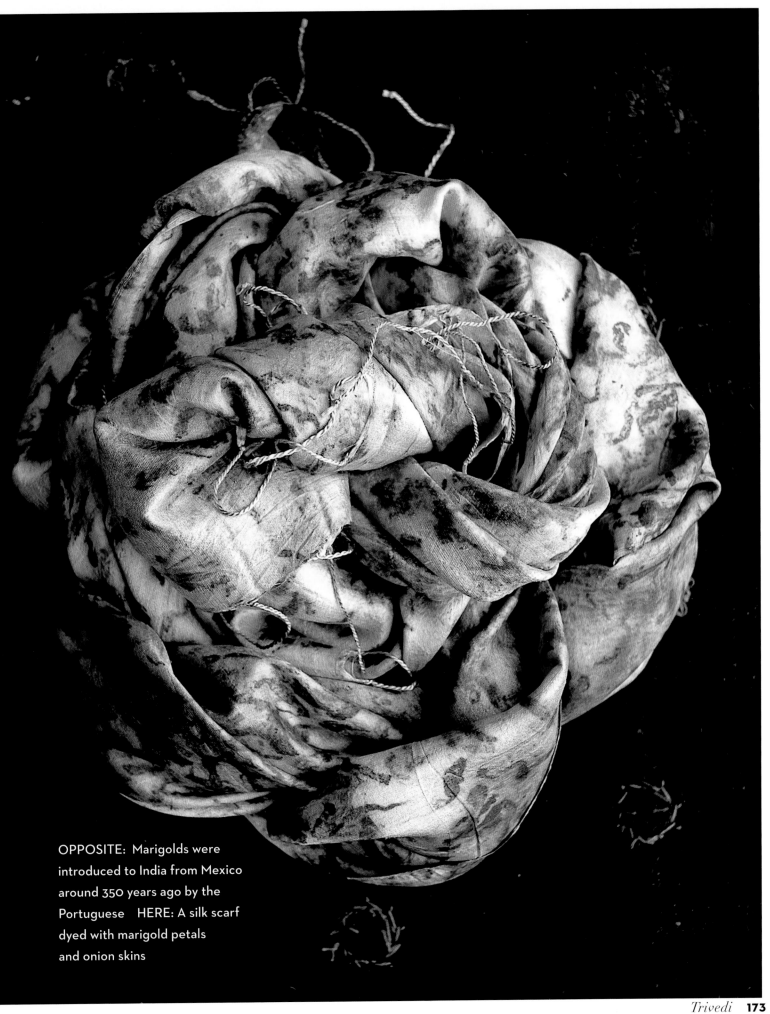

OPPOSITE: Marigolds were introduced to India from Mexico around 350 years ago by the Portuguese HERE: A silk scarf dyed with marigold petals and onion skins

reach of people's doorsteps in the distant agrarian or forest-dwelling past—are universally present, alongside pure, simple foodstuffs like ghee, milk, honey, and rice. These elements are combined in ways that may vary by region and occasion, but they are shared cultural touchstones rich with meaning.

The most revered flower of Hinduism is the lotus, whose role in Hindu cosmology is all-important: the lotus inspired the inception of the Universe, just as it symbolizes the divine potential of each human spirit. It is associated with Lord Brahma, the Creator. Jasmine, abundantly present in India with over 100 varieties, is also meaningful as a symbol of love, marriage, and sensuality. Goddess Sita signaled her choice of Lord Rama as husband with a jasmine garland. Other flowers mentioned in the Vedas include the fragrant blossoms of many trees including champak, pomegranate, ashoka, and Indian ash.

Interestingly, the marigold, though it appears in prodigious quantities in temples and homes across India, is not mentioned in the Vedas or in any other ancient text from the subcontinent. Bred for showiness by the Aztecs, the marigold is a Central American plant introduced to India by the Portuguese just 350 years ago. Almost ubiquitous today, it may have struck a chord for several reasons: it grows prolifically, it's sturdy and noticeable, and its saffron hues—the colors of flame, associated with purification of self and spirit—make it a heartfelt offering to the gods. It is used every day, thousands of times a day, to make garlands for statues of deities or in bouquets placed at their feet. It's also used in decoration for wedding altars, thresholds to homes and shops, and more.

"In dense, busy, urban Mumbai, most people have lost a lot of their connection to nature," Rupa observes. "Temple flowers, including marigolds, are one of the few ways to feel that relationship come alive."

NATURAL DYES AND NEW DIRECTIONS

"Soon after my marriage, I worked with my husband to establish our high-tech ultrasonic business.

Still, in the back of my mind, I had a hunger to work with nature and handmade things. I suspect that natural dyes were in the back of my mind since those early days in Ganeshpuri," Rupa recalls. "In 2004, after my daughter moved to the US, I was ready for a new chapter. I saw city life with new eyes, reawakened to the struggles of the people living around me, the harsh challenges they face in Mumbai. Combining all these past and present thoughts really fueled me to set up a business which would touch the also-restless souls of my fellow twenty-first-century humans."

Beginning with two cooking pots and an intern, Rupa began to experiment with natural dyes in her office kitchenette. Like the scientist she was trained to be, she sought out books and manuals on Indian natural dyeing traditions in their purest form, only to find very little precise information. Undaunted, Rupa dove into online research, and with much trial and error gradually came to understand the principles of natural dyes. Soon she was using food waste such as onion skins and coconut rinds as well as floral waste and other natural materials to create a palette of Indian natural colors. The sense of self-invention that energized her then still does. "Perhaps my lack of formal training and no 'dye guru' to follow is one of the main reasons why I am still experimental and adventurous in our work."

In 2006, Rupa started her business, Adiv Pure Nature, and received her first international customer.

A SOCIAL PATH

Today, Adiv Pure Nature's thirty employees include skilled dyers and tailors from some of Mumbai's most challenging neighborhoods. Without exception, they arrived at the Adiv workshop in the East Andheri district of Mumbai without any previous experience with textiles but looking for a way to make a living with pride and dignity.

In 2007, Mukhtar, a tall, handsome motorcycle mechanic of few words, came to Adiv still in the grip of alcohol and drug addiction. Working with Rupa, he found a place to focus his intense emotions, and he has matured into a master dyer and family man. His substance abuse is a thing of the past. His eye for detail, his knowledge of all Adiv recipes and techniques, and his diplomatic way of managing the dye rooms put him in a key role in everything that happens at the workshop.

"Another beautiful example of the lovely human gems that make up Adiv is Tabussum, Tabu to many," Rupa recounts. "She is one of our early dyers, brought to Adiv by her father, a fine embroiderer whom I had known. In a bad marriage, she had been thrown out by her husband with the three utterances of Talaq![1] Her father requested that Tabu be allowed to come to Adiv to help her combat her severe depression. At first the other dyers teased her, and she ended in tears each day. However, things changed when she fell ill with typhoid and malaria. The dyers who had initially teased her took care of her during her recovery, making sure she took her medicines and ate enough.

HERE: Marigolds darken as they dry and produce a mustard yellow
BELOW: Marigold garlands adorn a statue of Lord Ganesha at Siddhivinayak Temple
OPPOSITE: Vinod Mahadeshwer sorts flowers at the temple

As she got stronger, she began to take up dyeing. She enjoyed experimenting, and one of her very first shibori textures has been in demand with buyers since it was first shown. We named it after her: the Tabu texture. Tabussum has become a strong advocate for her children and for women in her community, helping them navigate challenging local bureaucracies."

Mukhtar and Tabu and their colleagues produce 4,000 to 5,000 meters of cloth a month in more than seventy colorful shades as well as dozens of shibori clamp-dyed, contact-dyed, dipped, and splattered textures. Every pattern or texture originates from the workshop. Every color is the subject of testing

and replication. Every product is laundered, pressed, and inspected for perfect quality. It is obvious to everyone involved that Rupa has turned her human and social impulses into a vibrant business, a nexus she keeps in her mind at all times. "I always want anyone appreciating our work to see that underneath something beautiful is someone's love, someone's effort, someone's heart and someone's life." Here, sales and success are never decoupled from person and principle.

Adiv principles extend into environmental responsibility. Plans are forming to compost all botanical waste on site. A small water recycling system reprocesses all dye water. Rightly proud of Adiv's thor-

oughness, Rupa says, "At the end of the day, we're making a small sustainable world that is a beautiful example of environmental friendliness, as well as a social enterprise for the benefit of its workers and their sense of self-worth."

THE TEMPLE FLOWER PROJECT

During the first two years of developing Adiv Pure Nature, Rupa's long desire to combine her spirituality with natural dyeing began to materialize. Just as they did long ago in Ganeshpuri, the rituals at her temple were speaking to her. "Interestingly, it all became clear in 2008 during the annual Ganesh festival, when statues of the problem-solving deity are ritually immersed, flower garlands and all, in the sea. The coast is littered with flowers for many days. I began my experiments with temple flowers not long after, during the nine-day Navratri festival, which celebrates the Mother Durga, who was brought forth by the ancient gods to fight evil and to teach the language of love to all beings. Full of ideas about flowers, dyeing, loving our fellow Man, and growing an all-natural business, I went on the sixth day to pray at the temple of my goddess, Lakshmi, one of the manifestations of Durga. The clear blessings of the powerful feminine energy at work during those days put me firmly on the path that I walk now. I began to dream of working with the flowers of temple offerings. Many, many thousands of garlands and bouquets are brought to temples all over India every day. They are full of dye potential—especially marigolds."

Custom dictates that these offerings be disposed of by being cast upon water rather than mixed with other refuse. As a result, floral waste often chokes waterways around the country, creating a contami-

LEFT and ABOVE: Marigold petals are sprinkled on silk and cotton fabrics, rolled into packets, and steamed. After steaming, the petals are shaken off and composted.
BELOW: Temple Project scarves in marigold petal textures

nation issue. Rupa knew that she could relieve at least some of this refuse problem by bringing petals to her workshop and dyeing with them.

All she needed was a temple to agree to partner with Adiv in this project. Rupa made the rounds of Mumbai, starting at smaller temples where she imagined she would find friendly ears. Worried that they would be breaking religious tradition, all the priests said no. By that time, Rupa realized that the number of petals she would need to conduct a meaningful and dependable dye business was too large for these sites. Eventually, a friend recommended her project to the world-famous Siddhivinayak Temple, dedicated to Ganesha. Though she entered her meeting with apprehension, she exited with a firm "yes" in a matter of ten minutes: Adiv was formally authorized to collect flower petals from the temple every other day. As for concerns about breaking religious tradition, the priest saw Adiv's dyeing as a form of casting the flowers on the water and dispersing their blessings to the Universe.

These days, an Adiv employee, a deaf-mute man, works full-time at the temple to collect and sort heaps of flower petals and coconut husks. Between 100 and 300 kilograms are transported to the workshop two or three times a week, depending on customer de-

"The human touch of love. The beautiful energy of the temple blessing. These are the soul of Adiv, and they're irreplaceable."

Rupa Trivedi

mand. "Seasonality has its effects, too; in summer, the petals rot faster and are less useful," observes Adele Mattern, a US-based designer, marketer, and all-around Adiv Pure Nature advocate.

"The workshop has developed techniques to dry and pulverize petals for use as dyes," Adele continues. "However, when they're steamed fresh into silks using a contact-dye technique, it's exciting to see how different color values emerge. During monsoon season, the moisture content of the flowers is high, which makes for juicy bright yellows. If the petals are dried before steaming, earthier straw-yellows appear. Petals that are a few days old and beginning to darken can leave a darker mustard shade."

These variations are attractive to work with, but when one of Adiv's larger customers from the US, France, Germany, or Switzerland unpacks an order, they are not interested in wide variations from whatever color they have approved.

As Rupa remembers it, "Until we came along, flowers were not majorly used for commercial-level dyeing, especially in textiles, so there were no known parameters to define precise extraction and application. With time and serious focus on color control, we managed to set some standards for our work. Around this time, I established a relationship with the Institute of Chemical Technology, a world-renowned college with a commitment to environmental conservation, to work toward further regularization of the tones and variation of the shades achieved from the flowers. We studied, among many variables, the impact of the pH of the water used in dyeing and steaming, along with different levels of flower drying and different weather conditions. Every lot of marigolds brought in must be tested to see what shade it will make. This is a lesson we learnt the hard way."

URBAN ARTISAN

"Like most of us in India, I associated the idea of 'artisan' with someone who lived in harmony with nature according to traditions handed down over centuries by ancestors who pursued their art at every stage," says Rupa. It was a leap of imagination for her to become an "urban artisan," a step out of the rulebook of traditions and old ideas and into the freedom to explore, experiment, invent, and create using the tools of art and science and everything in between.

Gratifyingly, her new status has brought Rupa back full circle to where the link between nature and spirituality was first forged. "Thirty years later, I returned to Ganeshpuri and felt reconnected to its energies again. We're working with a farmer there now to grow organic flowers and herbs for our work. So the nature-inspired urban artisan is really connecting back to nature."

Marigold petal textures on cotton and silk fabrics

A Season of Marigolds

The range of marigold yellows
varies with the season,
the water, the freshness of
the petals, and with modifiers
such as iron or alum.

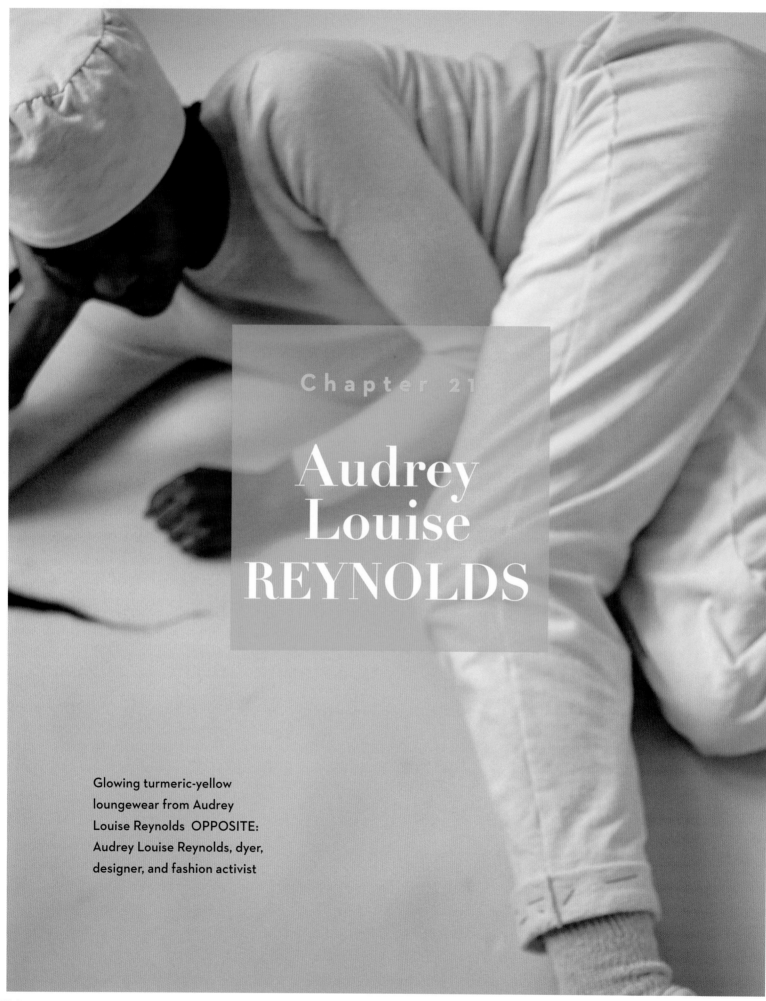

Chapter 21

Audrey Louise REYNOLDS

Glowing turmeric-yellow loungewear from Audrey Louise Reynolds OPPOSITE: Audrey Louise Reynolds, dyer, designer, and fashion activist

GOLDEN GIRL

At age three, Audrey Louise Reynolds painted her parents' walls with turmeric, as high as her little arms could reach. When asked how that went over with the neighbors in her hometown of Charlotte, North Carolina, Audrey replied, "Well, we never really fit in down there."

Charlotte might be a bit more receptive these days now that turmeric, employed extensively in Ayurvedic herbal medicine for millennia, is gaining the attention of modern medicine for its anti-inflammatory and antioxidant properties. Taken internally or used as a poultice, turmeric is reported to be beneficial to the digestive system and effective in treating psoriasis, fungal infections, wounds, and even sprained ankles. Other more wondrous claims are out there about turmeric and Alzheimer's disease, multiple sclerosis, and cancer.[1]

Thirty years later, Audrey is still into turmeric, along with a mastery of so many other botanical color sources that she's sought after by clients like Rogan, Jigsaw, Nike, and Roman and Williams. She's challenging, guerilla-style, the fashion industry's skepticism around the scalability and suitability of natural dyes in a mainstream production context. She frequently puts her natural dyes into "old school" dyeing machines and gets fantastic results. "We don't need to set out to reinvent all the dye houses in the world. We can work with existing infrastructure, in scalable quantities, at accessible prices," she says.

Outside the realm of big fashion, Audrey is developing an online audience with her own clothing line, dyed with turmeric, of course, as well as with wildflowers and organic rose petals. She's confident that garment-to-skin transfer of turmeric's virtues is a proven fact, but even if you doubt it, there might be other benefits to wearing turmeric. Kyle Roberts, an Ayurvedic herbalist based in Jacksonville, Florida, claims that wearing yellow foments a certain mental-spiritual heat and focus within us.

Beyond the dye vat, Audrey has also been known to colorize one-of-a-kind garments by rubbing stripes and stains into them with florist's waste, seaweed, algae, turmeric, and more, a technique she says was inspired by the grass stains on Darryl Strawberry's Yankee uniform. You may be inspired to try this on your own after watching her in action in online demonstrations.[2]

OPPOSITE: Turmeric and rose petals from one of Audrey Louise Reynolds's dye packets HERE: An example from Audrey Louise's naturally dyed clothing collection

Chapter 22

Catharine ELLIS

A weld dye pot in Catharine
Ellis's studio   OPPOSITE:
Dyer and natural color
innovator Catharine Ellis
harvesting weld in her garden

PRECISE YELLOWS

Catharine Ellis was just starting out in the 1970s, and she remembers the spirit of the times well. "People were moving to the country, living off the land in communes, growing vegetables, exploring, and enjoying themselves. We wanted to get back to the essence of things." Embracing (or re-embracing) all things natural and authentic included a revived interest in not just natural foods but also natural dyes.

"My first introduction to natural dyes was during my year on the Navajo reservation in Arizona, where I was a student at the Navajo Community College. We gathered alum right from the ground. Leaves, alum, and wool were all put in a pot together and cooked," she recounts, but information on natural dyes and the best techniques to achieve beautiful colors was superficial.

"There was no science to it, and plenty of misinformation. Can dandelion roots give you red, as the first book on natural dyes I bought said they would? No, they can't."

Natural dyes were not especially exciting to Catharine at that point. "Eventually, I got tired of all the yellows and beiges I was getting from the plants around me," she recalls. "I felt I had to become more professional—to master synthetic dyes. I enjoyed the discipline and the science and the specificity of work-ing this way, and I became very adept at using acid dyes, fiber-reactive dyes, and more." Beyond her expertise in dyeing, Catharine developed what she calls "woven shibori," which involves adding supplementary threads to a textile on the loom and using them to gather and shape a cloth during the shibori process.

Catharine shared her passion for weaving and dyeing over a long career as a teacher, and it was, in part, her students who asked for her to return to natural color. But it was retirement from teaching in 2008 that brought her fully back to natural dyestuffs. "When I set up my studio at home, where we have a well and a septic system and a creek, I knew that I couldn't continue using the chemical dyes that were my forte. I had to explore more natural ways of working."

Ever committed to mastering whatever discipline she pursues, Catharine went to an expert in her search for natural-dye knowledge. Michel Garcia, a French citizen born in Algeria, is renowned worldwide for his careful and artful exploration of historical natural dyes and printing techniques and for his generous workshops. "He showed us cottons printed and dyed in brilliant colors with natural dyes and hinted at a body of information I did not know. Michel showed me it could be done, which pushed me to go home and test, test, test! But I admit that I was still confused."

The confusion began to settle in 1997 when Catharine met Joy Boutrup at the Penland School of Crafts in North Carolina, where she was teaching technical aspects of printing and textile finishing. Joy's technical expertise, developed since the 1970s when she earned a textile degree in Germany, centers

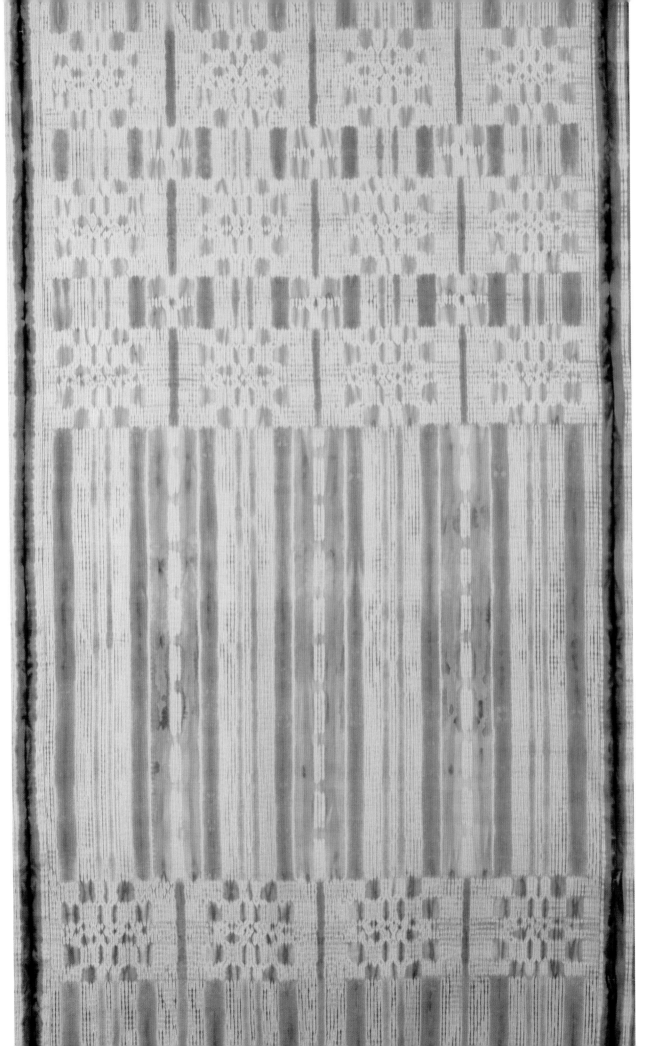

OPPOSITE:
Weld turns
olive under the
influence of iron
post-mordants.
HERE: Weld
shibori on cotton,
from Catharine
Ellis's Garden
Series

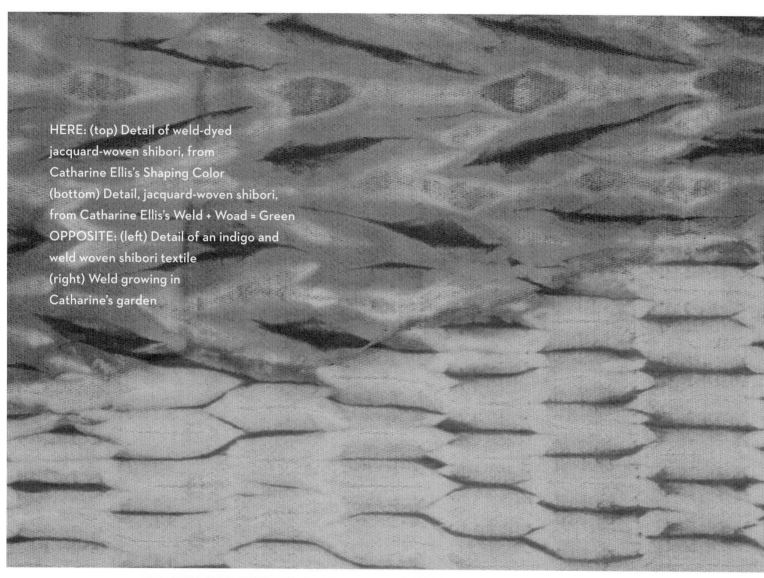

HERE: (top) Detail of weld-dyed jacquard-woven shibori, from Catharine Ellis's Shaping Color
(bottom) Detail, jacquard-woven shibori, from Catharine Ellis's Weld + Woad = Green
OPPOSITE: (left) Detail of an indigo and weld woven shibori textile
(right) Weld growing in Catharine's garden

on the study of historical textiles, particularly early twentieth-century commercial work produced when natural components were still in use. "Joy became my teacher. She's a linear thinker who knows how to explain process and science. She will often hint at the 'why' behind a dye phenomenon or at an historical solution to a color challenge, and off I go to test it out in the studio."

June. Archaeological evidence shows that weld has been used to make yellow dyes since at least 1000 BC. Traditionally employed to color silks and wools, weld can also be used in the production of lake pigments (with the addition of alum or calcium). Dutch master Johannes Vermeer evidently used weld-derived paints in his *Girl with a Pearl Earring*.

"I bought weld only once, from Maiwa in Van-

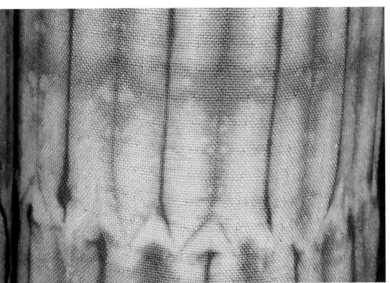

Their working partnership resulted in the 2019 publication *The Art and Science of Natural Dyes: Principles, Experiments, and Results*, which explains the scientific principles of natural dyeing and goes deep into hundreds of combinations of dyestuff, mordant, time, temperature, and other variables.

What is Catharine's favorite natural dyestuff? "Weld is the rock star flavonol of the natural dye world," she answers with surety. "Based on everything I have observed, it produces the clearest, most lightfast yellow of the commonly available natural dyestuffs."

The stems, leaves, and flowers of weld, known botanically as *Reseda luteola* and commonly as Dyer's Rocket, contain luteolin, a flavonol compound that yields yellow color. This biennial grows up to five feet high, with spikes of pale yellow flowers blooming in

couver," says Catharine. "Then I started to grow it on my own. There's always a patch of it in the garden now, big enough to do dye work, share with students, and produce seeds for the following year. It keeps indefinitely when dried. It smells good. It's easy to grow. It likes poor soil, and it seeds itself readily."

The key to successful weld dyeing, she says, is hard water. "I once tried to dye some wool with weld and got almost no color. The yarn might have been processed with an acid, which is sometimes used to remove plant debris from the raw wool. Once I added chalk to the dye bath, the color simply blossomed."

These days, Catharine can be found in her studio, dyeing with plants, weaving, and always experimenting toward mastery of something new.

Chapter 23

AVANI

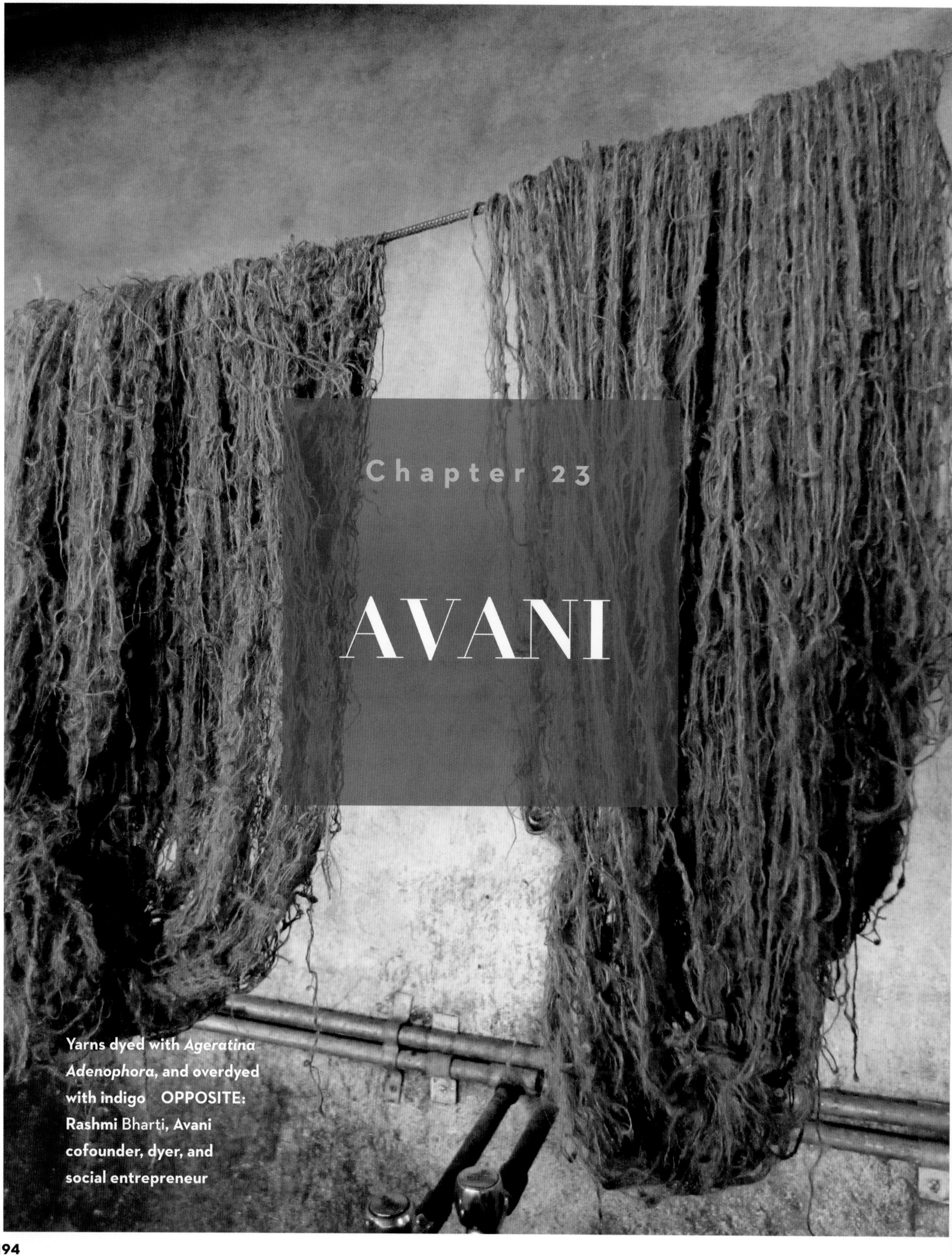

Yarns dyed with *Ageratina Adenophora*, and overdyed with indigo   OPPOSITE: Rashmi Bharti, Avani cofounder, dyer, and social entrepreneur

INVASIVE COLOR

As is sometimes the case with a pretty face, there's more to *Ageratina adenophora*[1] than meets the eye. While the plant does have lovely features—daintily scalloped leaves, long multibranch stems, and adorable white tufted blossoms that appear in the fall—its Nepalese name suggests the rest of the story. There it is called *ban mara*, which means "forest killer."

A native of Mexico, it started to make its way about the world in the 1800s as an ornamental plant. Two hundred years later, *Ageratina adenophora* is now a well-known pest in approximately two dozen countries,[2] including parts of the United States. Its impact in Australia was especially calamitous: during the 1940s and 1950s, its invasion, along with changing climate conditions, forced some farmers to give up cultivating their crops.

In the Kumaon region of Uttarakhand, located in India's Central Himalayan range just west of the Nepal border, *Ageratina adenophora* has crowded out local plants to the point of establishing a near-monoculture on the floor of local forests. Social entrepreneurs Rashmi Bharti and Rajnish Jain decided to put up a fight.

The couple moved from Delhi to remote Uttarakhand in 1996 in search of a simpler life. Recognizing that the traditional spinning, dyeing, and weaving practices of local Shauka and Bora communities were disappearing, they established their nonprofit organization, Avani, three years later. Their goals were to bring back the quality of local textiles and to help the artisans compete successfully in fashion and textile markets seeking responsibly made goods. What started with twenty families has grown to involve over 1,400 people, almost 80 percent of them women. All of these community members are engaged in some aspect of silk, wool, and linen textile making—always naturally dyed and always produced in adherence to ecologically and socially sound principles.

Rashmi describes the dyes they use: "Our first colors were yellows and browns from rhubarb and walnut. We expanded from there into many different dyestuffs and colors, including indigo. It was not traditionally grown here, but we focused on altitude-appropriate varieties of *Indigofera tinctoria*, *Persicaria tinctoria*, and *Strobilanthes cusia*. We now make indigo pigment in a decentralized way that is available for sale."

OPPOSITE: (top) *Ageratina adenophora* originated in Mexico and is now invasive in many parts of the world (bottom) Harvesting the weed helps native plants reestablish the forest understory
HERE: *Ageratina adenophora* yields yellow-greens, which deepen into greens with the addition of iron

Handspun local fibers create delicious textures OPPOSITE: Avani makes and sells only handloomed fabrics

"We also set up a research space where we looked at local plants for their dye-yielding properties, wanting to use only plants that were plentifully available." When their research revealed that *Ageratina adenophora* could produce beautiful yellows and greens, from a bright pale lemon to a deep olive, a path forward seemed obvious.

"Our daughter inspired us to create nontoxic art supplies," Rashmi recalls. "We made 100 percent beeswax crayons with plant-based colorants as well as watercolors that could be used by children, and by artists, without adversely affecting their health."

That's not all. "We also set up a research space where we looked at local plants for their dye-yielding properties, wanting to use only plants that were plentifully available." When their research revealed that *Ageratina adenophora* could produce beautiful yellows and greens, from a bright pale lemon to a deep olive, a path forward seemed obvious. "There were entire forests of this plant all over the region. We thought it would be wonderful, too, if we could encourage communities to remove it from the woods and process it into dyes for use in our workshop and others in India and abroad. This has been our innovation, to create a use for something that is damaging the ecosystem."

After a decade of using *Ageratina*'s yellows and greens in luscious textiles, Rashmi, Rajnish, and their team introduced these colors into crayons and watercolors. "Our daughter inspired us to create nontoxic art supplies," Rashmi recalls. "We made 100 percent beeswax crayons with plant-based colorants as well as watercolors that could be used by children, and by artists, without adversely affecting their health."

The addition of healthful art supplies is part of Rashmi and Rajnish's desire to expand their work to reach at least 2,500 families in the next five years, adhering to their ecological ideals while bringing opportunity and income to the talented textile makers of this remote rural area.

All-natural dyeing and crayon making are part of the work of the Avani organization

Avani team member Nitin Gupta arranges silks dyed with invasive *Ageratina adenophora*

Chapter 24

NILDA
Callañaupa

Yarn dyed blue-green with the symbiotic combination of *hongo negro*, a parasitic fungus, and its host plant *Baccharis genistelloides* OPPOSITE: Nilda Callañaupa, social entrepreneur, writer, weaver, and Andean textile expert

FRESH GREENS

Nature's prodigious green finery notwithstanding, botanical sources of green dyes are rare. Most leaves will yield some degree of tan or yellow, if treated properly, and the leaves of a few dozen species contain the precursor to indigo. But only a scant handful of plants will yield green, usually helped along with an iron mordant. It's not surprising that two green-yielding species of the broad-ranging genus *Baccharis*—one common and one less so—can be found in the phenomenal biodiversity of Peru, home to 84 of our world's 103 ecosystem types.

The more common species is the shrubby plant known in Quechua as *chillca* and as *Baccharis latifolia* to botanists. It grows best along mountain streams at 12,500 feet above sea level, but still flourishes at 15,000 feet. (That's quite a bit shy of Peru's highest peaks, which are in the low 20,000-foot range.) Boiled in the dye vat for about an hour with *collpa*, a mineral-rich clay found in formerly volcanic areas of the Andes, the chillca is ready to transfer its color to yarn.

On dark gray wool, chillca looks almost black. On white wool, it is light green. Varying the amount of leaves will change the intensity of the color. Chillca is also used in traditional Quechua healing as an anti-inflammatory. It can be taken as a tisane for kidney stones, infused into a warm bath to treat swollen hands and feet and soften the skin, or used in a poultice on rashes.

The other green often seen in Andean textiles is a magical color somewhere between celadon and teal. It comes from a symbiotic relationship between a host plant and a fungus. The host, called *kinsa q'uchu* in Quechua, is *Baccharis genistelloides*. Its leaves grow flange-like along its long stems, giving it the appearance of a fern. Its habitat is the eastern side of the An-des in a middle-altitude zone called the "eyebrow of the jungle," whose moist microclimate re-sults from jungle humid-ity ascending the moun-tains to form soft clouds and gentle rain as it hits cooler altitudes. This mi-croclimate is perfect for the plants and the black fungus—*hongo negro*—that grows on them.

The combination of plant and fungus is es-sential to the making of green. Without the fun-gus, the leaves produce only a pallid yellow. Without the fern-like kinsa q'uchu, the dye bath lacks the tannins that help the wool take up the color.

According to Nilda Callañaupa, founder of the Center for Traditional Textiles of Cusco (CTTC), "We go, or we send some-one, to the one place we know of to find the plants. Only the leaves with fungus growing on them are useful, and they're found near the Amazon headwa-ters of the Manú National Park."

CTTC's weavers, who are spread out across ten communities in the Cusco area, value the beautiful blue-green celadons and teals they derive from the fungus. "We get the paler greens by reusing the dye water. Each reuse gives us a lighter color," Nilda ex-plains. No additional mordant is necessary because the acidity of the ferns does the job.

OPPOSITE: Women in Chinchero, Peru, members of the Center for Traditional Textiles of Cusco, prepare a mordant bath with alum. HERE: Dried fronds of *Baccharis genistelloides* alongside yarns that have been dyed with the plant

The color is most beautiful when the leaves and fungus are fresh, just after harvesting in March and April. Dried leaves work well enough, however. Nilda says the key to a successful dye vat is to keep the yarn moving. "The fungus has to come into contact with the yarn in order to give color. We stir constantly. Sometimes we will add a little bit of chillca at the end to create a beautiful layering of green colors."

This lovely range of greens, which contrasts beautifully with the reds and ochres so prevalent in Andean weaving, is an important part of the spectrum of natural colors produced by CTTC dyers and weavers. Reviving the natural dyes of the region has been an important initiative of CTTC, and the skills and knowledge they have mastered are shared throughout the ten communities that make up the organization.

OPPOSITE: A dyepot with *Baccharis genistelloides* and *B. latifolia*, called *chillca*   HERE: Varying combinations of CTTC's two green-producing botanical dyestuffs BELOW: A range of warmer greens comes from chillca

Chapter 25

Atelier NL

Small ceramic vessels show the mineral signature of various sands from around the world, each of which produces unique colors and textures when fired in a kiln OPPOSITE: Atelier NL cofounders Lonny van Ryswyck and Nadine Sterk

MINERAL SIGNATURES

By uncovering the colors hidden in clay and sand, Atelier NL designers Nadine Sterk and Lonny van Ryswyck give a new visual dimension to the farm fields and dunes of the Dutch landscape—and now to beaches around the world. Their spectacular spectrum of earthenware chocolates, reds, and yellows and glassy blues, greens, and bog-browns, each the manifestation of the mineral signature of its place of origin, is simultaneously seductive and informative.

"When I look at sand, I see different sizes and grains, structures and colors. Then I think that the sand is brought here by rivers, seas, and winds. It has its own background and has traveled for years."

Lonny van Ryswyck, Atelier NL

Carafes and glasses from Atelier NL's ZandGlas collection. Sand sources from left to right: Terschelling, Savelsbos, Knokke, Savelsbos, Brabantse Duinen, Savelsbos, and Knokke OPPOSITE: Glass tiles show regional variations in color

Their sensitivity to what most of us overlook came not from their sea-level Dutch hometowns but from the highlands of the Peruvian Andes, where Nadine and Lonny worked with the ceramic artisan collective Allpa. "Digging for clay in the highlands of Peru, carrying it back to the town of Chulucanas on horseback, and dancing on it with my Quechua colleagues to remove the air bubbles—that's when we saw clay for the first time," remembers Lonny. "Our hands-in-the-dirt experience, the physicality of it, gave the clay more importance to us. When we got back home, we said to each other, 'How can we even think of buying clay from the shops now?'"

FARM TO TABLE

Instead, they headed to the Northeast Polder, 181 square miles of land reclaimed from the IJsselmeer between 1935 and 1955 and intended for mostly agricultural use. The design duo convinced eighty of the Polder's farmers to let them dig for clay. There was some skepticism among these practical-minded growers of fruits and vegetables about what the designers would produce. But when they ate strawberries or potatoes grown in the same earth that the bowl was taken from, *their* earth, they saw the connection. The land they work on every day acquired new virtues of beauty, color, potential, productivity. "Over a lunch where we served farm-grown food in farm-sourced clay vessels, one farmer said, 'Well, even if my harvest fails, this land can still give me ceramics,'" Lonny recalls.

Polderceramics evolved into Atelier NL's Kleiservice ("clay service" in English), an assortment of plates, bowls, and cups whose clays are sourced from six locations throughout the Netherlands. The shapes are utterly simple, letting the color and character of the clay-bodies come through. From dark cinnamon to brick red and pinkish adobe, from ochre to pale yellow, the range of color is a function of each individual locale ornamented only by an Atelier NL stamp declaring the source of the clay. Originally made by venerable porcelain company Royal Tichelaar Makkum from 2009 to 2015, the collection is now sold directly from the Atelier NL Earth Alchemy workshop.

WILD SANDS

"As we worked with clay and ceramics, we came across the glass process," Lonny recounts. "We learned quickly that this industry uses only white sands, and there is already an awareness that one day the sources of this pure sand will be exhausted by over-mining." Exploring the "wild sands" found in most ecosystems on the earth became a fixation for the artists, not merely to identify their aesthetic and design potential but also to better understand the links between location, mineral content, and plastic properties. Tracking and presenting data is integral to this project, as is pairing didactic information with sand and glass samples in meticulously crafted specimen boxes.

"Each grain of sand has a story to tell," Lonny reflects. She sees grains of sand much like people—arriving at their destination after long journeys, influenced by their surroundings, combining their origins with their histories in unique ways. "Melted at high temperatures, natural sands fracture, foam, and crystallize according to their unique mineral signature," she says, noting the surprising variations that emerge in the kiln, each one the visual expression of a distinct narrative.

Shown under magnification, sand samples reveal differences in color and texture OPPOSITE: Bottles of sand sent from around the globe form the "To See a World in a Grain of Sand" library.

"In the case of computers and circuitry, the purest silica is needed or you get errors. In the making of other things," she asks, "could we look at the impurities of wild sands, their trace elements, their pollutants, as *enrichments*?" If we see the "impurities" of wild sands as a kind of *terroir*, as authentic marks of distinctness and distinction, perhaps the variations they engender make the final product more, rather than less, valuable. Perhaps the story and sense of place they contain are more worthy of consumer buy-in than their bland and standard counterparts? Perhaps the enrichment of narrative, of history, renders objects less disposable?

ZandGlas, Atelier NL's line of carafes and drinking glasses, traces the narrative of the Dutch landscape in distinct sand-derived colors. Coastal sands from the North Sea towns of Terschelling and Knokke ren-der airy, cool greens and blues. Sands from the pine barrens of Brabantse Duinen make a crisp, pale yellow-green, while iron- and nutrient-rich sands from the Savelsbos forest in the south turn into a luscious, dark bronze-green. Are the colors inherent in these sources of sand an obstacle or an opportunity? Do their variations send us fleeing back to the colorless glass made with industrially mined pure white sands?

IN A GRAIN OF SAND

Is it possible that our future as consumers is written in a grain of sand?

The habits of modern manufacturing demand total uniformity of product so that mass-marketing techniques can make identical promises to the largest possible number of consumers to create the highest possible sales at the highest possible profit margins.

But these habits require that we give up narrative, connection, individuality, and variation in the name of "efficiency." Their work in clay and sand has helped Nadine and Lonny see a "quantity versus quality" problem: Do we need so much, and so much sameness? Or would we be better satisfied with objects that spoke to us not with the cheapest but perhaps with the deepest voices? Can we rebalance the system with more and better values incorporated into the products we design, make, and consume?

Not content with narratives only from the Netherlands, Nadine and Lonny launched "To See a World in a Grain of Sand" in 2017. The project encourages people from around the world to submit sand samples—along with location data and a brief narrative—from places that mean something to them. If desired, the sample can be turned into a specimen box with a sealed glass tube of sand and a clay cup whose vitreous finish comes from firing the sand in a kiln. Purchase of the specimen box melds sand, location, and memories into an evocative permanent object.

From palest blue to murkiest brown-black, with every color in between, their collection of mineral signatures grows every day. And every sample establishes another path forward for the development of narrative-rich sourcing and making.

"When we understand our journeys, where we come from and maybe even where we're going, we make beautiful colors."

Lonny van Ryswyck, Atelier NL

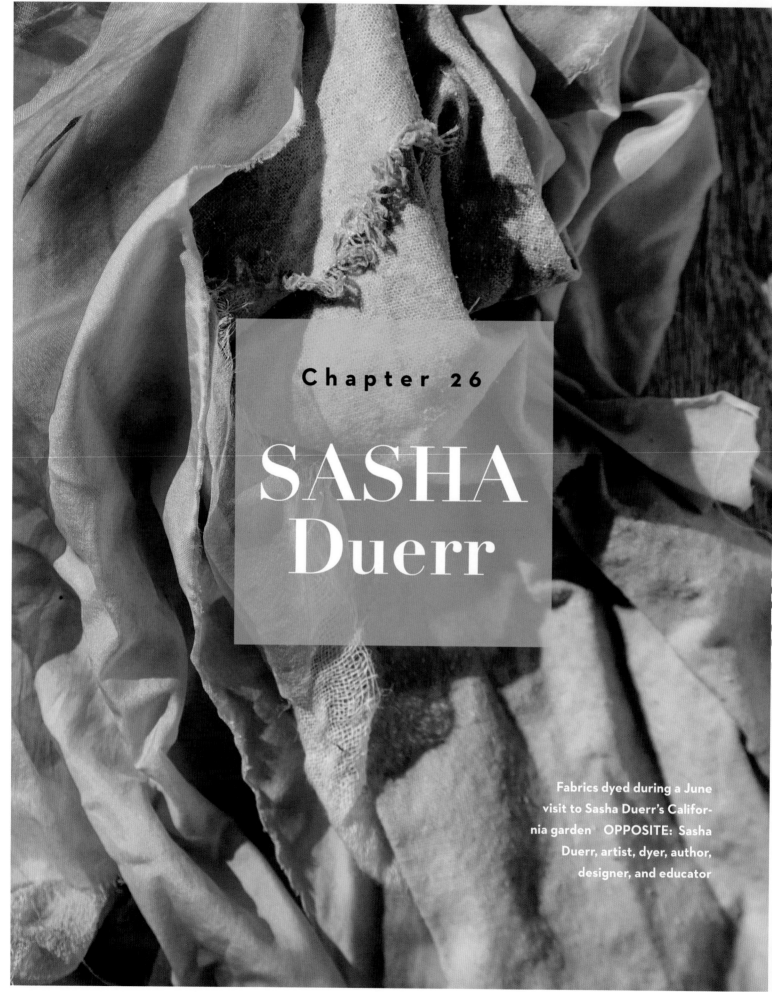

Chapter 26

SASHA Duerr

Fabrics dyed during a June visit to Sasha Duerr's California garden   OPPOSITE: Sasha Duerr, artist, dyer, author, designer, and educator

BACK to the GARDEN

Every conversation with Sasha Duerr is like walking through a lush garden at peak bloom. All of her ideas are in full flower, each attracting its own universe of pollinating satellites, each colorful leaf, petal, and seed promising something colorful or useful or nourishing, or all three. If you listen carefully, her garden's roots quietly expand outward in rich run-on sentences, not just toward new ground but toward every corner of consciousness.

We've got to get ourselves back to the garden.

—Joni Mitchell, "*Woodstock*," 1969

The very soil in which Sasha's intoxicating ideas grow is her sense of the connection between plant, color, and experience and how connection creates a sense of value and belonging within us. Connection is everything to her, because if we do not deepen our relationship with our environment and with each other, she sees little possibility of change in our approach to people and planet living in harmony.

One of Sasha's many ways of describing the sense of unity she seeks for herself, as well as for everyone in her ken, is ecoawareness. As she uses the term, it refers not only to a macro- consciousness of the biosphere in all its strength and fragility but also to the intimate sense--driven experiences that guide us toward understanding and keeping that understanding fresh and alive within us.

Ecoawareness combines past and future, memory and intention, knowledge and action. For Sasha, botanical color is a physical means to a metaphysical end— one of many paths toward seeing ever more clearly our responsibilities as stewards of our environment.

HOW HER GARDEN GREW

Sasha lives on an urban farm in Oakland, California, where she grows flowers and herbs and vegetables and other plants. And two children. It's hard to tell for sure whether any given plant she raises will be used as food, medicine, ornament, or dyestuff, be-

cause to her, these categories are entirely intertwined.

Her multilayered view of plants stems from her early upbringing on the back-to-the-land farmstead Sasha's family established in Maine in the 1970s. "The farm was very formative for me. Playing outside in all seasons, running through the veils of coastal fog, smelling the wet earth, the damp moss, the pine needles, the roses, the salty air. I was immersed in my environment, and this is still part of my creative flow and how I come to my work," she recounts.

At the age of nine, she and her family began to spend half the year in Hawaii, which in short order became their home. Hawaii only deepened Sasha's immersion in Nature. "It rains a lot in Hilo. It's one of the rainiest places on earth, in fact, and the warmth of tropical rain meant that we could be out all day, no coat, free in our yard, in the woods, anywhere. Our house was at the top of a cliff overlooking the ocean, and being surrounded by rain and waves was a little like being in a dye bath."

Were her schoolyard forays into making shampoo out of awa'puhi ginger (first brought to Hawaii in the canoes of early Polynesian settlers) an early indication of her path? "I was always foraging for food, materials for fort building and art making, and soaking things in puddles to see what would happen. That does seem a little predictive, doesn't it?" she says with a smile.

OPPOSITE: Sasha Duerr
checks the progress of a
natural dyepot HERE: Fresh
mint yields dreamy greens

FROM PUDDLES TO PAINTINGS

As a student at Middlebury College, Sasha simultaneously explored painting, religion, ethics, screenwriting, and ecology. Even as her abstract art practice continued to draw upon her fascination with Nature's near-magical transformation of sunlight and earth into Life itself, her outlook expanded with exposure to the field of environmental ethics.

Steven Rockefeller, then dean of Middlebury College, brought a complex view of ecology and society into the classroom. His decades-long study of religion blended with extensive advocacy for environmental sustainability to form a perspective at once deep and broad. He worked for many years to help birth the Earth Charter Initiative, intended to guide the formation of sound environmental policy at the national and global level in its expression of "a consensus of values and principles among diverse cultural, economic, religious, and scientific interests."[1] Forty-five national committees and twenty-three international members were involved in its formation, with Rockefeller serving for three years as chair of the drafting committee.

One of the planks in the charter's platform, endorsed by UNESCO in 2000, sets an important goal for institutions like Middlebury: *Integrate into formal education and life-long learning the knowledge, values, and skills needed for a sustainable way of life.*[2] Perhaps because of her back-to-the-earth upbringing, perhaps because of Rockefeller's comprehensive and persuasive thinking, Sasha absorbed this notion, along with another formative idea. "Rockefeller taught us that people aren't going to change through facts alone. We need an emotional response to see the need and urge for change into germination, into flower, into action." The goal of blending information and emotion into ethical action remains a cornerstone for Sasha's work today.

While mind and soul were thriving in the heady mix of paint and policy, the body suffered. "My work in the studio with oil paints left me feeling chemically sensitive, experiencing headaches and nausea. I began to be aware of the disconnect between the caustic materials I was using and the ideas I was absorbing about the environment," Sasha remembers. "My research into nontoxic alternatives led me to natural pigments, but there was little information in the library to help me, and my professors didn't have much to give there, either."

The search for healthy color started with grinding earth pigments for paint and naturally led to boiling plant matter. A dyer was born.

HYBRID IDEAS, HYBRID PRACTICES

After Middlebury, Sasha was drawn to the San Francisco Bay area for its ethos of community action, its progressive tilt, and the California College of Arts and Crafts (now CCA). In 1999, she began the MFA program at CCA, where she "saw art and plants as integral to my process, and my process as connected not only to Nature but to community." Sasha was, perhaps, a puzzling hybrid of art, craft, performance, and environmentalism for CCA faculty, but this did not deter her.

Berkeley's Edible Schoolyard program gave Sasha a two-year grant to conduct natural dye workshops

OPPOSITE: Sasha Duerr with a handful of rhubarb leaves
HERE: The vivid color of fresh indigo leaves, and the mellow greens of mint

It's hard to tell for sure whether any given plant she raises will be used as food, medicine, ornament, or dyestuff, because to her, these categories are entirely intertwined.

OPPOSITE: Working with fresh indigo HERE: (from lower left to upper right) Green tones made with rhubarb root, dyer's chamomile, and rosemary clippings

The stems and leaves of roses, plus a little iron, deliver gray-greens
OPPOSITE: Steeping mint prior to a dyeing session

and to write curriculum around plant-based color for the schoolkids flocking to their one-acre community garden. The links between natural color and food, and teaching and community solidified for Sasha. Her descriptions of this period of growth sound very much as if she was collecting and combining ideas in hybrid form to develop her own original sort of *ecoliteracy*. Her comprehension of the language of plants, with their myriad capacities to yield color, food, fiber, and more begat a desire not just to communicate her insights but to better understand how to engage individuals and communities to move them closer to ecoawareness. And thus closer to being participants in solving our ecological problems.

This integrated way of thinking eventually brought Sasha to the 2007 founding of the Permacouture Institute, a nonprofit supporting education and research into dye and fiber plants, as well as into social practice for sustainability in fashion and textiles. Even as permaculture aims to work with nature instead of against it in the production of foods, permacouture

seeks to meld the interests of the entire ecosystem with the design, sourcing, production, care, and composting of clothing. It's a sort of "unified field theory" of fashion consumption that aims to forge new solutions to age-old problems: How do we satisfy our need for clothing and our passion for beauty, while incorporating Nature's opportunities and limits into the process? How can we make, and use, truly responsible fashion, taking all factors into account?

Some early examples of how Sasha envisioned it all working appear in the clothing of the now shuttered Adi + George, a fashion line she cofounded with designer Casey Larkin. For example, oxalis, a weed endemic to much of California, provided a stunning lemon-yellow hue to designs meant to be produced while oxalis was in bloom (November through April), and sold accordingly. Year-round colors like a Millennial Pink hue derived from avocado pits sourced from Bay Area restaurants were less seasonally constrained. Making and selling when botanicals are in season would ground design and marketing cycles to the cycles of Nature in an industry hardly accustomed to any constraints at all.

Lest permacouture sound altogether too idealistic, Sasha's view of the fashion industry clearly reflects awareness of the waste built into the current business model, as well as an accurate assessment that we consumers have been trained over a few generations to have very little thought about or involvement in what we wear. "It's nearly impossible for us to comprehend how time- and resource-intensive clothing really is," she says, before reeling off the many steps that are part of garment making: farming animal and plant fibers, harvesting and processing the yield, spinning, designing, weaving, dyeing, cutting, sewing, embellishing, finishing, packaging, shipping, selling. Sasha would add laundering, mending, redyeing, remaking, and eventually composting to that list. And she'd like to see all of it happening in sync with the annual cycles of Nature, as well as within the greater arc of environmental health.

Permacouture could bring sound social practices and fresh information into trans-

"I was always foraging for food, materials for fort building and art making, and soaking things in puddles to see what would happen. That does seem a little predictive, doesn't it?" she says with a smile.

forming one of the most polluting industries on earth.[3] But, to put it mildly, response from the fashion industry has been slow. There is so much profit at stake, and so little immediate reward for virtue over sex appeal or responsibility over sales results. "There is more desire for progress, and more collective goal-setting now than in the past, even among larger players, but there's only so much the industry can do right now. But you can see a shift in understanding. Priorities are changing. Consciousness needs to come from so many different angles. Students, for example, see that sustainability is truly multidimensional and ever-learning."

Students see the situation. And teachers like Sasha, now on the faculty at CCA, help them see more. It's not hard to imagine Sasha stirring a dye vat of, say, wild fennel, surrounded by undergrads and grads, calling for awareness of the sense-memories elicited by the smell, the color, the plant itself, extolling all the while the possibilities and eventual scalability of low-impact botanical dyeing. It's not hard to hear her pushing along the bigger issues

ACROSS THE TOP: A dye session with oxalis flowers and stems BOTTOM: Raspberry brambles in the dye pot

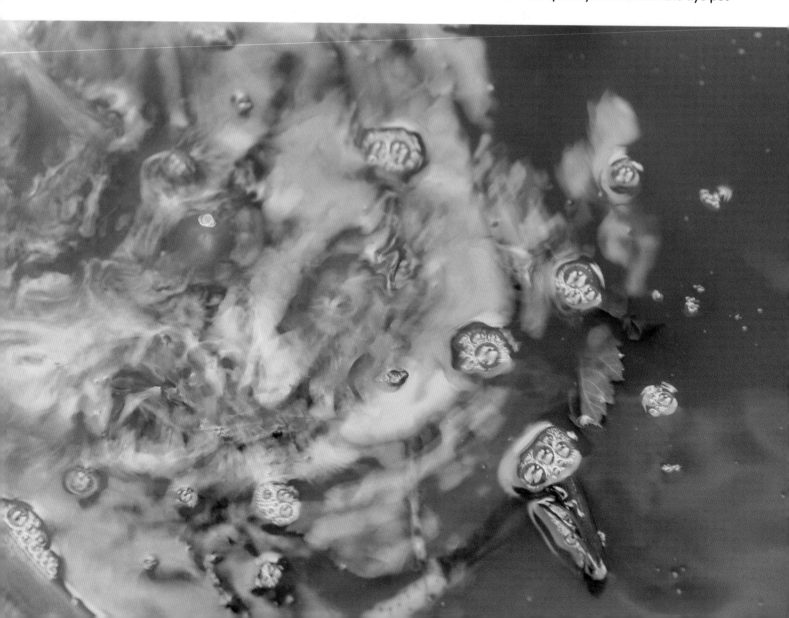

around cradle- to-grave textile production methods.

It's not at all difficult to imagine what a compelling teacher Sasha must be at CCA, at the dozens of workshops she holds around the US, and among the planters and cultivators of the many dye gardens she's helped into being in the last five years.

NATURAL DYEING IS A GATEWAY DRUG

"Natural dyeing is a gateway drug," Sasha asserts with humor, meaning that the thrill of seeing textiles soak up fresh plant color is a memorable sensory experience, and as such, a step along the road to her overall goal of fostering ecoawareness in students, clients, colleagues, friends, and family. "Nobody is going to change their thinking about color and textiles without an experiential connection."

Sasha treats botanical dyeing very much like cooking, offering a few rules and a base of necessary information to stay safe and on the right track. The color recipes she sets forward in her books are not complicated and convey clear ratios of dyestuff to fiber, easy instructions on how and when to employ nontoxic mordants, and so on. Although some of her dye knowledge comes from delving "into the textile history of many cultures around the world,"[4] most stems from personal experimentation. It's not hard to imagine the internal calculations that must happen every time Sasha first encounters a sidewalk weed or a roadside plant: when to harvest what color, and how to extract it onto what fiber with what mordant and when?

Years of research and experimentation have created a spectacular natural-color library. Windfall tree leaves and seeds (Japanese maple and acorns are favorites), various barks and a few roots, food waste (avocado pits, onion skins, olive leaves), waste from the floral industry, and foodstuffs (herbs, beans, berries, coffee, tea) produce colors from deep black all the way through the spectrum to an alluring, pale yellow-green. Nontoxic premordants, mordants, and aftermordants multiply the possibilities exponentially. Add explorations with traditional dye plants, such as fresh indigo leaves milled in a food processor and soaked with silk to make a luminous daiquiri green, and Sasha's library becomes encyclopedic.

But that breadth is not broad enough for Sasha. Her commitment to sustainability extends traditional hot-water dyeing into cold-water and solar-heated techniques. A desire to go deep into the color potential of a particular place compels Sasha to create intricate color wheels where she captures the natural hues available locally on a seasonal and year-round basis, as well as the tonal variations created with basic mordanting techniques. And for still more possibilities, she often looks beyond dyeing textiles and into transforming yarns, papers, wood, shells, leather, and even the occasional pair of shoes with botanical color.

Lately, Sasha has worked to take the transformative properties of her discipline still further. Along with her CCA students, Sasha has been exploring links between color and medicine. "We can have a more connected understanding of what we put against our skin. The ancient notion of poultices, which placed plant matter directly on the skin so that our body could absorb botanical medicines—we're exploring that with dye. Why couldn't we absorb the healing properties of plants through dyed textiles?" Audrey Louise Reynolds, who uses turmeric-dyed fabric, would agree (see page 185). So would Aboubakar Fofana's grandmother (see page 19). But Sasha takes the concept further. "Perhaps we could extend Ayurvedic herbal techniques by dyeing cloth with plant blends specific to an individual. Personally, I've been looking at comfrey, once known as bone-knitter, to help me with some strengthening after an ankle break."

The roots of her garden are indeed constantly expanding outward.

There's rosemary, that's for remembrance.

Hamlet, Act 4, Scene 5

Rosemary, fragrant and roughly cut, goes into the dye pot OPPOSITE: Lovely blue-greens are the result

Sasha cuts back a rampant rosemary bush for our dyeing session. OPPOSITE: When iron is added to the steeping rosemary, a gorgeous blue-green appears

SYMBIOSIS

We visit Sasha in Oakland in early June 2018. She's gathered rosemary, mint, sage, oxalis, and wild fennel so that she can show us how this natural dyeing thing is done. Aside from mordanting, the dyeing process is, as promised, like cooking, with pots warming on the stove or steeping off to the side. A few jars of fabric, liquid, and dyestuffs sit on the shelf like pickles, marinating into saturated-color maturity. Always at home in the kitchen, I'm already hooked.

The dyeing starts to happen with nothing more than a few pots of water, heat, fresh herbs, and some iron powder to coax the yellows released by today's dyestuffs into varying shades of green. We begin with rosemary.

"Rosemary is associated with remembrance," Sasha says, calling up one of Ophelia's botanical references in Shakespeare's *Hamlet*. The lore around this may come from rosemary's reluctance to shed its fragrant leaves, as well as from its ancient use at funerals, as referenced by Friar Laurance in *Romeo and Juliet*. The herb was also used widely across northern Europe at betrothals and weddings as an expression of fidelity.

Nicholas Culpeper's 1653 *Complete Herbal* assigns rosemary many healing and strengthening properties, including the ability to shore up a "weak memory."[5] This particular notion endures in the twenty-first century, with many students in the UK relying on rosemary oil's memory-strengthening properties at exam time.[6]

My own associations are more prosaic and personal. Rosemary's scent summons the camaraderie of Thanksgiving preparations and the green of my own rosemary bushes, among the last plants to fade in winter in the US Northeast. The colors Sasha makes from this herb, from dark greens to browns, take me immediately to the satisfaction and slight melancholy of a late autumn session in the garden when I'm preparing my perennials for winter.

Sasha moves on to mint, from which she extracts a wonderful array of greens, appropriately brighter and more extroverted than rosemary. According to the Greeks, the lovely nymph Minthe was trampled to death by jealous Persephone when she discovered her husband's infidelity. Hades turned the poor thing into mint. The herb is also said to have been a key ingredient in *kykeon*, a hallucinogenic taken as part of the Eleusinian mysteries.

More lighthearted tropes include hospitality, in ways that link to mint's modern "fresh and clean" reputation. Both ancient Greeks and Romans scrubbed their tables with it before a party. It's these associations that resonate with me: a childhood love of peppermint gum and an unreasonable grown-up fondness for the several varieties rampant in overgrown corners of my garden. They grow, ergo I love them.

I realize that I've entered Sasha's symbiosis of nature and culture.[7] I'm in the continuum of cultural and personal associations. I'm seeing and reseeing the natural dyestuffs in front of us, and the colors they produce gain depth and importance. They belong to me and I to them. I'm wanting to go home to my own garden and mint-dye linen for a shirt, and rosemary-dye some worn napkins so that I can be reminded of, and retell, their stories. So that I can patch and care for these things across their long lives.

So that I can share my evolving ecoawareness with family, friends, and colleagues, not just with the words of this book, but also with the very-much-alive practitioners of natural color whose lives and motives make me feel more alive and more hopeful about our future as a species.

Garden-Variety Greens

Sasha Duerr dyed the five silvery-gray fabrics on the left with rosemary and iron. The six warm tones in the middle come from rhubarb root. The six pale greens on the right are also made with rosemary. All plant material was harvested from Sasha's garden.

NOTES

A POINT OF SILENCE

1. From an essay by Birgitta de Vos published in 2013 on www.pantoneview.com, no longer available online. Text provided by Birgitta de Vos.

TRADITION AND PROGRESS

1. https://en.wikipedia.org/wiki/Groupe_Bogolan Kasobané

BACK TO BLUE AND BEYOND

1. Jenny Balfour-Paul, *Indigo: Egyptian Mummies to Blue Jeans* (Richmond Hill, Ontario: Firefly Books, 2011), 26–27; Rita Bolland, *Tellem Textiles: Archaeological Finds from Burial Caves in Mali's Bandiagara Cliffs* (Amsterdam: Tropenmuseum/Royal Tropical Institute, 1991).
2. Balfour-Paul, *Indigo*, 142.
3. Marcella Echevarria, "Pre-Columbian Purple," *HAND/EYE Magazine*, 06/Global Color (Fall 2011), 52.
4. https://www.ncbi.nlm.nih.gov/pubmed/21717088.
5. Michele Wipplinger, http://hand-eyemagazine.com/content/inside-indigo.
6. Balfour-Paul, *Indigo*, 118.
7. https://www.ncbi.nlm.nih.gov/pubmed/20695891.

NEVERTHELESS, WOAD PERSISTED

1. John Edmonds, *The History of Woad and the Medieval Woad Vat* (Little Chalfont, Buckinghamshire: John Edmonds, 1998.
2. http://www.woad-inc.co.uk/history.html.
3. http://www.woad-inc.co.uk; http://www.bleu-de-lectoure.com/en/.

THE LAST PURPLE

1. Marta Turok, "Pre-Columbian Purple," *HAND/EYE Magazine*, 06/Global Color (Fall 2011), 58-59.
2. Eric Sebastian Mindling, *Oaxaca Stories in Cloth* (Loveland, Colorado: Thrums, 2016), 38-42

SERIOUS SYMBOLS

1. http://www2.palomar.edu/users/warmstrong/ecoph4.htm.

STALKING WILD COLOR

1. https://www.namyco.org/history_mushrooms_for_color.php.

AUTHENTIC VOICES

1. Lynn Stephen, "Export Markets and Their Effects on Indigenous Craft Production: The Case of the Weavers of Teotitlán del Valle, Mexico," in *Textile Traditions of Mesoamerica and the Andes* (Austin: University of Texas Press, 1996), 392.
2. Patricia Rieff Anawalt, *Indian Clothing Before Cortés* (Norman: University of Oklahoma Press, 1981),
3. Stephen, "Export Markets," 392.
4. Because of the lack of any mention of Teotitlán weaving activity in the text of a 1777–1778 report to the Spanish court, *Relaciónes Geograficas*, it is possible that the tradition of weaving is not unbroken in the community.
5. Stephen, "Export Markets," 383–384.
6. Ibid., 385.
7. https://blogs.missouristate.edu/arthistory/contemporary-mesoamerican-textiles/.
8. PBS, *Craft in America*, "No Borders," Season 9, Episode 1, 2018.
9. http://entheology.com/plants/tagetes-lucida-marigolds/.
10. https://www.ncbi.nlm.nih.gov/pmc/articles/PMC4328766/.
11. https://digitalcommons.unl.edu/cgi/viewcontent.cgi?referer=https://www.google.com/

&httpsredir=1&article=1043&context=tsaconf.

12. Ibid.
13. Van Dam, Alex et al. "Point of Origin: Genetic Diversity and the Biogeography of the Cochineal Insect." in Carmella Padilla and Barbara Anderson, eds., *A Red Like No Other: How Cochineal Colored the World* (New York: Skira Rizzoli, 2015), pp 90-93.
14. Amy Butler Greenfield, *A Perfect Red* (New York: Harper Collins, 2006), p. 36
15. Stephen, "Export Markets," 382.

RED RISES AGAIN

1. http://www.peopleandtheplanet.com/index. html@lid=30256&topic=27&section=32.html.
2. Pamela Ravasio, "Tradition, Wisdom, Inspiration." *HAND/EYE Magazine*, 10/Craft and Compassion, 2012.
3. Kikuo Morimoto, "Traces of War: The Revival of Silk Weaving in Cambodia." *Textile Society of America Symposium Proceedings*, 528, 2002: 199. http://digitalcommons.unl.edu/tsaconf/528.
4. http://www.peopleandtheplanet.com/index. html@lid=30256&topic=27&section=32.html.

LIKE A PRAYER

1. Talaq is a 1,400-year-old practice among some Sunni Muslims that gives a husband the right to divorce by repeating "I divorce you!" three times.

OLD WAYS, NEW TECHNIQUES

1. India Flint, "Out of the Woods," *HAND/EYE Magazine*, 02/Future of Folk: Fall/Winter 2009: 2.
2. https://www.organicgardener.com.au/articles/ ethical-threads.

IN THE WATER

1. https://www.uv.mx/personal/megalindo/ files/2010/07/GalindoTovar_325_334_V21. pdf.

GOLDEN GIRL

1. http://www.ayurvedacollege.com/articles/students/turmeric.
2. https://vimeo.com/88530951.

INVASIVE COLOR

1. The plant is also known by an older botanical appellation: *Eupatorium adenophora*.
2. https://www.cabi.org/isc/datasheet/23243.

BACK TO THE GARDEN

1. Julie Newman, *Green Ethics and Philosophy* (Los Angeles: SAGE, 2011): 119.
2. Ibid., 122.
3. http://www.wri.org/blog/2017/07/apparel-industrys-environmental-impact-6-graphics.
4. Sasha Duerr, *The Handbook of Natural Plant Dyes* (Portland: Timber Press, 2011): 14.
5. http://mrssymbols.blogspot. com/2015/04/rosemary-for-remembrance.html.
6. https://www.theguardian.com/life-andstyle/shortcuts/2017/may/23/rosemary-herb-choice-students-memory.
7. Duerr, *Handbook*: 14.

BIBLIOGRAPHY

Anawalt, Patricia Rieff. *Indian Clothing Before Cortés: Mesoamerican Costumes from the Codices.* Norman, Oklahoma: University of Oklahoma Press, 1981.

Balfour-Paul, Jenny. *Indigo: Egyptian Mummies to Blue Jeans.* Buffalo: Firefly Books, 2012. Original edition British Museum Press, 2011.

Bessette, Arleen Reinis. *The Rainbow Beneath My Feet: A Mushroom Dyer's Field Guide.* Syracuse, New York: Syracuse University, 2001.

Bessire, Lucas. *Behold the Black Caiman: A Chronicle of Ayoreo Life.* Chicago: University of Chicago Press, 2014.

Bolland, Rita. *Tellem Textiles: Archaeological Finds from Burial Caves in Mali's Bandiagara Cliff.* Amsterdam: Royal Tropical Institute, 1991.

Boutrup, Joy, and Catharine Ellis. *The Art and Science of Natural Dyes: Principles, Experiments, and Results.* Atglen, Pennsylvania: Schiffer, 2019.

Brett-Smith, Sarah C. *The Silence of the Women: Bamana Mud Cloths.* Milan: 5 Continents Editions, 2014.

Cardon, Dominique. *Natural Dyes: Sources, Tradition, Technology and Science.* London: Archetype Publications, 2007.

Carman, Jean K. *Dyemaking with Eucalypts.* Kenthurst, New South Wales: Kangaroo Press, 1985.

Chenciner, Robert. *Madder Red: A History of Luxury and Trade.* Richmond: Curzon, 2000.

Culpeper, Nicholas. *Culpeper's Complete Herbal,* 1653.

De Vos, Birgitta. *Out of Fashion: The New Fashion.* Amsterdam: Birgitta de Vos, 2017.

Deutscher, Guy. *Through the Language Glass: Why the World Looks Different in Other Languages.* New New York, Metropolitan Books, 2010.

Duerr, Sasha. *The Handbook of Natural Plant Dyes.* Portland, Oregon: Timber Press, 2010.

———. *Natural Color: Vibrant Plant Dye Projects for Your Home and Wardrobe.* Berkeley: Watson-Guptill, 2016.

Eckstut, Joann, and Arielle Eckstut. *The Secret Language of Color.* New York: Black Dog and Leventhal Publishers, 2013.

Edmonds, John. *The History of Woad and the Medieval Woad Vat.* Little Chalfont, Buckinghamshire: John Edmonds, 1998.

Finlay, Victoria. The Brilliant History of Color in Art. Los Angeles: J. Paul Getty Museum, 2014.

Flint, India. *The Bundle Book.* Mount Pleasant, South Australia: Prophet of Bloom, 2014.

———. *Eco Colour: Botanical Dyes for Beautiful Textiles.* Loveland, Colorado: Interweave, 2010.

———. *Second Skin: Choosing and Caring for Textiles and Clothing.* Sidney, Australia: Murdoch Books, 2012.

———. *Stuff, Steep and Store.* Mount Pleasant, South Australia: Prophet of Bloom, 2013.

BIBLIOGRAPHY *(continued)*

Green, Gillian. *Traditional Textiles of Cambodia: Cultural Threads and Material Heritage.* Chicago: Buppha Press, 2003.

Greenfield, Amy Butler. *A Perfect Red: Empire, Espionage, and the Quest for the Color of Desire.* New York: Harper Collins, 2006.

Hilu, Sam, and Irwin Hersey. *Bogolanfini Mud Cloth.* Atglen, Pennsylvania: Schiffer Publishing, 2005.

Kirby, Jo, et al., eds. *Natural Colorants for Dyeing and Lake Pigments.* London: Archetype Publications, 2014.

Legrand, Catherine. *Indigo: The Color That Changed the World.* London: Thames and Hudson, 2012.

Mabey, Richard. Weeds: *In Defense of Nature's Most Unloved Plants.* New York: Harper Collins, 2011.

Maxwell, Robyn. *Textiles of Southeast Asia: Tradition, Trade and Transformation.* Hong Kong: Periplus Editions, 2012.

McHugh, James. *Sandalwood and Carrion: Smell in Indian Religion and Culture.* New York: Oxford University Press, 2012.

Mindling, Eric Sebastian. *Oaxaca Stories in Cloth: A Book About People, Belonging, Identity, and Adornment.* Loveland, Colorado: Thrums Books, 2016.

Newman, Julie, ed. *Green Ethics and Philosophy: An A-to-Z Guide.* Los Angeles: SAGE, 2011.

Padilla, Carmella, and Barbara Anderson, eds. *A Red Like No Other: How Cochineal Colored the World.* New York: Skira Rizzoli Publications, 2015.

Pete, Lynda Teller, and Barbara Teller Ornelas. *Spider Woman's Children: Navajo Weavers Today.* Loveland, Colorado: Thrums Books, 2018.

Phipps, Elena. *Cochineal Red: The Art History of a Color.* New York: Metropolitan Museum of Art, 2010.

Rice, Miriam C. *Mushrooms for Color.* Eureka, California: Mad River Press, 1980.

Rieske, Bill. *Navajo and Hopi Dyes.* Salt Lake City, Utah: Historic Indian Publishers, 1974.

Rovine, Victoria L. Bogolan: *Shaping Culture through Cloth in Contemporary Mali.* Washington, DC: Smithsonian Institution, 2001.

Sacks, Oliver. *Oaxaca Journal.* New York: Vintage Books, 2012.

Sandberg, Gösta. *The Red Dyes: Cochineal, Madder, and Murex Purple.* Asheville: Lark Books, 1996

Scheville, Margot Blum et al., eds. *Textile Traditions of Mesoamerica and the Andes: An Anthology.* Austin: University of Texas Press, 1991.

St. Clair, Kassia. *The Secret Lives of Color.* New York: Penguin Books, 2016.

Varichon, Anne. *Colors: What They Mean and How to Make Them.* New York: Abrams, 2006.

Weiner, Annette B, and Jane Schneider, eds. *Cloth and Human Experience.* Washington, DC: Smithsonian Books, 1989.

Wipplinger, Michele. *Natural Dye Instruction Booklet.* Seattle: Earthues, 2017.

INDEX

Page numbers in *italics* indicate photos.

A

Adeyemo, Gasali, 24–25
Adiv Pure Nature, 168–181
African textiles
    indigo-dyed, 24–31
    mudcloth, 8–17
Ageratina adenophora, 194–203
Ahmad, Mishael Aziz, 42, 44
ajunao tree, 157
Akiyama, Masazuku, 26
Allen, Alissa, 124–129, *125*
Artemisia tridentata, 164
Atelier NL, 210–215
Avani, 194–203
Avendaño, Habacuc, 66–73, *67*, *72*
Avendaño, Margarida, 66–67, *67*
de Ávila, Alejandro, 84
avocado pits, 118–123, 224
Ayoreo people, 152–161

B

Baccharis genistelloides, 204–209
Baccharis latifolia, 206, 209
Bharti, Rashmi, *195*, 196–200
Balfour-Paul, Jenny, 22, 24
batik, 36
Beard, Antonia, 117
beige and tan. *See also* brown
    from desert plants, 164
    from tree moss, 86, 87, 164
black
    from bark and berries, 157
    from bark and sapwood, 157
    from *dajudie*, 158
    historical perspective, 75–76
    from logwood, 76–79
    in mudcloth, 11
Bleu de Lectoure, 64
blue. *See also* indigo
    from flowers, 136, 140
    from sand, 210–215
    from woad, 60–65
bogolanfini, 8–17
Boutrup, Joy, 190, 193
Bromelia hieronymi, 154
brown
    from bark and sapwood, 157
    from *dajudie*, 158
    in mudcloth, 11
    ochre pigments, 142–151
    from rosemary, 231

from sand and clay, 210–215
from walnut hulls or canaigre, 164
from *zapote* fruit, 86
Bukhara Red, 102–109
Burgundy, Duke of, 75–76
Buro Belén, 74–79

C

cactus leaves, 90–91, *92*
California College of Arts and Crafts
    (CCA), 220
Callañaupa, Nilda, 204–209, *205*
CARE Social Ventures (CSV), 43–44
Carman, Jean K., 133
carpet making, 102–109
Cavendish, Sue, 20
Center for Traditional Textiles of Cusco
    (CTTC), 206, 209
ceramics, 213. *See also* tile making
chamomile, *223*
Charles V, 76
Cheque Oitedie, 152–161
chillca, 206, 209
Chrysothamnus spp., 164
Clark, Sarah, 126
Clarke, Irene Hardy, 162–167, *163*, *165*,
    166
clays and sands, 210–215
Clé Tiles, 50–53
cochineal, 80–99, 100–101
Contreras, Javier, *86*
Contreras, Juana Gutiérrez, 80–94, *81*,
    82, *86*, *89*, *90*, *91*
cotton
    African, 28–29
    mudcloth, 10–11
    tixinda-dyed, 66, 67
Culpeper, Nicholas, 231
cupesí tree, 157

D

Dactylopius coccus, 90–91, *92*
dajudie plant, 154
Dermocydes, 129
Design Academy Eindhoven, 6
de Vos, Birgitta, 4–7, *5*
dheu sewing technique, 48
dissa, 26, *31*
Documenta 14, 31
Dogon people, 24
Dosape, Gladys, 154
Doumbia, Boubacar, 8–17, *9*, *17*

Dragonby (United Kingdom), 62
Duerr, Sasha, 216–231, *217*, *218*, *220*,
    230
Dufour, Jean, 3
Duijf, Brecht, *75*, 78–79
Dusenbury, Mary, 3

E

Earth Charter Initiative, 220
ecoprinting, 130–141
Edelkoort, Li, 6
Edible Schoolyard program, 220, 224
Elizabeth I, 62, 64
Ellis, Catharine, 188–193, *189*
Enamul, Mohammad, *41*
Etacore, Ique, 160, *161*
eucalyptus leaves, 130–141
Eyck, Thomas, 79

F

fashion industry
    ecoprinting, 130–141
    permacouture, 224–225, 227
    turmeric, use of, 184–187
    water pH, influences of, 118–123
Flint, India, 3, 130–141, *131*
flowers
    iris and violets, 136, 140
    lotus, 174
    oxalis, 224, *226*
    roses, *224*
    temple flower project, 168–181
    weld, 193
Fofana, Aboubakar, 18–31, *19*
Fragmentario, 122

G

Garcia, Michel, 3, 190
Ghana Paper Project, 56
Girl with a Pearl Earring (Vermeer), 193
glass, 210–215
green
    from *Ageratina adenophora*, 194–203
    from chamomile, *223*
    from *hongo negro*, 204–209
    from *maruush* leaves, 86
    from mint, *219*, *221*, 231, *232–233*
    from rhubarb, 220, *223*, *232–233*
    from rosemary, 223, 228–230, 231,
        232–233
    from sagebrush, 164, *166*
    from sand, 210–215

from weld, 188–193
Groupe Bogolan Kasobane, 9–11
Gupta, Nitin, *203*
Gustafson, Heidi, 142–151, *143, 146*
Gutiérrez, Porfirio, *81, 86,* 94–99, *97*

H

Haeatoxylum campechianum, 74–79
HAND/EYE Magazine, 3
Han dynasty, 36
Han Shan, 34–39, *35*
Hapsburg, House of, 76
Hark, Mary, 54–59, *55*
head wraps *(tagelmousts),* 25
Hedstrom, Ana Lisa, 59
hibiscus, *168*
Hinojosa, Ines, 158, 160
hongo negro, 204–209
Hormuz Island, Iran, *149–151*
Hydnellum peckii, 129
Hypomyces lacticluorum, 128, 129

I

ikat
    Khmer, 110–117
    Uzbek, 102
indigo
    dye process, 25, 26–28, 42–43, *46–47*
    growing and harvesting, 42–43, *46*
    historical perspective, 22, 24, 36, 42
    Indogofera tinctoria, 41–43, *46–47*
    linguistic origins, 24
    medicinal qualities, 25
    papermaking with, 54–59
    Strobilanthes cusia, 34–39, 196
    tile making with, 50–53
    twelve shades of, 32–33
Indigofera tinctoria, 41–43, *46–47,* 196
Institute for Khmer Traditional Textiles
        (IKTT), 110–117
Institute of Chemical Technology, 180
International Folk Art Market, 108
invasive species. *See* weeds/invasive
        species
Isatis tinctoria, 60–65
Iwamoto, Midori, 117

J

Juglans major, 164

K

kantha stitching, 48, *49*
Kasobane, 9–11

Kendjaev, Fatillo, 102–109, *103, 108*
Kendjaev, Firuza, 105, *108*
Kendjaev, Zarina, 105, *106*
kinsa q'uchu, 206
kozo, 56
Kwame Nkrumah University of Science
        and Technology (KNUST), 56

L

Laccifer lacca, 112
lac dye, 112–117
Langenhuijsen, Lenneke, *75,* 78–79
Larkin, Casey, 220
Leigh, Aviva, 60–65, *61*
lengua de vaca tree, 88, 94
Living Blue, 40–49
logwood, 74–79
lomassa, 24, 26, *33*
Lonchocarpus cyanescens, 21–23, 25, 26
lotus flowers, 174

M

madder, 102–109
Malian textiles
    indigo-dyed, 24–31
    mudcloth, 8–17
mantas, 82
marigolds, 168–181, 182–183
maruush leaves, 86
medicinal plants
    African, 20
    comfrey, 227
    gala, 20
    indigo, 25
    pericón, 87–88
    soukolan, 20
    turmeric, 20, 186
    woad, 64
Memariani, Alireza, 149
mescal, 88
Metropolitan Museum of Art, 56, 94
Miao indigo, 34–39
Middlebury College, 220
Millennial Pink, 120, 224
Mindling, Eric, 68, 71, 73
mint, *219, 221, 225, 231, 233*
Mixtec sea snail, 66–73
Mohenjo Daro, 42
mokume, 48
Monte Albán ruins, 82
Morimoto, Kikuo, *111,* 111–112, 117
mudcloth, 8–17
mushrooms, 124–129
Mycopigments, 126

N

Naematoloma fasciculare, 126
Navajo people, 162–167
Ndomo, 14
nglama tree, 11
Nijera Cottage and Village Industries
        (NCVI), 43–44
nopales, 90–91, 92

O

ochre, 142–151
onion skins, 105, 122, *173, 175,* 227
Opuntia cactus, 90–91, 92
orange. *See also* red
    from avocado pits, 118–123
    from eucalyptus, 130–141
    from lichens, 164
    from mushrooms, 124–129
    ochre pigments, 142–151
Osburn, Deborah, 50–53, *51*
Osburn, Luca, 50–53, *51, 53*
oxalis, 224, *226*

P

papermaking, 54–59
Parmelia molluscula, 164
patola, 112
pericón, 86–87, 88
Perillie, Patrice, 68, 71, 73
Permacouture Institute, 220
Persicaria tinctoria, 196
petates, 95, 98
Philip III, 75
Phipps, Elena, 94
Picanere, Ata, *153,* 157
pink. *See also* red
    from avocado pits, 118–123, 227
Polderceramics, 213
Pombo, Maria Elena, 118–123, *119*
porcelain tiles, 50–53
posahuancos, 69, 71
Prosopis cf. *alba,* 157
Pterogyne nitens, 157
purple
    from flowers, 136, 140
    from logwood, 76, 78, 79
    from mixtec sea snail, 66–73
Purpura pansa, 66–73

R

Rajnish, Jain, 196–200
Rana, Masud, *41*
Rani, Shiuli, *48*
Rani, Soptomi, *41*
raspberry brambles, *226*
red
 from cochineal, 80–94, 100–101
 from eucalyptus leaves, 130–141
 from lac, 112–117
 from madder, 102–109
 from mushrooms, 124–129
 ochre pigments, 142–151
 from sand, 210–215
Reseda luteola, 188–193
Reynolds, Audrey Louise, 184–187, *185,*
 227
rhubarb, *220, 223, 232–233*
Roberts, Kyle, 186
Rockefeller, Steven, 220
rosemary, 223, *228–230, 231, 232–233*
Roy, Sona Rani, 44
Rubia Natural Colours, 78–79
Rumex hymenosepalus, 164

S

sagebrush, 164, 166
samphot hol, 112
sands and clays, 210–215
Sean Kelly New York, 31
shibori
 indigo-dyed, 40–49
 on linen, *30*
 woven, 190–192
Siddhivinayak Temple, *176*, 180
Silk Road, 108
silk weaving, 110–117
soukolan, 20
SPINDIGO (Sustainable Production of
 Plant-derived Indigo), 64
Stephen, Lynn, 94
Sterk, Nadine, 210–215, *211*
Strobilanthes cusia, 34–39, 196
suzani, *104, 109*

T

Tagetes lucida, 87–88
Take Time Press, 56
Tamayo, Rufino, 94
Tellem people, 22
Teotitlán, 82, 84, 94

TextielLab, 78–79
tile making, 50–53
tixinda, 66–73
Toledo, Francisco, 94
"To See the World in a Grain of Sand"
 project, 214–215
tree moss, 86, 87
Trivedi, Rupa, 168–181, *169*
Tuareg groups, 25
turmeric, 184–187
Turok, Marta, 68, 70

U

utebatai bags, 152–160
Uzbek ikat, 102

V

van Ryswyck, Lonny, 210–215, *211*
Vásquez, Juan Isaac, 94
Vermeer, Johannes, 193
Villa Medicis Hors les Murs, 26

W

Watermark tiles, 50–53
water pH, effects of, 119–120, 122
weaving
 Andean, 206, 209
 Bukhara carpets, 102–109
 Buro Belén, 74–79
 Mexican, 70–71
 Navajo, 162–167
 silk, 110–117
 utebatai bags, 152–160
 woven shibori, 190–193
 Zapotec, 82, 84, 94–99
weeds/invasive species
 Ageratina adenophora, 194–203
 oxalis, 224, *226*
 woad, 60–65
weld, 188–193
white, 4–7
Wipplinger, Michele, 3
woad, 60–65
Woad-inc, 64

Y

yellow
 from *Ageratina adenophora,* 194–203
 marigold color range, 182–183
 from mushrooms, 124–129

from onion skins, 105
from oxalis, 224
from *pericón,* 86–87, 88
from rabbitbrush, 164
from sagebrush, 164, 166
from sand, 210–215
from temple flowers, 168–181
from turmeric, 184–187
from weld, 188–193
Yoruba indigo, *21, 22, 23, 24, 25, 26*

Z

ZandGlas, *212,* 214
Zapotec people, 80–99
zapote fruit, 86

PHOTOGRAPHY CREDITS

COVER

TOP AND BOTTOM: *Keith Recker*
CENTER, FAR LEFT, NEAR LEFT & FAR RIGHT: *Joe Coca*
CENTER, NEAR RIGHT: *Heidi Gustafson*

V.	*Riley Salyards*
VII.	*Adriaan Louw for DNA*
VIII.	*Griffin Moore*
12.	*Keith Recker*
4	*Birgitta de Vos*
5	*Courtesy of Birgitta de Vos*
7	*Birgitta de Vos*
8	*David Crookes for DNA*
9	*Adriaan Louw for DNA*
10	*Davod Crookes for DNA*
11	*Adriaan Louw for DNA*
12	**TOP ROW:** *Adriaan Louw for DNA* (LEFT AND CENTER), *David Crookes for DNA* (RIGHT) **MIDDLE ROW:** *David Crookes for DNA* **BOTTOM ROW:** *David Crookes for DNA*
13	*David Crookes for DNA*
14	*Adriaan Louw for DNA*
15	*Adriaan Louw for DNA*
16	*David Crookes for DNA*
17	*David Crookes for DNA*
18	*Riley Salyards*
19	*Francois Goudier*
20	*Aboubakar Fofana*
21	*Francois Goudier*
22	*Aboubakar Fofana*
23	*Aboubakar Fofana*
24	*Joe Coca*
26	*Riley Salyards*
27	*Francois Goudier*
28	*Francois Goudier*
29	*Riley Salyards*
30	*Keith Recker*
31	*Joe Coca*
32	*Riley Salyards*
34-39	*Joe Coca*
40-49	*Courtesy of Living Blue*
50-53	*Courtesy of Cle Tiles*
54-59	*Courtesy of Mary Hark*

60-62	*Holly Davie*
63	*Joe Coca*
64-65	*Holly Davie*
66	*Marcella Echavarria*
67	*Michael Benanav for IFAM*
69	*Marcella Echavarria*
70	*Marcella Echavarria*
71	*Eric Mindling*
72-73	*Eric Mindling*
74	*Thomas Eyck*
75	*Boudewijn Bollman*
76-77	*Thomas Eyck*
78-79	*Thomas Eyck*
80-95	*Joe Coca*
96	*Courtesy of Porfiro Gutiérrez y Familia*
97-101	*Joe Coca*
102	*Elyor Nematov*
103	*Michael Benanav for IFAM*
104	*Edward Addeo*
105-106	*Elyor Nematov*
107	*Keith Recker*
108	*Elyor Nematov*
109	*Edward Addeo*
110-113	*Courtesy of IKTT and Harvey Morrison*
114-117	*Magali An Berthon*
118	*Joe Coca*
119	*Griffin Moore*
120	*María Elena Pombo*
121	*Joe Coca*
122	*Luis Corso*
123	*Griffin Moore*
124	*Joe Coca*
125	*Courtesy of Alissa Allen*
127-129	*Joe Coca*
130	*Courtesy of India Flint*
131	*Sharon Blomgren*
132-141	*Courtesy of India Flint*
142-148	*Heidi Gustafson*
149	*Alireza Memariani*
150-151	*Sheena Callage*
152	*Joe Coca*
153	*Ines Hinojosa*

154	*Ines Hinojosa*
155	*Tom Wool*
156-157	*Joe Coca*
158-159	*Ines Hinojosa*
160-161	*Edward Addeo*
162-167	*Joe Coca*
168	*Adele Mattern*
169	*Michael Benanav for IFAM*
170-171	*Julie Hall for Adiv Pure Nature*
172	*Prarthna Singh*
173	*Keith Recker*
174	*Prarthna Singh*
175	*Julie Hall for Adiv Pure Nature*
176	*Prarthna Singh (petals)* *Julie Hall for Adiv Pure Nature (Ganesh)*
177	*Julie Hall for Adiv Pure Nature*
178	*Julie Hall for Adiv Pure Nature*
179	**TOP:** *Julie Hall for Adiv Pure Nature* **BOTTOM:** *Adele Mattern*
180-181	*Michael Benanav for IFAM*
182-183	*Joe Coca*
184-187	*Courtesy of Audrey Louise Reynolds*
188-193	*Courtesy of Catharine Ellis*
192	**TOP:** *Tim Barwell* **BOTTOM:** *Kent Stewart*
194	*Ana Paula Fuentes*
195	*Didier Binetruy*
196	**TOP:** *Didier Binetruy* **BOTTOM:** *Ana Paula Fuentes*
197	**TOP & BOTTOM LEFT:** *Didier Binetruy* **BOTTOM RIGHT:** *Ana Paula Fuentes*
198	**TOP:** *Didier Binetruy* **BOTTOM:** *Ana Paula Fuentes*
199-203	*Didier Binetruy*
204-209	*Joe Coca*
210	*Mike Roelofs*
211	*Martin Dijkstra*
212	*Blickfänger*
213	*Courtesy of Atelier NL*
214	*Courtesy of Atelier NL*
215	*Blickfänger*
216-233	*Joe Coca*

In *True Colors*, Keith Recker explores one of the earliest forms of communication and creative expression: color. He takes us on a stunning journey of discovery, documenting techniques that evoke equal parts science and magic. You will become entranced by both the colorful traditions and the many-hued innovations that are shared so intimately within this book.

COLLEEN NEWELL, *Executive Vice President*, **ABC Carpet and Home**

Through his exhaustive research from Mexico to Mali, from the red earth used to create Adam to the TextielLab in Tilburg, Keith Recker has uncovered stories of human endeavor that connect us to the myth and magic of colour.

POLLY LEONARD, *Founder*, **Selvedge Magazine**

Captivating and engrossing, *True Colors* takes you on a poetic stroll across the natural color spectrum, pausing at each hue for an in-depth look at the creative process and personal exploration of each of the featured artists. This book is more than an in-depth exploration of an ancient art: it makes a strong, timely case for embracing sustainable sources of color.

VERA VANDENBOSCH, *Photographer, stylist, and writer for **blog.CalicoCorners.com***

True Colors is an absolutely fascinating look at the incredible artistry achieved when creative and visionary individuals from all over the planet interact with their environment in a respectful and mutually beneficial way. The colorful results are uplifting, healing and energizing – just what the doctor ordered!

SUZANNE TUCKER, *Founder of **Tucker & Marks Design***

Keith Recker takes us on a dazzling visual journey around the world that deepens into a seductive and educational reportage of 21st century eco-awareness. This is truly a soulful narrative worth reading and adding to every design library.

SHERRI DONGHIA, ***international design and color specialist***

Keith Recker has created a masterpiece, a unique account of the alchemy of color as defined by master artisans around the world. He documents the colors of nature, the colors that always existed, revealing a very old, and at the same time very new, palette that is very much needed in this world.

MARCELLA ECHAVARRIA, Mexico City-based *journalist and photographer*

"No one will protect what they don't care about, and none will care about what they have never experienced," says Sir David Attenborough. *True Colors* is an ode to natural dyeing, its endless palette and the inspiring people who continue the practice. The book will make the uninitiated in natural dyes fall in love with their magic. The book's important argument for natural dyeing and organic agriculture will, hopefully, jolt us out of the chemical dye addiction that poisons our homes and selves.

KAVITA PARMAR, designer and founder of **The IOU Project**

Vivid in every sense, *True Colors* locates natural dyes as an unexpectedly rich intersection between past and present. Capturing the voices of both traditional practitioners and innovative designers from across the globe, the book covers the full spectrum of a fascinating subject.

GLENN ADAMSON, Senior Scholar, **Yale Center for British Art**

The countless voices and stories surrounding color have never been so compellingly and lyrically expressed. The people, their passions, their processes and their cultural traditions are captivating. You thought you knew color? Think again.

CHARLOTTE MOSS, **designer and author**

It's always stunning to look through the lens of Keith Recker's creative eye: the pages of *True Colors* vibrate with beauty, wellness, wisdom, and love.

PAULETTE COLE, CEO, **ABC Carpet and Home**

This book interweaves literature, philosophy, art and religion with the traditions, manufacture and enjoyment of color. The breadth and depth of the stories behind each color makes this a compelling resource to any student of color, craft, art, nature and history.

KATHARINE KUHARIC, Professor of Art, **Hamilton College,** *and Diebenkorn Fellow,* **San Francisco School of Art**

Linking textile dyeing to massive problems with pollution in the wet processing of contemporary textiles, *True Colors* elevates the value and beauty of traditional dye practices. The book venerates traditional cultures with long histories of natural dyeing, as well as contemporary practitioners and applications, acting as an antidote to mainstream fashion's wasteful and polluting processes. By highlighting dye masters from around the world, Keith shows that natural color can be a means to affect positive change – a welcome challenge to the system.

SASS BROWN, Assistant Lecturer and PhD Candidate, **Manchester Metropolitan University**

Keith Recker introduces us to artisans all over the world—from hereditary craftspeople in indigenous communities to millennial fashion designers—dedicated to harvesting the color by fermenting plants or boiling flowers or pulverizing beetles or milking snails. It is shocking how little most of us know about how the natural world has yielded its colors to us for millennia, even though it's only been a tiny blip of time in human history that we have been relying on synthetic dyes. What's even more shocking is that nearly every one of the methods Recker highlights—from indigo to cochineal—had all but died out in the very communities where people had once practiced them for generations. The makers in this book have diligently reclaimed older techniques and practices, bringing back essential aspects of their own cultural identities. The current revival in creating color from nature is an act of imagination, and an expression of our shared humanity.

DEBORAH NEEDLEMAN, writer and former editor of **T: The New York Times Style Magazine,** **WSJ Magazine,** *and founding editor in chief of* **Domino Magazine**

From indigo leaves to purple sea snails to ebony silt to bright orange mushrooms, Keith Recker offers an insightful and personal exploration of dyestuffs and pigments found in our natural surroundings. In this beautifully photographed volume, Recker invites readers into a vibrant and inspiring world of color, and the lives of diverse practitioners around the globe who are dedicated to making this world a reality. Scholars, designers, artists, and enthusiasts who share Recker's passion for traditional craftsmanship, sustainable fashion, and the handmade should make this book a touchstone in their libraries.

Cristin McKnight Sethi, Ph.D., Assistant Professor of Art History, **The Corcoran School of the Arts and Design, George Washington University,** *and Editorial Board Member of* **The Textile Museum Journal**